Humanities China

Volume 1   Issue 1

Fall 2024

World Chinese Publishing

New York

Advisors

Ba Huang	*artist, writer*	Torbjörn Lodén	*scholar of Chinese studies*
Cao Jun	*artist*	Wang Molin	*art historian*
Chen Bing	*Buddhist culture scholar*	Wang Qingyu	*historian*
Chen Feipeng	*writer, calligraphy researcher*	Wang Shan	*historian*
Chen Min	*writer, media professional*	Wu Shiping	*haiku poet, media professional*
Chen Tushou	*historical writer*	Wu Si	*scholar and media professional*
Deng Shurong	*stage director, actor, educator*	Xu Bing	*contemporary artist*
Fu Zhengming	*writer, translator*	Xuan Shuzheng	*writer*
Gao Falin	*writer, poet*	Xu Youyu	*philosopher, writer*
Gao Minglu	*critic, curator, scholar of art*	Yang Qianwu	*drama critic*
Guo Shixing	*playwright, director, writer*	Yang Peng	*philanthropist, scholar*
Hao Jian	*film studies scholar*	Yang Zuoren	*scholar of Confucianism*
Huang Jisu	*sociologist, playwright*	Yu Ning	*scholar of English, literary critic*
Lin Kehuan	*drama critic*	Zhang Lange	*drama critic*
Liu Zhengcheng	*calligrapher*	Zhang Shuguang	*economist*
Ma Guochuan	*scholar, media professional*	Zhang Yiqi	*writer, literary researcher*
Qin Hui	*historian*	Zhong Qiao	*poet, playwright, drama director*
Shen Heyong	*psychoanalyst, scholar*	Zhong Wen	*journalist*
Sun Huizhu	*playwright, director, educator*	Zhou Qiren	*economist*
Su Xinping	*artist and art scholar*	Zhu Dake	*cultural critic, writer*
Teresa Buczacki	*writer*	Zhu Linhang	*scholar of intellectual history*

Editorial Team

Editor-in-Chief	Chen Jianli
Executive Editor	Luo Weinian
Staff Editors	Wang Jinli
	Ding Minshuai
	He Fa
	Yang Lexiao
	Yang Hongfeng

Cover Arts

Cover Design	Chen Yuanjun, Chen Yi
Front Cover Art	Chen Yuanjun, "The Earth Temple of Zhenhai Village", 2024
Back Cover Art	Ba Huang, "Portrait of a Tibetan Woman"

Distribution: Google Play (electronic version), Amazon (Paper Version)
Price/Issue: $38.00
Subscription: $70.00 for one year two biannual issues
Email: humanitieschina@gmail.com – feedback and subscription is most welcome.

Content

EDITORIAL NOTE

For the Inaugural Issue of Humanities China

CHEN Jianli

After the avalanche,
A surviving fox contemplates the cause:
Was it the golden eagle's flight?
Or the sigh of the tribal elder?
Every rock retains a memory.

We typically understand "culture" as the advanced and core parts of human civilization, distinguishing humans from beasts. The ancestors of the Chinese, like those of other peoples on this planet, held the torch of civilized belief, often ending savagery and ignorance either resolutely or through great struggle. In this way, we have attained what is spoken of in ancient Chinese maxims— "observing culture to transform the world" and "benevolence and righteousness are the expressions of broad love and generosity." Chinese culture has an unchanging and steadfast side, as well as an inclusive and assimilative side. These aspects are intertwined, spanning from its inception to its flourishing throughout East Asia, experiencing cycles of cultural prosperity and decline. This dynamic demonstrates that Chinese culture has never been and can never be isolated from the world, nor from humanity's pursuit of freedom and dignity. The birth of *Humanities China* during the challenging and painful pandemic era embodies our humanistic ideal of exploring truth and seeking future directions following the beacon of civilization.

This publication esteems the "spirit of independence," dedicated to highlighting original art and scholarship. The originality in these fields is the source of human spiritual life. We also uphold the "freedom of thought," aiming to establish a greenhouse of free thought amidst the current intellectual desert, nurturing seeds of independent thinking and expanding the intellectual space of China. We also believe in the "power of faith," striving to illuminate universal values and beliefs belonging to all humanity in a place that disregards natural laws and faiths, hoping to lead our people from barrenness to the promised land of modern civilization.

Our contributors come from the global Chinese-speaking and China studies communities, uniting intellectuals committed to writing for truth, to build a thought haven in the Chinese-speaking world. Here, there are no distinctions between ancient and modern or East and West in scholarship. Both cultural radicalism and cultural conservatism will be treated with equal respect. We reject nihilism and promote positivism; we discard materialism and advocate humanism; we refuse to abandon the spiritual pursuits for mere techniques, preferring to replace materialism with transcendental principles; we oppose neglecting the fundamental for the superficial, aiming to replace short-sighted utilitarian practices with the foundation of faith.

We engage with poetry. Without learning poetry, one cannot speak well. As descendants of the ancient kingdom of poetry, we deeply believe that the existence of poetry and poets creates a tension against technological progress and the free market. We advocate for poetry to redeem modern Chinese language, which has been simplified, standardized, and vulgarized.

We engage with drama, this ancient and noble art, the pillar of human intellect and emotion. In response to the call of drama, we gather, weep, and cheer; through the baptism of drama, we gradually attain freedom and face fear and loneliness with determination.

We engage with films, not out of adherence to Lenin's assertion that "cinema is the most important art form." When sincere and courageous filmmakers attempt to engage with life through fictional or non-fictional films, eliminating unhealthy habits, celebrating beauty as beauty, and elucidating evil as evil, we are glad to support and encourage them.

We engage with classical and contemporary arts, paying tribute to outstanding minds that understand human nature and cognitive patterns, and honoring bold acts of genius that break from tradition. However, we maintain a restrained critical attitude towards individuals or institutions that stifle creativity and monopolize discourse.

We engage with philosophy, law, history, religion, psychology, education, sociology, political science, economics, anthropology, literary studies, and any fields related to the human spirit and social practice. From a humanistic standpoint, we are interested in all effective and vivid expressions of ideas but remain vigilant against academic formalism in any guise.

More than five centuries ago, the Oirat cavalry, victorious at the Battle of Tumu Fortress, advanced on Beijing. Yu Qian (于谦, 1398–1457), with immense courage and wisdom, reversed the tide of defeat, rallying all available forces to win the Battle of Beijing's defense. In this battle, the citizens and soldiers of the capital united against the enemy, with reinforcement troops from both capitals, Henan, Shandong, and coastal regions of Nanjing contributing to the effort. The so-called "king" they were willing to sacrifice for was not just the Emperor Zhu 's family, but their cherished way of life. Buddhists venerate Shakyamuni as the "King of Emptiness," and Zen practitioners risk their lives to comprehend the "King of the Mind," which is the essence of our existence and universal truth. "Turning the declining tide starts with turning the declining heart" – once the heart is turned, the tide will follow.

Though their approaches were vastly different, both *New Youth* (《新青年》) and *Xue Heng* (《学衡》) enlightened an era and profoundly influenced their successors. Martin Luther and Thomas More fiercely criticized each other, but no force could diminish their brilliance in intellectual history. We do not speculate whether Father Sergei's achievements lie in the battlefield, monastery, or heaven, but we clearly see Tolstoy encouraging him to leave and never look back. We see the old count insisting on not dying in his immoral estate, changing the way humanity loves and says no through his writing.

Humanities China emerged in the spring of 2023. Spring is the time of renewal. It is like a mustard seed, heralding the news of spring; it is a ray of sunlight, shining at the tunnel's end; it is the grand sound of a bell at the end of an age, playing the divine music of heaven; it is the hope we hold, singing the universal melody of the future. *Humanities China* is ready to make its mark. If you can sing loudly, the world will hear.

About the author:

Chen Jianli is a film director, playwright, poet, and the Editor-in-Chief of *Humanities China*.

ART REFLECTIONS

Ah Cheng's Memory and Expression of the Times

SUN Yu

Wang Zengqi (汪曾祺, 1920-1997) once spoke about Ah Cheng (阿城, 1949-)'s works, feeling that his knowledge structure was unique and that there was an internal beauty in Ah Cheng's work that he himself could not match. He made similar remarks more than once. Rather than self-deprecation, it is more akin to an inner resonance [1]. Both are writers I admire, and they share similarities, such as being eclectic in their interests, with an understanding of the arts of leisure writing. They are also sensitive to literary style, inheriting the flow of ancient Chinese prose. In their works, there's often a resistance to the tradition of moralistic dogma, and the ideological tones post-May Fourth Movement are rarely seen in their fictional works. They apply a non-mainstream discourse to life, showing us a different landscape.

Speaking of the literature of the 1980s, Ah Cheng cannot be omitted. However, from any perspective, he was an exception in the literary world of that era. His scholarly knowledge was rare among writers. Wang Zengqi recognized the internal strength in Ah Cheng, which precisely represented a tradition that had long disappeared. Chinese literature is closely related to prose, but the old scholars had ruined prose, and it was the secular novel that liberated literary styles, reviving the prose. Not many understood this fact; Wang Guowei saw the vitality of art in the dramas of the Song and Yuan dynasties, but unfortunately, the new literati abandoned this tradition, leading to overly moralistic writings and an increasingly narrow path. Those advocating populism rejected intellectuality and were assimilated by the masses, resulting in a loss of

historical depth behind the words.

In 1981, Wang Zengqi emerged from the Beijing's literati circle, his style of writing as clear as if washed by water. His works remind us of Fei Ming, Shen Congwen, and of course, the note-style novels of the Ming and Qing dynasties. Ah Cheng, on the other hand, was different. He was outside the Beijing literati circle and rarely carried the vibe of bookishness. The Beijing circle was a product of modern education, while Ah Cheng grew wildly, with knowledge and prose that didn't conform to ivory tower standards, bringing the true essence of ancient Chinese language. Bypassing the tone of the May Fourth Movement and directly reaching back to the veins of pre-Qin era, with the writing essence of the Song, Yuan, and Ming, he produced works that were spirited and cool. This was not the old sound of nostalgia, but also contained the warmth of modernity, a rarity since the May Fourth Movement. In the realm of the spirit, he went further than Wang Zengqi.

Upon its release, "The King of Chess" (《棋王》) immediately astonished the audience, its narrative thrust reminiscent of a return to traditional novel writing that strikes directly at the heart, like a refreshing breeze that brings delight. "The King of Trees" (《树王》) reveals the chaotic ignorance of the "sent-down youth" life, surpassing common motifs and subtly satirizing the societal choices made since modern times. "The King of Children" (《孩子王》) is a narrative filled with absurd descriptions, yet within this absurdity, it unveils the irrational nature of existence, providing a compelling explanation for what makes the unconventional, unconventional.

At that time, Ah Cheng handled the collective memory of people in a highly individualized manner, offering a distinct perspective. When people were confined to expressing thoughts in public discourse, he saw the possibility of individualized existence among those out of sync with the times. "The King of Trees" portrays a failed hero, making those ignorant youths from outside appear extremely pale in comparison. The lack of intelligence in collectivity stems from blind following, leading to the natural desolation and the desolation of humanity.

For the author, the process of writing is a way to overcome this desolation. What earned him widespread acclaim was "The King of Chess," a novel about the pleasure a marginalized young man named Wang finds in chess throughout his life. The years depicted by Ah Cheng flow with warmth from a life of dreariness, but this warmth doesn't stem from popular thought or trending theories; it's an ancient cognitive movement that roams in the realm of art. The narrative style of "The King of Chess" is not novel in modern literature, except for its use of old vernacular. It describes the lonely lives of several sent-down youths, days as monotonous as the desert, yet their inner worlds sparkle with divine intelligence. Ah Cheng believes that in an era devoid of paths, if one can still enter the realms of aesthetic and spiritual pleasure through skill and art, then the spirit is far from barren and salvation is within reach. This ancient ethos from Taoism and Zen flourishes even in chaotic times. The indomitable spirit, even miraculously flickering, allows for a tranquil and regretless existence.

Ah Cheng grew up in a unique era, where literature pursued pure and grand perfection. However, he chose to write about lives that were neither grand nor perfect. He knew that the fake literature, which strayed far from humanity, was not the essence of life. Only in the everyday could true meaning be found, and the great power of the spirit could also be obtained from the mundane. Several scenes in "The King of Chess" are unforgettable: one is the depiction of eating, where the fragrance wafts through, the profundity in simplicity is quite appropriate, much like the remnants of *Dream of the Red Chamber*. This aesthetic presentation of appetite is a contemplation of the Eastern view of life, occasionally found in old note-style novels. Yet, in terms of vividness, Ah Cheng is no less than the ancients. Another scene describes the state of playing chess, a completely self-forgetting contemplation, where one metaphorically inhales and exhales the sun and moon, encompassing the energy of sky and earth, with the vast universe and the cosmos rotating under the hero's wrist. Beneath the novel's overall common tone, there is a transformation of worldly sounds, making the ordinary extraordinary. Yet, in its elegance, there are phrases like those from a fairyland, with a divine solemnity and exquisite charm. Third, it portrays the extraordinary flavor of people, shrouded in mystery, such as an old man picking up trash, resembling a hermit with a mysterious aura. These are all marginal figures, looked down upon by society, but the more marginal, the deeper the thought, perhaps what Zhuangzi (Chuang-tzu, 庄子) meant by "the use of the useless" (无用之用).

The most captivating aspect of the novel is not the sanctification of the mundane, but rather the desolation that lies behind the sacred. After Wang's dazzling performance on the chessboard, he wounded in spirit and wept, still ensnared in the worldly web, and all of us remain in this pitiable world. Concluding here, one can't help but inhale sharply; the misfortune of the cosmos, as always, remains unshakable. This melancholic sentiment, how could we possibly forget? The ending of the novel merits profound reflection, teeming with endless implications. Wang Zengqi, upon reading this novel, was full of praise, yet also remarked on certain flaws, suggesting that revealing all the mysteries was somewhat regrettable. However, I feel it is not so; by writing in this manner, the novel returns to the mundane, bringing its gaze back down. Otherwise, if literature of the Cultural Revolution only sought to elevate its characters, rendering them almost ethereal, untouchable by worldly concerns, that would leave one cold at the heights. What Ah Cheng desired, it seems, was precisely this outcome.

Those who appreciate Ah Cheng will notice that his essays are concise, and his works are mostly short stories. His essays are to the point without unnecessary embellishment. In his writing, he often uses fragments and glimpses to record his experiences. *Flowers Everywhere* (《遍地风流》 writes of early memories, taking a unique path and serving as a scan of humanity. Describing these series of works as ethnographic sketches is not an exaggeration. Whether it's the fleeting impressions of the capital city or the livelihoods of rural areas, they are vividly presented. However, writing such texts does not immerse in the folk charm as Wang Zengqi does. Instead, there is a deep spirit of critique buried in his works, reflecting the legacy of the May Fourth Movement in a non-May Fourth manner. Thus, it can be said that there is the essence of the May Fourth Movement that is not explicitly of the May Fourth, recording forgotten history accurately.

His novels *Young Then*(《彼时正年轻》) and *Miscellaneous Colors* (《杂色》) mostly document the lives of ordinary people: craftsmen, bookstore workers, waiters, hunters, rightists, educated youths, soldiers, etc., each with their own difficult paths. How these people lived in the 50s and 60s is rarely documented officially, and revolutionary literature often overlooks them. Ah Cheng's materials are precious for understanding the people and events of that era. Sometimes his works seem like legends, or records of the extraordinary, encompassing all sorts of characters. Some stories are thrilling, others are satirical, evoking sighs from the readers. He has a keen understanding of human malice. But in writing about these people and events, he does not complain but naturally reveals them, showing readers the true nature of life. Some thoughts are deeply buried. Through stories, he subtly reflects on the joys and sorrows of life and understanding of situations, with a hint of Lu Xun (鲁迅, 1881-1936)'s legacy, yet more implicit.

Although the revolution took place, the servility among people did not diminish; instead, the bitterness deepened. Those who labored at the bottom frequently faced unexpected disasters, their spirits groveling on the ground, unable to rise. In his series about ordinary people, he mocks the distorted human mentality with sharp and piercing insight, filled with implicit meanings.

Ah Cheng excels at depicting deformed individuals or the suffering people within distorted lives. In "Nightmare" (《噩梦》), Old Yu loves to laugh, even at inappropriate times at work, which makes others think he is not serious. It turns out he has been having nightmares and only laughter brings some relief. In "Old Books" (《旧书》), Wu Qingxiang, a book delivery man for an antique bookshop during the Republic of China, had his unique life but committed suicide in 1950. The author does not explain why, leaving readers pondering.

"Reminiscence" (《回忆》) narrates the experiences of a soldier during the Cultural Revolution, with multiple layers of implication. The laughable moments are the heaviest, lingering with the absurdity of time. In an era dominated by a single color, he saw a multi-colored scene, where different people made their choices out of helplessness, often becoming numb. Yet, there were special individuals among them, like Old Guan in "Rehabilitation" (《平反》). Though the organization wanted to rehabilitate her, she insisted on her own characterization, her spirit remaining unyielding.

Ah Cheng's novels are not as constrained by the entanglements of men and women as Eileen Chang's, presenting a broader and more complex life. Nor are they as gentle as Wang Zengqi's, who finds comfort in the Confucian legacy within everyday life. He resembles an interrogator of the world, uncovering the terrifying ancient ghosts in secular society, seeking to restore these remnants, all done in a calm and understated manner. Behind these stories stands the narrator "I," seeing unease amidst tranquility, revealing bitterness in laughter. In the twisted space-time, all aspects of humanity are exposed.

Regarding life in the 1960s, today's youth know very little. The authenticity of those areas covered by moral discourse is instead inscribed in time by Ah Cheng's alternative penmanship. How people survived in uncontrollable environments, and all the facets of the lives of the lower class, cannot be described by the grand terms of the era. Yet he records these abnormal lives with an alienating vocabulary. In "Records" (《唱片》), Zhao Heng listens to records during turbulent times, the exquisite musical notes dancing in the mundane years, inadvertently bringing solace to ordinary people's hearts. "Arson" (《纵火》) describes the fear of a stamp collector during the campaign against the Four Olds, where art is destroyed by fire, along with dreams. The death of Zhang Wuchang in "Blanket" (《被子》) is something not seen in his earlier works. These unrelated pieces form a three-dimensional human tableau, each part of an interconnected chain. These are fragments not recorded by newspapers, nor are they the imagery praised by fashionable poets. In "Erecting This for Future Reference" (《立此存照》), Ah Cheng leaves behind images of life in special years that sociologists seek.

I believe this is his most valuable writing. Although the author does not place much importance on the texts of that time, compared to those who evade memory, everything he depicts holds undeniable value. Works of nostalgia by Beijing literati often carry a sense of identity, or the habitual revelations of professionalism, or the emotions within their circles, their spirits often confined within the discourse of epistemology. Ah Cheng's work lacks these traces, thus his descriptions of folk culture differ from the refined literati, imbued with the breath of the fields and the colors of the mountains and forests. He consciously resists the habits of the intellectual community, external to the tones of the academic and writer groups, thus the landscapes of the city and countryside are exposed to the wind and rain. Yet, unlike the poignant renderings of rural writers, he maintains a distance from the subject world. It is as if he is an outsider of our era, yet so close to the life on the ground. Those breaths, laughs, and colors face us vividly. And in his mirror, we also see our own reflections.

When discussing his novels, Ah Cheng candidly admits that he is deeply influenced by "Records of the Grand Historian" (《史记》). His concise and powerful works, with their skill in conveying spirit through form, are connected to the Han dynasty's legacy. Sima Qian reached the pinnacle of Chinese historiography and biographical writing. Although later generations made advancements, these were mostly extensions of the branches and leaves, with little progress in the main structure and overall spirit. Sima Qian's simple yet profound prose encapsulates vastness within limited space, which is also the path Ah Cheng follows.

From the perspective of composition, Ah Cheng's works are marked by clear and deeply imprinted lines and dots, possessing "structural strength" without "charming appeal," more "ancient simplicity" and less "modern prettiness." New literature writers often possess more "charming appeal" and "modern prettiness," but often lose the ancient style. Beijing literati after the May Fourth Movement frequently start with the Six Dynasties' aesthetic, subtly influenced by

Buddhist elegance. However, Ah Cheng appreciates the demeanor of the Zhou, Qin, and Han dynasties—straightforward and skillful without being contrived. This distances him from the soft tones, reflecting thoughts in detail, subtly hinting at history, vivid, lively, and distinct from various expressions in translation styles.

Due to the influence of ancient styles, his writing is restrained, controlled with ease, often leaving blank spaces. Sometimes, it flows with distant thoughts. In the deeper realms of aesthetics, it also carries a wildness, reminiscent of the dance between humans and gods in Han dynasty stone carvings, with a spirit that is soaring. He writes about the mountains and eagles of the borderlands, where coldness is imbued with flowing heat, and amidst the desolate hues of the world, a vast spirit bursts forth, embodying heroic sentiment. The unleashing power like the mythical Qilin, with an aura akin to that of a dragon and tiger. Consider how "Zip Line" (《溜索》) is written with such thrilling, majestic boldness:

The leader didn't believe the sound could be the Nu River. He said nothing, just nudged his horse. But the horse hesitated more, and the oxen slowed too.

A large eagle circled, then dove into the sound from the other side of the mountain. The mule caravan, as if signaled, stopped. The men dismounted, walked to the oxen, and began shouting, cursing, punching, and kicking. The bells rang out in panic, and the caravan, like thick porridge, slowly moved towards the pass.

An hour earlier, they heard a faint, muffled thunder. At first, they ignored it, thinking it was rain from a hundred miles away. But as the thunder continued, they grew suspicious and asked about it. The leader lazily replied that it was the Nu River, and they were about to cross the zip line.

The mountain wasn't high, and the pass was narrow, only wide enough for one and a half oxen. They tensed up, ready to see the river that runs through western Yunnan. But as they turned out of the pass, the thunder still rumbled. The oxen in front refused to move, so they dismounted and walked to the riverbank. When they reached the edge, they took a breath and their legs trembled, just like the oxen, not daring to take another step.

A sheer cliff dropped away. The mule caravan was on top of this precipice. They had been winding their way around all day, thinking the mountain was low and the wind cold, never realizing they had been hovering at such a great height [2].

These are words carved like a knife, not elaborated like typical literary works, yet within these sparse phrases, a grand atmosphere emerges. Contemporary writers who describe treacherous mountains and rivers are often influenced by Western art. Zhang Chengzhi (张承志)'s pasture is like a Repin's oil painting, dazzling in its colors; Wang Meng (王蒙)'s portrayal of Xinjiang's storms has the andante feel of Tchaikovsky; whereas Ah Cheng's work resembles Han Dynasty sculptures, exuding a majestic simplicity. His depictions of natural scenes carry meaning (意) within form (象), and when describing human emotions, they embed form within meaning. This flavor is only found in the ancient Chinese poetry and prose.

Realizing this, we suddenly understand that without a background in painting, it might be impossible to achieve such effects. Ah Cheng is a painter, and his essays carry a painter's touch, compensating for the limitations of words in conveying imagery. His essays and notes are not just visual but also rich in scholarly insight. Chen Danqing greatly admires his perceptive abilities, finding much ingenuity in his words. When I read his *Venice Diary* (《威尼斯日记》) years ago, I marveled at his diverse writing style. Historical relics came to life one by one, presenting the myriad facets of time like a movie. He understands the strengths and weaknesses of the Chinese language, writing freely yet knowing when to stop just right. In the foreign towers and pavilions, history's mirrors reflect the shapes and shadows of his homeland, revealing secrets in the dust. At such moments, our author becomes a painter, a photographer, and an archaeologist. Yet in fleeting moments, he transforms into a poet, capturing the essence of the ancients in his musings, with vast skies and broad lands where people find comfort, and distant spirits are gently summoned back.

What attracts Ah Cheng is the warmth within human relics. Why are we like this, where is the road ahead, where do we want to go? These questions arise. Although *Venice Diary* seems to discuss Italy's past and present, it actually provides insights into Chinese history. Reading about China from afar makes the world transparent, light and shadow intertwine. For example, the development of Tang poetry might be related to West Asian music, and his descriptions feel natural without exaggeration, with many accurate observations. Additionally, his discussions on the history of Jews in China are well-documented, revealing a scholarly approach, blending human suffering with the colors of history. The diary entry comparing Venice and Yangzhou, and the interpretation of *Record of Painted Boats in Yangzhou* (《扬州画舫录》), could only be done by a historian, yet it is not rigid, flowing with colors—perhaps due to the author's experience with ink and brush. Ah Cheng's discussions on landscapes are knowledgeable, interesting, and

imbued with a philosophical touch, reminiscent of Kafka and Sartre's thoughts. One day, his diary wrote:

In Venice, I once saw a stone plaque on a wall by a bridge, inscribed with the words 'Mozart stayed here.' However, for some reason, I was never able to find that bridge again later on. [3]

Remnants of history within the fabric of time move and blur, twist and turn, and quickly fade away, layering multiple images. Mu Xin was also skilled at conveying this kind of feeling, but he filtered it too cleanly, with a slightly heavy touch of rhetoric. Ah Cheng, on the other hand, is more understated; the rust of history and the scent of earth still linger deep within his prose. His subtle thoughts invite readers to pause and observe, much like old artifacts displayed in museum cases.

I enjoy his conversational prose, which intertwines narration and commentary, with landscapes, scholarship, and insights interspersed throughout. His talent is fully expressed in this form. Although *Venice Diary* (《威尼斯日记》) is brief, it encapsulates his essence. The elements of film, painting, and scholarship flicker casually within. Despite its short length, it traces a long historical path, reminiscent of ancient writing styles. Sometimes, this frugal use of words creates a sense of distance from the reader, as if he is not catering to the audience but walking his own path, regardless of whether the reader can keep pace. In those moments, he stands on one shore while we stand on the other.

After the May Fourth Movement, intellectuals sought to establish a new modern vernacular, but few succeeded. Wang Zengqi and Ah Cheng both disliked the May Fourth style, feeling that Hu Shi and others had disrupted the ancient literary tradition. Wang Zengqi aimed to restore the rhythm of classical prose, paying attention to the harmony between sentences and words, incorporating classical language, dialects, and formal language into his writing. Unlike Wang Zengqi, Ah Cheng prefers a more forceful expression, with a brisk and vigorous style. He believes that pre-Qin thinkers possessed a literary spirit, but later scholars could not carry on that legacy, losing the original tone. However, this spirit can still be found in folk expressions. He senses this heritage in Han Dynasty sculptures and utensils. The beautiful objects from the court initially had roots in the folk traditions, possessing a certain taste. Over time, as they became detached from their origins, they fell into desolation, which is a cultural tragedy.

Whether in his novels or essays, Ah Cheng lets objects speak for themselves, using his own words sparingly. These people and objects reveal their meanings naturally. Not everyone has this skill; the simplicity of ancient China flows gently through his work, bathing our pallid selves. Ah Cheng believes that the liveliest aspect of Chinese novels is their secular nature, from Ming and Qing novels to the works of Zhang Ailing. But in his eyes, this secular nature is not vulgar but a vibrant landscape. If we say that Dream of the *Red Chamber* (《红楼梦》) imbues the secular with a poetic soul, and Zhang Ailing captures coldness amidst the splendor, then Ah Cheng adds intellectualism to the portrayal of the masses. His writings are not rooted in Tang poetry or Ming essays, but in the radiation of knowledge and reason. There are few scholarly novelists, with only a handful like Jin Yong and Wang Zengqi possessing this skill. Ah Cheng's scholarship is both broad and deep, covering history, literature, sociology, and aesthetics—a rarity in the literary world of the past seventy years.

The issue of ancient and modern in literature has been a challenge for a century. The May Fourth generation believed they had solved this problem, but it is not so simple. This brings to mind Zhang Taiyan's legacy; one of Mr. Taiyan's academic spirits in the late Qing was to revive literature through a return to the past. This revival was not a mere return to Confucian order but an exploration of the gems of Han civilization. After being overshadowed by utilitarianism, the wisdom of the ancients became stunted and diminished. In his essay *On Style* (《论式》), Zhang Taiyan wrote:

Late Zhou Dynasty's discussions exhibit both profound insights and elegant expressions, their words neither excessive nor deficient. During the Han dynasty, beginning with Jia Yi, writings became more elaborate and gradually merged with the style of rhapsodies. Lengthy discourses of thousands of words often conveyed ideas that could be summarized in just a few phrases.

Only the Shi Qu Discussion Records *(《石渠奏议》) from the Han dynasty maintain a balance between substance and style, with concise and precise language, making them exemplary models. The later Han scholars proliferated, and by the early Wei dynasty, there were hundreds of works. However, those that truly grasped essential principles were few: on critical examination of affairs, none surpassed* Lun Heng *(《论衡》); on political discourse, none exceeded* Chang Yan *(《昌言》); and on character analysis, none outdid* Ren Wu Zhi *(《人物志》). These three works can be compared to those of the late Zhou period. The rest, though elegant and refined, are mostly trivial discussions.[4]*

Ah Cheng also holds the pre-Qin writings in high esteem, saying:

Discussing philosophy, Zhuangzi used prose, Laozi used verse, and Confucius employed dialogue. In the two thousand years since, there have been no works in Chinese that similarly address both the metaphysical and the physical with such excellence. Nowadays, regardless of whether something makes sense, it is narrated in a way that puts people to sleep. Occasionally, when three good articles are found, they are read repeatedly, as if rereading them would make more good articles appear. [5]

From this perspective, Ah Cheng values the ancient style, believing that the further back in time one goes, the more unrestrained the expression becomes. The Confucian scholars after the Han dynasty did not understand this principle, focusing on contemporary writings, leading to a gradual decline in spirit and authenticity. Zhang Taiyan (章太炎) once wrote a letter to Qian Xuantong (钱玄同), mocking the then-popular literary style and criticizing the works of Liang Qichao and Lin Shu for their artificiality. In his view, the writings before the Six Dynasties were superior because they contained genuine expectations and anxieties, not pretentious declarations. This perspective greatly influenced Qian Xuantong's generation. The rhetoric of Zhang's disciples during the New Culture Movement often drew from *Qiu Shu* (《訄书》), making it intriguing and unique. Lu Xun's later success lay in avoiding the discourse of that era, even changing his way of thinking. This pattern is also evident in Wang Zengqi and Ah Cheng. Their mutual understanding seems inevitable.

Art that retains its primal energy is rarely seen in the writings of the Tongcheng school. Qing dynasty scholars' understanding of the ancients was often superficial. The formulas in literary studies easily became part of the rigid eight-legged essay structure. Therefore, those with a keen sense do not fall for the traps of pedantic scholars. The Chinese language is a unique entity; its logographic nature determines the variability of prose. The beauty in this variability is not in the accumulation of ornate words but in the presence of a mystical structure. Primitive expressions lack external embellishments. Ah Cheng enjoys discussing shamanism and Nuo rituals, all of which relate to the primal beauty of strength. His research on Miao totems also reveals these elements. Engaging in archaeological studies is perhaps a search for that vigorous spirit. In literary expression, using a bit of clumsy, earthy language is not a bad thing, as it is closer to the true nature of humanity. Ah Cheng says:

A good article does not have to be composed of good sentences throughout. There should be some clumsy and awkward sentences, seemingly incomprehensible ones, so that the good sentences that follow appear exceptionally brilliant. Life is the same; constant cleverness can be tiresome. [6]

This also explains why he refers to his own writing as "tuoqiang" (脱腔, offbeat), because in a world dominated by a single tone, an individual's unique voice is incredibly important. In his casual conversations, he is similarly unhurried, with his thoughts sometimes leaping, weaving in and out of idle chatter. Amidst his nonchalant expressions, a brilliant phrase might suddenly appear, becoming the highlight. At times, it seems as if his words are not aimed at the reader but spoken to the universe.

Few contemporary writers possess cultural self-awareness, and thus the elements behind their words are scarce. Ah Cheng values knowledge structure and cultural composition, which is insightful. In mainstream thinking, one cannot see another corner of the world, and it is often in those abandoned realms that the brightest aspects of civilization are preserved. Writers benefit greatly from a broad range of knowledge. Ah Cheng spent his childhood in Liulichang, among antiques, developing a keen eye for history. Since the 1980s, most people have only taken a few steps forward, returning to the Seventeen Years or the May Fourth period. However, he looked back to the Ming dynasty and earlier, studying architecture, furniture, painting, and prose. His recent publication The Origins of Civilization's Forms in the *Luoshu and Hetu* (《洛书河图——文明的造型探源》) delves into ancient civilizations. By examining artistic issues through the lenses of anthropology and archaeology, he reveals the breadth of his thought. Reflecting on how Chen Mengjia transitioned from poetry to archaeology and Shen Congwen immersed himself in the history of clothing, one sees a profound sentiment. Writers escaping the hustle and bustle of city life are often much wiser than us common folk, possessing an all-seeing eye that perceives the finite and infinite aspects of existence. Many of today's scholars have lost this ability.

One year, a friend and I invited Ah Cheng to give a lecture at Renmin University, where he discussed Han dynasty folklore and rural art, showcasing his aesthetic preferences. He admired the extraordinary imagination in Chu culture's folk songs and customs. He specifically addressed the issue of tradition versus the avant-garde, revealing a mindset detached from contemporary trends, embodying an avant-garde consciousness even on an apparently retro path. Ge Fei once said that in the 1980s, Wang Zengqi's works were truly avant-garde. This statement also applies aptly to Ah Cheng. Reflecting on how Nietzsche drew inspiration from the legacies of ancient Greece and India, changing the structure of the German language, it becomes evident that recovering lost spiritual elements can spur new art forms.

I believe Ah Cheng's late-life fascination with archaeology and anthropology may be an effort to maintain his spiritual vitality. His late lectures and writings show that his quest for ancient styles has never ceased. Writers venturing into archaeology have been around since the early Republican era, some transitioning from epigraphy and others from book collecting. Zheng Zhenduo introduced foreign archaeological ideas during his active literary period; Lu Xun's involvement in the 1927 Northwest field investigations is also a fascinating story. Lu Xun's research on Qin and Han tiles, Han sculptures, and Japanese archaeological reports was linked to his writing, with some elements of his cultural perspective deriving from this. Ah Cheng's later literary works became scarce as his interest in archaeology grew, which could be seen as an aesthetic shift. Limiting cultural understanding to words alone is problematic; painting, architecture, and music can also provide spiritual pleasure. However, these intellectual elements did not continue to extend into his novels, which I see as a pity. Excessive calmness reduces poetic expression; Ah Cheng, filled with scholarly ideas, restrained his talent as a novelist, which might have been a loss for readers.

Yet, what we expect of him may not be what he values. In a culturally moralistic context, Ah Cheng is difficult to approach. He might be one of the few in our era who are most distant from contemporary trends. In retrospect, Ah Cheng does not care about being labeled as a writer, as labels can assimilate one into dull words. Understanding Ah Cheng requires seeing his cultural ideas in their entirety; only by placing his novels, essays, films, and paintings in one space can we see his full scope. His worldview spans different art forms, and his ambitions may not be immediately apparent to us. China has always had a secular folk society where genuine cultural elements are often hidden. Still, these cannot be discovered in a false context, only illuminated through the eyes of the ancients. In a strange wilderness, he found those references, imbued with a primal energy belonging to both the distant past and the seekers of today. Ah Cheng values the secular folk but does not belong to them. This complex entanglement sparks meaningful aesthetic light, offering a place where modern people can renew themselves.

About the author:

Sun Yu was born in 1957 in Dalian, China. He graduated from Shenyang Normal University and has served as the director of the Lu Xun Museum. He is currently the Dean of the School of Literature at Renmin University of China and is a renowned literary critic.

Endnotes:

[1] Wang Zengqi, "The Reason People Are Human - Reading 'The King of Chess' (《棋王》)," in Solitary Essays (《独坐小品》), p. 287, Henan Literature and Art Publishing House, 2017 edition.

[2] Ah Cheng, "Crossing the River by Rope" (《溜索》), in The Collected Works of Ah Cheng (Volume Two) (《阿城文集（之二）》), p. 5, Jiangsu Phoenix Literature and Art Publishing House, 2016 edition.

[3] Ah Cheng, "Venice Diary" (《威尼斯日记》), p. 116, Writers Publishing House, 1997 edition.

[4] Zhang Taiyan, "On Style" (《论式》), in Critical Essays on Ancient Matters (《国故论衡》), p. 117, The Commercial Press, 2010 edition.

[5] Ah Cheng, "Venice Diary" (《威尼斯日记》), p. 5, Writers Publishing House, 1997 edition.

[6] Ah Cheng, "Venice Diary" (《威尼斯日记》), p. 10, Writers Publishing House, 1997 edition.

A Brief Discussion on the Relationship between Xiang Thinking and Chinese Art

LIU Qian

At the beginning of the last century, Western Imagism in literature, drawing extensively from the rich tapestry of Chinese culture with texts such as the *Yijing* (*Book of Change*s 易经), Zhuangzi (Chuang Tzu 庄子), along with Tang Dynasty poetry and Song Dynasty lyrics, intricately linked the use of imagery with the distinctive features of Chinese art. Imagism, absorbing Henri Bergson's intuitionism and his philosophy of life, which explores perceptions of the world, life, and time, found parallel resonance with traditional Chinese views on the world, concepts of space-time, and the consciousness of life. Central to this intercultural synergy is Xiang Thinking (象思维, image/metaphorical/analogical thinking), a concept intrinsic to Chinese culture.

Xiang Thinking in Chinese culture diverges from Martin Heidegger's assertion that "where words break off, no thing may be" (a phrase from Stefan George's poetry), by precisely utilizing Xiang to fill the gaps left by words, thus unveiling another perspective to understand and express the world.

Like Ludwig Wittgenstein, ancient Chinese thinkers were keenly aware of the relationship between language and meaning. However, their strategy was not to "remain silent" as Wittgenstein suggested, but to "establish Xiang" for articulation of thoughts and ideas.

1. What is "Xiang Thinking"

The concept of "Xiang Thinking" was introduced by Mr. Wang Shuren (王树人) in the 1980s.

His major contribution was in distinctly identifying a unique mode of thinking in traditional Chinese culture, different from Western conceptual thinking. The fundamental traits of Xiang Thinking, as defined by Wang Shuren, are its "non-substantial, non-objectified, and non-ready-made" nature (非实体性、非对象性、非现成性). This mode of thinking mirrors the distinctive ways in which the Chinese nation observes, comprehends, and interprets the world and is evident in various cultural phenomena, from Chinese characters to the concepts of Yin-Yang (阴阳) and the Five Phases (Wuxing 五行), undeniably impacting Chinese culture and art.

The essence of Xiang Thinking is encapsulated in the principle of "establishing Xiang to fully convey meaning" (立象以尽意), as stated in the "Xici Shang" (系辞上) chapter of *the Book of Changes*. This encompasses two significant aspects: first, an awareness of the limitations inherent in language and words; and second, the creation and validation of advanced cognitive activities through the medium of Xiang.

The first aspect is succinctly captured in the expression "words cannot fully convey meaning" (言不尽意) from the "Xici Shang" of the Book of Changes. Conceptual thinking, characterized by its reliance on vocabulary, concepts, and logical reasoning, while enhancing thought efficiency, also replaces reality with an abstract conceptual framework, consequently altering our perception of the world. In the Bible, Adam's act of naming animals represents the establishment of a linguistic (conceptual) world, setting a human-centric standard for understanding all things. This approach suffers from intrinsic flaws in both cognition and expression. The conceptual systems we devise often warp our perceptions and limit our expressiveness, resonating with Laozi (Laotzu 老子)'s saying: "The name that can be named is not the eternal name" (名可名，非常名).

The second aspect highlights the distinctive Chinese approach to understanding and articulating the world. The ancient practice of "observing the celestial imageries and scrutinizing the terrestrial principles" (仰则观象于天，俯则观法于地) from the "Xici Xia" (系辞下) of the *Book of Changes* reveals a quintessentially Chinese method of cognition. Here, "imageries" (象) and "principles" (法) are not concrete goals for studying the world as an object but are patterns and laws grasped holistically, rooted in the philosophy of unity between heaven and humanity. The "imageries" in astronomy and the "principles" in geography are understood in this context. Ancient Chinese thinkers recognized the limitations of language and concepts. Consequently, except for schools like the Logicians (名家) and the Mohists (墨家), mainstream culture did not adhere to the same precision in conceptual application and logic as in the West. In contrast, the core concepts of major philosophical schools—Confucianism, Buddhism, and Taoism—such as "Dao" (道), "Ren" (仁), and "Tathātā" (真如), are indefinable and inexpressible in our limited, experiential language. Xiang Thinking, therefore, sidesteps the absoluteness and restrictions of concepts, utilizing "Xiang" as a pivotal method and tool in thought. Besides the hexagrams in the Book of Changes, the most basic and frequently employed images include Yin-Yang (阴阳), and the Five Phases.

2. Examples of Xiang Thinking from Traditional Chinese Culture

The essence of "Establishing Xiang," a core principle in Chinese thought, lies not in the replication of natural forms but in the human ability to create symbols beyond nature's own constructs (non-substantial, non-objectified, and non-ready-made). These symbols serve as tools to comprehend, interpret, and navigate the world. Amongst the plethora of symbols fashioned by the Chinese, Yin-Yang stands as the most fundamental. This binary, unique to Chinese culture, embodies a relationship of mutual opposition, dependence, and transformation. Unlike the Western penchant for static, absolute, and isolated linear logic, Yin-Yang presents a fluid interplay, marked by their capacity to contain elements of each other and transform upon reaching their respective zeniths. Their use in understanding the world exemplifies a dynamic equilibrium found in all aspects of life, a unity in opposites.

If Yin-Yang offers a one-dimensional dialectical symbolism, then the Five Phases expand this into a two-dimensional network of symbols. While Yin and Yang suffice to understand a single entity, the Five Phases map out a richer tapestry of interrelations among multiple entities. This is achieved through dualities of action - active and passive, positive and negative - forming a grid of generating, being generated, overcoming, and being overcome. The Five Phases - Wood, Fire, Earth, Metal, and Water - serve not as substances but as dynamic symbols in this relational network in the pattern that "consecutive elements generate one another, alternate ones overcome one another", forming a pentagram (alternate, overcoming) within a pentagon (consecutive, generating).

If only the overcoming relationship is involved, then three elements will form a full circle, as in the commonly played game "Rock, Paper,

Scissors". To establish a full circle involving both generating and overcoming relationship, however, requires five elements, fully encapsulates four relational dynamics without redundancy. Each element participates in generating, being generated, overcoming, and being overcome. The generating and overcoming cycle, depicted as a pentagon within a pentagram, illustrates an endless cycle, further complicated by the intersecting nature of these relationships. Thus, the relationships between any two elements are never absolute, static or simplistic but a complex, systemic interplay.

The choice of the Five Phases to complete the two circles of generating and overcoming, although not perfect, is really a genius work done. The Five Phases, then, are not physical substances but symbolic representations of dynamic dialectics, as explored in my article "Five Phases, Four Elements, and 2×2 Matrix: An Exploration of the Cultural Value of the Five Phases Through Comparison of Chinese and Western Ways of Thinking" published in Review of Natural Science Studies in Chinese Classics and Culture, vol. 5.

This network, once established, extends its influence through another layout of the Five Phases with "earth" in the middle and the other four phases to the four directions. It links to time (four seasons) and space (four directions and the middle), the senses (five colors, five tones, five flavors), human physiology (five organs) and psychology (five feelings), and even morality and ethics (five eternal values) through analogical reasoning, becoming a comprehensive framework that integrates all aspects of existence. Thus, the two-dimensional network of the Five Phases not only capture all existence of the world but also embody a systemic approach to understanding it.

To convey the dynamic interplay of dialectical relationships through time and space, the Book of Changes' 64 hexagrams come into play. These hexagrams, with their six lines each, represent a progression through time and space, from low to high, the proximate to the distant, the past to the future.

In sum, Yin-Yang, the Five Phases, and the Eight Trigrams (Bagua 八卦) exemplify the essence of Xiang Thinking, a testament to the unique cognitive landscape of Chinese culture.

3. The Nature of Xiang Thinking

The essence of Xiang Thinking lies in utilizing a non-conceptual "imagery" system, created by humans, to understand the world and articulate meaning. Significantly, meaning is not inherent but is imbued by people. Xiang Thinking represents a vital method of subjective engagement and interaction with the world. When we view the world through a dichotomous lens, such as "one divides into two," all things can be perceived in terms of Yin-Yang. Yin and Yang are exhaustive and inclusive, pervading every aspect of existence. Similarly, categorizing the world into five parts aligns everything with the Five Phases, elucidating the complex and ubiquitous relationships among them. Dividing temporal and spatial processes into six, as with the six lines (Yao, 爻) of the Book of Changes, allows for an exploration of the unfolding of events. Summarizing all scenarios into 64 types encapsulates them within the 64 hexagrams. This is a complete system in terms of mathematics and universally applicable in practice. The early development of these systems was likely not entirely deliberate or instantaneous, but they evolved and matured over time, gradually reflecting and aligning with the intrinsic laws of development, thus fully harnessing the latent meanings and functions of these symbols.

Lou Yulie (楼宇烈) summarizes the characteristics of Chinese culture as "holistic association, dynamic balance, natural rationality, and intuitive thinking." These traits are vividly embodied in the concepts of Yin-Yang, the Five Phases, and the Eight Trigrams. It can even be argued that it is precisely the Xiang Thinking represented by Yin and Yang, the Five Phases, and the Eight Trigrams that has shaped and reinforced the holistic, dialectical, natural, and intuitive aspects of Chinese cultural identity. These conceptual frameworks not only illustrate but also significantly contribute to the unique features of Chinese culture, demonstrating an inherent preference for a more interconnected, dynamic, and intuitively grasped understanding of the world.

3.1. The Instrumental Nature of Xiang Thinking

In daily life, Xiang Thinking employs symbols as a medium to observe, comprehend, address, and solve problems. Traditional Chinese medicine (TCM), as a complete domain, serves as an excellent example to understand Xiang Thinking. The core of TCM, the doctrine of Zangxiang (脏象, organ Xiang), is founded upon the Xiang Thinking of Yin-Yang and the Five Phases (五行). TCM employs this cognitive toolkit to interpret the human body, understand diseases, administer treatments, and maintain health.

Xiang Thinking, as a conceptual tool, is characterized by its dialectical and open nature. For instance, Yin-Yang can be infinitely subdivided. Everything possesses aspects of Yin and Yang, and each aspect can be further divided into Yin and Yang. The *Taiping Jing* (太平经) states, "Though Heaven (天) moves upward without limit, it still has its Yin and Yang, pairing in twos"(天虽上行无极，亦自有阴阳，两两为合) and "Earth (地) also moves downward without limit, having its Yin and Yang, pairing in twos. Thus, one Yin and one Yang, endless above and below, without termination on the sides" (地亦自下行何极，亦自有阴阳，两两为合。如是一阴一阳，上下无穷，傍行无竟). Zhu Xi (朱熹) expressed this idea as: "In terms of Heaven and Earth, there is Taiji (太极, Yin and Yang) within them; in terms of all things, each has its Taiji" (在天地言，则天地中有太极；在万物言，则万物中各有太极). Similarly, each of the Five Phases contains aspects of all five (一行当体即有五义), as noted in Xiao Ji's (萧吉) The Fundamentals of the Five Phases (Wuxing Dayi 五行大义) and Zhang Jiebin's (张介宾) commentary on its application in the TCM: "Each of the Five Organs contains the Five Phases" (五脏各具五行之妙).

By avoiding the rigidity and absoluteness of conceptual thinking, this holistic and dialectical framework encompasses a broader set of correct answers. This openness and flexibility allow different TCM schools to develop entirely unique theories and treatment principles and methods based on the same Zangxiang doctrine.

This flexibility, however, also imparts a certain ambiguity to the tool. As Mr. Lou Yulie questions, "Is clarity or ambiguity closer to the true nature of things?" Given the limitations of human cognition and the complexity and infinity of the world, precise expressions based on human experience often become one-sided, losing much information, connections, and meanings. He observes, "The development of science increasingly recognizes that fuzziness is closer to the true nature of things, while clarity often represents a more fragmented understanding." The ambiguous nature of symbols provides a more inclusive framework for thinking, presenting multi-referential approaches to health and disease within an integral, interconnected, and dialectical mindset. In TCM, not only are Yin-Yang and the Five Phases considered symbols, but also concepts like deficiency and excess, cold and heat, and Qi and Blood. These should not be solidified, conceptualized, or fixed, but dynamically understood in different contexts.

When facing complex systems like society and life, the advantages of Xiang Thinking as a cognitive tool become even more evident compared to linear logical thinking.

3.2. The Transcendental Value of Xiang Thinking

Chinese culture, rooted in the fundamental belief of unity between heaven and man ("Tian Ren He Yi", 天人合一), contains a transcendent dimension, a pursuit towards a higher plane, metaphorically referred to as the path upward ("Xiang Shang Yi Lu", 向上一路). In this context, Xiang Thinking (象思维), as a thought tool distinctively characteristic of Chinese culture, plays a crucial role in the elevation of life.

In Chinese philosophy, humans and the external world share a common origin, known as "Dao" (道). However, as a transcendent concept, Dao defies definition by language. Thus, Laozi in the Daode Jing states: "The Dao that can be spoken is not the eternal Dao" ("Dao Ke Dao, Fei Chang Dao", 道可道，非常道). Instead, Dao is described through terms like "the mystery of mysteries, the door to all wonders" (玄之又玄，众妙之门) and "vague and elusive" (恍兮惚兮). Similarly, in Buddhism, ultimate concepts like "Tath ā t ā " (True Nature, 真如) defy mental conception and verbal expression, leading Zen Buddhism to advocate a non-reliance on words or texts, as expressed in the teaching: "Cut off the way of speech, extinguish the place of thought" (言语道断、心行处灭). This is evident in Yunmen's three phrases (云门三句), "encapsulate the universe", "sever all streams", and "follow the waves" (函盖乾坤句、截断众流句、随波逐浪句), as well as the metaphorical exchanges in Chan Gongans (koans), often relying on Xiang to convey various states of being.

The inherent nature of Xiang Thinking transcends conceptual (linguistic) thinking. It focuses on the whole rather than getting lost in parts and details. Its dynamic nature avoids stagnation in rigid concepts and ideologies, always embodying a lively spirit. This is the charm of Chinese culture.

Transcendence, whether in personal life experiences or understanding the world, involves going beyond existing logical frameworks and cognitive systems. Undoubtedly, Xiang Thinking is better suited for intuitive grasping and epiphanic experiences. However, like conceptual thinking, it is merely a tool of human thought and should not be conflated with ultimate states of being. The "prime Xiang" (原象) and "Xiang of nothingness" (Wu Zhi Xiang 无之象) proposed by Wang Shuren as representative of the "Dao's Xiang" are arguably beyond the scope of Xiang Thinking. Their theoretical and practical significance warrants exploration. As tools serve a purpose, achieving understanding means not just "forgetting words" (De Yi Wang Yan, 得意忘言) but also "forgetting Xiang" (忘象), and as Mr. Lou Yulie suggests, citing Su Dongpo (苏东坡), ultimately "forgetting meaning to clear the mind" (忘义以了心), realizing the fulfillment of life.

For ultimate concepts that are "nameless and formless" (无称无名), and "without shape or imagery" (无形无象), language and imagery both reach their limits. As a tool with transcendental value, Xiang Thinking can be a bridge from this shore to the other, but it is not the other shore itself.

3.3. The Hierarchy of Xiang Thinking

Xiang Thinking is related to, but distinct from, image thinking (形象思维). As defined, Xiang Thinking is not merely a simple depiction of existing objects or limited to the intuitive image and appearance of things. It involves a process of refining and meaning-making in human cognition.

The development of Xiang Thinking evolved from using images as a basis for thought (以象为思) to using images to inspire thought (借

象来思). This transition marks a shift from passive reflection to active cognition, from perceiving concrete objects to grasping their holistic and interconnected nature. Legendary figures like Fuxi (伏羲) creating the Bagua (Eight Trigrams) and Cangjie (仓颉) inventing Chinese characters exemplify this shift. Their creations, inspired by observing and contemplating the world around them (仰观俯察), transformed physical observations into symbolic representations. As stated in The Commentary of Guliang (谷梁传), normal observation of familiar objects is called "seeing" (视), while contemplative observation of the unfamiliar is termed "observing" (观). This kind of observation involves an intuitive understanding of the unknown, not as a detached objectification but as a holistic and intuitive grasp, free from experiential bias and excessive analytical reasoning, akin to a child's innocent and curious perception. Both Bagua and Chinese characters are representative products of Xiang Thinking. "Observing Xiang" (观象) and "observing principles" (观法) demonstrate a typical cognitive mode in Chinese culture, where symbols are used for perception and expression. This activity of "obtaining Xiang" (取象) and "establishing Xiang"(立象) represents the core layer of Xiang Thinking being discussed. It differs from primitive image thinking that predates language and concepts, as well as from the general image thinking common in various cultures, being a higher level of cognitive function with creative recognition.

The function and value of symbols are directly proportional to their generality and integrative nature. Small symbols serve as substitutes or analogies for specific objects, while large symbols can provoke exploration of ultimate questions about the laws of nature and the essence of life. The symbols we've discussed, like Yin-Yang, the Five Phases, and the Bagua, all consider the whole and relationships: the relationship between Yin and Yang, the interrelations of the Five Phases, the relationships between the trigrams and within the hexagrams. The holistic, dialectical, and organic thinking characteristic of Chinese culture is a hallmark of high-level Xiang Thinking. Such thinking has long become a habitual mindset for the masses, "used daily without awareness" (百姓日用而不知 from the Book of Changes).

4. Xiang Thinking and Chinese Art

Chinese art is undoubtedly deeply influenced by Xiang Thinking, displaying a cultural style unique to the Chinese people in both aesthetic preferences and forms of expression.

Art and imagistic thinking are inseparable, involving perception with imagery, expression through imagery, and an intuitive grasp of aesthetics. When Alexander Gottlieb Baumgarten established aesthetics, he positioned it as the study of sensibility, also known as intuitionism, distinct from the study of reason in logic and the study of will in ethics. Beauty, too, is non-objectified and non-ready-made; it requires the infusion of human agency, not through logical rational reasoning, but through what is known as intuitive and emotional perception of beauty. Tang Yijie (汤一介) defined beauty as "the unity of sentiment and scene" (情景合一), while Ye Lang (叶朗) emphasized "beauty in imagery" (美在意象) and the intermingling of sentiment and scene (情景交融).

Chinese art, influenced by Xiang Thinking, has distinct characteristics compared to Western art and aesthetics. Western art focuses more on form and quantitative relationships, such as proportions, perspective, geometry, and lighting in painting. In contrast, Chinese art emphasizes subtler connections and feelings that transcend concrete physical forms, as described by Sikong Tu (司空图): "image beyond the image, scenery beyond the scenery, charm beyond the charm, and purpose beyond the style" (象外之象，景外之景，韵外之致，味外之旨). This is akin to the idea that "the best flavors often lie beyond the sour and salty in food." In this realm of "limited words but unlimited meaning" (言有尽而意无穷), Xiang Thinking particularly excels.

Just as logical thinking exists alongside Xiang Thinking in Chinese culture, Chinese artistic tradition also encompasses realism and representational fidelity. However, what most distinctively reflects the Chinese spirit, brought forth by Xiang Thinking, is its openness, interconnectivity, subtlety, ambiguity, and transcendence, forming a realm "between likeness and unlikeness" (似与不似之间) and "transcending the mundane to the magical" (出神入化). For example, "Yi (逸)" represents transcendence over the mundane while "Zhuo (拙)" signifies the avoidance of intricacy (precision). Many categories in Chinese art criticism, such as Qishi (气势, momentum), Fenggu (风骨, character), Shenyun (神韵, charm), and Yijing (意境, artistic conception), are difficult to express in Western languages.

Cognitively, the "upward observation and downward examination" (仰观俯察) of Xiang Thinking is not merely an aesthetic activity, but it possesses the core element of Western aesthetics, which is "intuitively grasping." However, in Chinese culture, Xiang Thinking involves "communicating with divine virtue" (通神明之德) and "classifying the emotions of all things" (类万物之情), encompassing both metaphysical pursuits and concerns for the material world. This intuitive grasp is a method of perceiving and interpreting the world, not just a perfection of sensory cognition as Western aesthetics might suggest. This kind of "observation" goes beyond visual perception to a holistic understanding, as exemplified by the butcher in Zhuangzi's "Butcher Ding slicing ox" (庖丁解牛), who grasp the ox with his spirit rather than perceptive organs, and Shao Yong's (邵雍) "Observing Things, Inner Chapter" (观物内篇), where understanding the laws of nature is perceived not with the eyes but with the heart and reason.

Functionally, in Chinese culture, art is never isolated, nor is there an abstract discussion of aesthetics. Traditionally, academia in China did not segregate into disciplines like sciences, humanities, and philosophy. Sensibility, rationality, and will are not strictly separated. For instance, the Book of Songs (诗经) embodies aesthetic, cognitive, ethical, and social functions. The ritual and music culture, with poetry, music, and dance at its core, encompasses politics, religion, ethics, art, education, military, and sports. Xunzi (Hsun Tzu 荀子) proposed that "beauty and goodness delight each other" (美善相乐), unifying the realms of aesthetic and moral. Confucian metaphors like "In the cold of winter, we see the pine and cypress are the last to fade" (岁寒而知松柏之后凋) and "The gentleman is like jade" (君子如玉) use Xiang to combine morality and aesthetics.

Regarding the relationship between beauty and truth in the concept of "Truth, Goodness, and Beauty," many Western studies, such as Subrahmanyan Chandrasekhar's Truth and Beauty: Aesthetics and Motivation in Science and Leonard Shlain's Art and Physics: Parallel Visions in Space, Time, and Light, have explored the significance of aesthetics in the discovery of objective scientific laws and theoretical breakthroughs. However, "truth" in Chinese culture is not the objective truth under the premise of subject-object dichotomy but the truth of returning to the original Dao in the unity of heaven and man (天人合一), as described by Tang Yijie. Ye Lang pointed out that "the world of imagery is a real world" in traditional Chinese aesthetics, representing the "manifestation of reality" and "direct experience" (现量). This concept of "direct experience" is borrowed from Buddhism, referring to intuitive perception before conceptual distinction. This world, unprocessed by thought differentiation, is also the most real present moment. Western cognition, being subject-object dichotomized and objectified, resolve the question of "what it is," whereas aesthetics and Xiang Thinking are intrinsic perceptions, addressing the question of "how it is."

Aesthetic activities and Xiang Thinking both avoid conceptual logic and perceive in unity with the object. However, the application of Xiang Thinking in Chinese culture is not limited to pure aesthetics but also encompasses cognition and ethics, melting truth, goodness, and beauty together.

Art and aesthetics themselves play an important role in the perfection of human nature, but in the context of Chinese culture, their expression and connotations differ. Confucian music cultivation was never solely for the enhancement of artistic education but for the elevation of overall personal character, an essential means of self-cultivation. Lou Yulie stressed "leading art with the Dao and achieving the Dao through art," as the Dao, although indescribable in words and concepts, can be experienced in the practice of body and mind unity. Calligraphy as the Dao of the brush, music as the Dao of the qin, and also the Daos of flowers, tea, incense, etc., are means of achieving the Dao through art. The highest realm of Chinese art is the transcendence of physicality, including both external physicality and the internal physicality of the self, reaching a state of detachment where self and object are forgotten. This transcendence inherent in Xiang Thinking is manifested in art. Inwardly, this process is the "humanization of the inner nature of man" and its transcendence, as Li Zehou (李泽厚) said; outwardly, it is the unity of heaven, earth, and humanity, the "three talents" (三才) in the form of achieving the state of heaven-man unity and oneness of all things.

The practice of achieving the Dao through art is practical, and Xiang only reveals its effectiveness and usefulness in practice. Compared to static concepts, Xiang is dynamic and infinitely rich. In dynamic balance, there is no dogma, and everything is lively. On the one hand, under the belief of "learning from below and reaching up," Chinese art characterized by Xiang Thinking constantly pursues an upward breakthrough in charm and realm; on the other hand, people enhance and improve their capability of Xiang Thinking through rich artistic practice. Artistic creation and Xiang Thinking promote each other.

Art is expressed through imagery, but there are profound and simple images. There are superficial physical images and profound metaphorical images. Xiang Thinking in art has different levels of expression. The analogy and evocative imagery in the Book of Songs and Confucian moral analogy are based on simple comparisons.

Xiang is not equivalent to form; good Xiang transcends form and expresses rich meaning. In art, this is reflected in "ancient paintings depict the idea, not the form" (古画画意不画形), as Ouyang Xiu (欧阳修) said. Xiang is also not equivalent to a symbol. Fixed symbols are rigid and dull, only producing formulaic and craftsman-like actions. Good Xiang however, is lively and endlessly charming, full of creativity and inspiration, opening the door of wisdom under Xiang Thinking.

"Using literature to convey the Dao" is a tradition of Chinese literature, but it does not mean that it must preach grand truths with a stern face. Precisely because the Dao cannot be spoken, it often needs to be expressed through Xiang. Yan Yu's (严羽) Canglang's Words on Lyrics (沧浪词话) criticized the Song Dynasty's approach of "using words as poetry, talent as poetry, and argument as poetry." But even in the poetry of Neo-Confucian scholars, there is no lack of vivid metaphorical expressions of abstract concepts, hence as Qian Mu (钱穆) compiled in Poetry Anthology of the Six Neo-Confucian Schools (理学六家诗钞), it demonstrates the ability to "embody and comprehend the Dao in everyday use, reaching ever more refined subtlety."

Aesthetic appreciation and artistic creation processes align with the processes of selecting and establishing Xiang, both being processes of imagistic thinking that exclude conceptual thinking. In aesthetic activities, Xiang exists as the object of appreciation, while under Xiang Thinking, Chinese art subtly elevates physical Xiang to a more enriched level of metaphorical Xiang. For instance, the physical Xiang of water and fire already encompasses multiple potential meanings like Yin and Yang, Kan (坎) and Li (离), north and south, heart and kidney in Xiang Thinking. These potential meanings are unique cultural resources that Chinese art can mobilize. This not only bridges the path from simple physical Xiang to profound metaphorical Xiang but also greatly shapes the lofty realm and extensive scope of Chinese art.

5. Conclusion

The prominence of imagery in Chinese art is not merely a reflection of aesthetic norms. The ancient tradition of Xiang Thinking, deeply embedded in Chinese history, has long been a part of various spiritual activities, including art. As a favored and adept tool of thinking for the Chinese, it has pioneered a holistic and dialectical mode of thought and contributed to shaping our integrated and interdisciplinary cultural characteristics.

The imagery of the Imagist movement mentioned at the beginning of this article predominantly dwells on the level of representations (images), reflecting the objects in the mind of the subject. Even the artists of the Italian Renaissance described by Hippolyte Adolphe Taine, who freely expressed their sensuous impulses in life and work, viewed things not just in parts or in words but "encompassing the whole, through the medium of the image." Their concepts emerged "not dissected, classified, or fixed into abstract formulas but in their entire, vivid, and vibrant reality" (from Philosophy of Art). Yet, their sensitive and intense vitality still remained at the level of representations. In contrast, the Xiang in Chinese art carries a much deeper cultural significance. Therefore, it should not be translated simply as "image" but should use the Chinese pinyin "Xiang," akin to Xiang Thinking.

Viewing Chinese art through the lens of Xiang Thinking allows for a more profound understanding of its unique characteristics. By consciously enhancing the utilization of Xiang Thinking, this ancient cultural tradition can be reinvigorated and flourish in the modern era.

About the author:

Dr. Liu Qian is the Vice Dean of Beijing San Zhi Cultural Academy and a former associate professor at the BiMBA Business School of the National School of Development at Peking University. He currently serves as the Executive Chair of the Global Youth Business Think Tank and is a researcher at the Institute of Modern Chinese Governance. Dr. Liu is also the author of *Quantum Leap* and the English-language book *Confucianism and Chinese Business*.

The Utilization of Chinese Narrative Systems in "Soulstealers"

The Poetics of Chen Li's Drama

ZHANG Lange

"Soulstealers" (《叫魂》) is the most distinctively Chinese play by Chen Li (陈力) and arguably one of the most thought-provoking and original works in the history of Chinese drama. By focusing on the soul-stealing case that spread across more than ten provinces in 1768, unsettling both the common folk and the court, the play delves deeply into the societal structures of mid-Qing China. The author's empathetic stance against injustice, his profound concerns for the nation and its people, as well as his sharp satire and keen observational skills, make this play a unique piece in the annals of Chinese theater.

A detailed analysis of the play's intellectual threads would require extensive discussion. This article aims to explore the poetic characteristics of Chen Li's drama, specifically how he seamlessly integrates the Chinese theatrical narrative system into the Western-imported art form of drama.

The Chinese narrative tradition encompasses the performance styles from the Song Dynasty's zaju (杂剧), Yuan Dynasty's sanqu (散曲), Ming Dynasty's chuanqi (传奇), to the modern and contemporary huabu (花部) opera. This rich tradition includes a comprehensive stage performance system featuring narrative, enactment, and allegory. In "Soulstealers," this tradition manifests in the following ways:

1. Latent Narrative Subject: This is evident as each character in the play, besides their identity within the narrative, also assumes the role of a narrator or even the author. Like how Shakespeare used heralds to convey high-level battlefield analyses, Chen Li's characters often exceed their immediate perspectives to deliver background information relevant to the plot. For instance, through Wang Er (王二) and Su Qi's (苏七) dialogue, we learn about an intricate network of folk organizations and their almost fanatical beliefs outside the Forbidden City. Through Ji Xiaolan's (纪晓岚) words, we gain insights into the emperor's private affairs and eccentricities. This latent narrator enhances the density of information and saves the need for scenes merely depicting the environment. Moreover, multiple perspectives enrich the characters, endowing them with typified and generalized traits. Writing about Wang Er and Su Qi also represents the lives of many impoverished people across various provinces. Characters also directly address the audience. The most notable example is Ji Xiaolan, who often comments on the emperor's collections and personality while facing the audience. These are things Ji would not dare say in public, representing his alternative self, but more accurately, these are the author's comments. These evaluations, reflecting contemporary perspectives, go beyond Ji's mental scope, transforming the play into a discourse. Although there are no introductory or exit poems typical of traditional Chinese plays, the extensive discussions reflect the author's stance and broad vision.

2. Illusionary Scenes and Role-Shifting Narration: Illusionary scenes transform narrative content into scenes. This is seen in the first act

where the beggar Wang Er persuades the female beggar Su Qi to join his path. To please Su Qi (by offering sacrifices to her parents), it appears as if Wang Er performs magic, causing papier-mâché figures to descend from the sky, which then serve tea and food, and even dress Su Qi, making her feel honored as if in a dream. In the subsequent story of Mr. Du and a certain Miss, characters temporarily take on roles, reminiscent of the role-shifting in Chinese opera (temporarily assuming another role). When the narrative involves crucial actions of the protagonist, Wang Er forces Su Qi into roles, particularly during her first reincarnation, where Wang Er considers himself Mr. Du and identifies Su Qi as his wife. When Su Qi faces fierce soldiers and throws her child to the ground, she becomes engrossed in the role, breaking down, earning Wang Er's rebuke. This scene-based narration clearly reflects the influence of legend storytelling and folk tales (Daoist folk tales featuring magic like turning stone into gold or planting and eating melons). Here, dialogues between two people transform into vivid theatrical scenes, with the papier-mâch é figures seen as either "deception" or live magic, making the narration more than just dry lines, but engaging theatrical performance. One of the characteristics of zaju is its allegorical and persuasive presentation. Early conscription plays (参军戏) like those of "Sun Shuao" (《孙叔敖》) or the "Two Saints Ring" (《二圣环》) use storytelling to deliver moral allegories. This traditional technique repeatedly appears in "Soulstealers." The play is woven together by numerous allegorical stories. From Wang Er and Su Qi's initial street tales to Ji Xiaolan's ghost stories and accounts of homosexuality and Xinjiang Taoists, to the emperor's stories of his favorite concubine Jinta (金塔) and frontier massacres, the narrative frequently employs storytelling to subtly express positions. However, the emperor's final brutal story of suppression during the soul-stealing case renders all other allegorical suggestions ineffective, as it starkly asserts his stance on the matter.

3. Variety Show Structure of Zaju: This structure subtly incorporates zaju's character configurations into the drama. For instance, in the second act, portraying high-ranking officials, the scene includes the emperor, eunuchs, favorites, and ministers, resembling the character setup in Song Dynasty zaju: an implicit composite performance group. Ji Xiaolan, akin to the end role in zaju, often steps out of the scene to narrate and comment on historical realities when facing the emperor's ostentatious street. The eunuchs serve as comic interjections, akin to the supporting clowns in zaju, providing comic relief, while the emperor and Gao Jin (高晋) perform as the primary figures presenting allegorical scenes.

4. Musical/Critical Structure and Variations Reflecting Musical Structure: Zaju integrates singing and discourse, creating a musical/critical structure. "Soulstealers" follows a similar pattern. Ostensibly, the external structure is the framework of the case play, but the courtroom scenes occupy less than a third of the play. Contrarily, an important palace scene, seemingly unrelated to the case (with minimal direct connection between Qianlong (乾隆), Ji Xiaolan, and the plot), occupies an equal proportion. This palace scene stands as a contrapuntal voice in the play, akin to another musical part, giving the play a symphonic or discursive structure. The author's broad vision and writing scope necessitate such an arrangement, juxtaposing the mid-Qing social panorama, encompassing both the high and the low, to present a comprehensive picture. In depicting the clash and entanglement of these forces, the play shapes vivid characters through what I call the "Ultimate Refinement Method" (九九归真法), akin to the ancient process of refining oil or smelting metals through repeated, intense heating, ultimately revealing the core of the characters. This method first appears in Wang Er's persistent psychological warfare against Su Qi, and is most successfully used in the combined interrogation by Gao Jin and his deputy against Wang Er. Gao

Jin's alternating soft-hard tactics and the deputy's brutal tortures showcase the harsh realities of survival for the lower classes. Yet, for the faith-driven Wang Er, these methods only incite a masochistic passion, ultimately leading to his death but also his ascension as a free, unrestrained soul. The most brilliant application of the "Ultimate Refinement Method" is seen in the interactions between the emperor and Ji Xiaolan. The emperor's sudden switch from casual chatting to ruthless denigration and suppression of Ji Xiaolan, only to restore his rank and reward him after breaking him down to the core, demonstrates the complete destruction of Ji's self-esteem, transforming him into a true servant. The use of variations is also evident, particularly in the final scene. With the protagonist dead and the plot concluded, this scene comprises entirely of "idle passages." Like film outtakes, it replays previous scenes. The emperor recounts the death of Nian Gengyao (年羹尧) in prison, interspersed with ghostly apparitions, followed by Ji Xiaolan's flattering new tune, Gao Jin's upgraded public executions, and finally, Wang Er and Su Qi's lament of their wanderings. These idle passages constitute a soul-stirring sonata, emphasizing the play's main theme and serving as a summary, compelling reflection on its central message.

The main theme is: in 1768, the land of China lost its soul. From the northern provinces to Jiangnan, from the government to the local counties, hundreds of people had their souls stolen. The skies of China echoed with the mournful cries of Wang Er and Su Qi, calling for the souls of those slaughtered, displaced, wrongfully killed or accused - those insulted and harmed. These calls, like the blood of the cuckoo, resonate endlessly, cursing the empire towards its downfall.

This structural analysis and detailed description vividly reveal that the real source of panic among the common people was not sorcerers or witchcraft but the racial subjugation and brutal suppression from the upper echelons. The officials' negligence in law enforcement and the people's prolonged exposure to oppressive despotism led to widespread panic among the populace.

The play's title references the work of American scholar Philip Kuhn (孔飞力). His extensive 270,000-character analysis covers various social strata in detail, yet remains superficial. This is not Kuhn's fault; the soul-stealing phenomenon is a complex historical and cultural issue, resulting from multifaceted social and psychological forces, embodying Lacan's "signifier" with the "Big Other" lurking behind it. Chen Li's concise 20,000-character play, through multi-layered dissection, unveils this hidden "Big Other," providing an unprecedented exploration of the Qing dynasty's governance from the perspective of national conquest and the Hegelian master-slave dialectic, uncovering the deep-seated maladies of cultural conquest over centuries. Moreover, Chen Li reveals the resilience of the lowly, as exemplified by the indomitable Wang Er, symbolizing the enduring spirit of the Chinese people.

Drama has been in China for over a century, with Chinese playwrights consistently following Western dramaturgy. Finally, a Chinese writer has integrated the Chinese narrative system into this imported art form, elevating and renewing the quality of drama. This is a fortunate development for Chinese drama and world theater arts.

About the author:

Zhang Lange, born in 1955 in Jiutai City, Jilin Province, graduated from the Central Academy of Drama with a degree in playwriting. He has worked as a professional playwright and journalist and later became a researcher at the Jilin Academy of Arts. Zhang has published over 200,000 words on drama theory in and authored books such as *The Humanistic Landscape of Chinese Drama* and *Drama Paradigms*.

Representation: Box, Grid, and Frame

Concepts in Western Art History: Preface to the 2nd Edition of "Representation and the Turn in Art History"

GAO Minglu

This book is a summary of work I have done intermittently over the past two or three decades, some of which comes from my research notes in China during the 1980s. At that time, I published an article titled "Contemporary Art History as General History" (《作为一般历史学的当代美术史》), which served as the preface to *A History of Contemporary Chinese Art (1985-1986)* (《中国当代美术史（1985—1986）》) completed in 1987. Although it reflects my thoughts after reading Western historical and art history works introduced in the 1980s, its more important purpose was to assert the legitimacy of writing contemporary Chinese art history. At that time, contemporary Chinese art had just started and had only developed for a few years, making both its creative practice and historical writing new and controversial.

In the early 1990s at Harvard University, I dedicated most of my time and energy to reading and researching Western art history theory. Having direct access to Western art historians and critics was a precious opportunity, and I attended many seminars and lectures, writing numerous research notes and papers. Harvard's libraries are among the best in the world, not just for their extensive collections but also for their ability to ensure access to books. Even if a book was checked out, you could usually find it in another branch. The campus was filled with bookstores, including many second-hand stores. By 1999, only two or three remained, but the basement of the Harvard Bookstore still thrived, offering great finds at half the original price. I visited daily and collected many old art history books.

One of the most beneficial courses I took was the "Methods and Theories of Art History" seminar for doctoral students, taught by Professor Joseph Leo Koerner from Harvard's Department of Art History. I still have the worn syllabus from over twenty years ago. At that time, Harvard's art history department was full of talent, with figures like William Norman Bryson and Yve-Alain Bois of the "October" group, as well as Henry Zerner, an expert in art history and theory. I participated in their seminars and wrote English research papers for each. Parts of these papers are included in chapters of this book, such as content in Chapter 7 on Romanticism, drawn from a paper for Zerner's seminar on Romantic art theory. Discussions on the avant-garde, especially the Russian avant-garde, come from papers written for Bois's modernism seminar. Bryson and others also collectively taught a visual culture theory course at Harvard, drawing students from various departments, filling large lecture halls with hundreds of students. I took detailed notes and recordings, which became valuable references for my research on Western art theory and criticism.

Since 2001, I have taught Western art history methodology courses to undergraduates and graduates at the State University of New York and Sichuan Fine Arts Institute (四川美术学院). Much of the content of this book comes from my teaching materials in the U.S., incorporating extensive reading selections. In China, I organized graduate students and young teachers to translate classic art history articles, and signed contracts with domestic publishers to publish a series called *Harvard Art History Classics* (《哈佛艺术

史经典系列》). However, due to heavy teaching loads and my commitment to contemporary Chinese art history and criticism, my health declined, leading to several hospitalizations. These plans were ultimately abandoned, but I greatly admire scholars like Fan Jingzhong (范景中), Yi Ying (易英), and Shen Yubing (沈语冰) for their work in introducing Western art history, which is crucial for Chinese academic teaching and research.

In 2006, editor Tan Yan (谭艳) from Peking University Press visited my Beijing apartment to discuss publishing my research on art history theory. We signed a contract, and over twenty years have passed since then. Regardless of the outcome, I am gratified that this book summarizes my work and thoughts in this area, fulfilling a long-held wish.

Many ideas in this book come not only from Western art history theory but also from my early research on ancient Chinese art and over thirty years of involvement in contemporary art history, criticism, and curatorial work. The issue of "representation" is deeply connected to my thoughts on contemporary art. I feel that art and theoretical practices since the 20th century have been derivatives of representation theory. Our art historians and artists have made their own creations and historical logic, but without understanding the development and implications of Western representation theory since the Enlightenment, we may never fully understand ourselves. The influence of postmodernism since the 1980s on contemporary Chinese art creation and theory is significant. For example, many stances and narrative methods in Chinese contemporary art criticism and creation over the past 30 years can be categorized into postmodern "cultural political linguistics," or what I call the "frame" theory model.

In writing this book, I published some preliminary ideas in the controversial book *On Yi Pai: A Theory Subverting Representation* (《意派论：一个颠覆再现的理论》). A thin volume, *On Yi Pai* aims to clarify Western representation theory, suggest the possibility of transforming tradition and establishing different theoretical perspectives, and integrate methodological approaches to art creation, criticism, and history. However, *On Yi Pai* was never meant to bear such a heavy burden alone. It should have been published after this current book to better explain why I criticize representation theory and propose the Yi Pai perspective, despite the term "subversion" seeming extreme. Its intent is reflection, inclusiveness, and transcendence. Given the constraints of its length, some critical issues were not fully explored.

On Yi Pai sparked significant reactions, including intense criticism. These critiques motivated me to complete the current book more quickly, as they did not address the issue of representation, which is the starting point of *On Yi Pai*. With this book, readers and academic peers can better understand why I critique representation theory in *On Yi Pai* and the reasons and basis for proposing the Yi Pai perspective.

What is representation? Why do I see it as the foundation of art history theory since the Western Enlightenment? These questions cannot be answered briefly or in a few articles. This book provides a basis for further discussion. Therefore, I did not immediately respond to the critiques of the Yi Pai because I realized that continued writing was urgent. In hindsight, the process may have taken too long, with many moments of silent contemplation and the writing of over 500,000 words, but it was an invaluable enjoyment for me.

This book does not categorize Western art theory from perspectives such as aesthetics, cultural studies, or sociology. Instead, its main narrative follows the historical development of representation theory. I referenced existing English-language publications on art history methodology, which commonly categorize by school of thought. For example, Donald Preziosi's edited anthology on art history methodology includes clear introductions and is comprehensive. He organizes the chapters by aesthetics, style, formalism, iconography, modernity, deconstructionism, and museology, introducing key theorists and their views. Vern G. Minor's "Art History's History" is not an anthology but a monograph that traces the origins of art history and introduces various modern art history theories. I used these two books as textbooks for my graduate seminar on art history methodology in the U.S., while supplementing them with additional articles not included in the original texts. These supplementary readings were compiled into anthologies for my students.

There are also many specialized studies on individual historians or schools of thought. For instance, *Michael Podro's The Critical Historians of Art* is an excellent book for understanding the development of early German (and European) art history theory. I remember Professor Koerner at Harvard once told me in 1993 that Podro's book should be translated into Chinese. This is not only because Podro's writing is excellent, but also because it was the first book to introduce early German art history theory to English readers. Koerner, being an expert in 18th and 19th-century German art history, naturally cherished this book. However, Bryson told me that Podro's book was "too outdated." From the perspective of new art history, this might be true. Indeed, from a postmodern art history research perspective, it may be considered "obsolete." Nevertheless, I still appreciate Podro's book for its clear explanations, and I have referenced many of his viewpoints in this book.

Another valuable resource is the two-volume *Key Art Historians*, which discusses the most important philosophers, art historians, and critics in Western history. Each entry provides an overview of their theoretical viewpoints and major works, making it an essential introductory book for art history and theory. However, it lacks an overarching summary, with each biography being independent and without interconnections.

There is an abundance of English-language publications and anthologies on modernism and postmodernism. For instance, Francis Frascina's anthology *Pollock and After: The Critical Debate* reflects the contentious viewpoints on modernism. Brian Wallis's edited collection "Art After Modernism: Rethinking Representation" is also suitable for readers, especially as it examines postmodernism from the perspective of "representation." Ultimately, researchers must engage with the seminal works of each art historian.

In my writing, I referred to existing classifications and frameworks in Western art history methodology books, as these classifications are clear and helpful. However, what relationships exist between these schools of thought? How did these relationships form the current historical logic and context? What are their internal driving forces? These questions require further exploration. Additionally, even though these classifications are clear, contradictions sometimes arise. For example, categorizing Clement Greenberg (1909-1994) as a formalist (opposed to sociology) might be accurate, but that does not mean Greenberg lacked a sociological perspective. His criticism has evident Cold War ideological elements, which many Western art historians acknowledge. Similarly, the stylistic classifications of Alois Riegl (1858-1905) and Heinrich Wölfflin (1864-1945) have issues, such as often overlooking the will principles they pursued. Structuralism, deconstructionism, and the New Art History all share a core focus on the relationship between verbal concepts and images, texts and contexts—issues of representation that stem from Enlightenment innovations.

Therefore, I attempt to break these classifications from the philosophical foundation of Western art history—the development history of representation theory. By following the historical logic of "representation," I aim to revise and re-organize these classifications, interpreting their internal relationships. This book is fundamentally intended to comprehensively introduce Western art history theories, using representation as the main thread to discuss these diverse theories. This approach is challenging but also represents a non-Western perspective interpreting the development of Western art theory, which is significant. Combining the introduction of theories with the concept of representation while maintaining a balance between narrative and critique is my main focus and biggest challenge. I must maintain consistency in certain core concepts to ensure logical and structural coherence.

Given this consideration, this book uses English publications as references. Even when consulting Chinese translations, I compare them to the English texts, adhering to the original English concepts and semantics. Chinese translations often contain conceptual ambiguities, not due to the translators but because of different interpretations. Thus, I strive to align my usage of concepts with the original English texts. Meanwhile, I include existing Chinese translations in the bibliography for the readers' convenience.

Why "Representation"?

I believe that when most readers see the subtitle "Representation and the Turn in Art History," they will immediately have questions: What does the concept of "representation" mean? Why use this concept to encapsulate the complex and rich history of Western modern art and art theory? This is a crucial issue. I argue that the philosophical foundation of Western modern art history and criticism is the Enlightenment-established "representation" or "representationalism." Western scholars also have two views on the issue of representation: one continues the ancient Greek notion of mimesis, using representation to indicate realistic art forms. However, in contemporary Western art history and criticism, this

view is mostly limited to general or non-theoretical popular expressions.

Most Western scholars and theorists regard representation as much more complex than mimesis, involving the intricate relationship between visual perception and verbal statements. They tend to view representation as part of philosophy and linguistics, thus surpassing the level of visual mimesis. Most philosophers and theorists discussed in this book, from Martin Heidegger (1889-1976), Walter Benjamin (1892-1940), Meyer Schapiro (1904-1996), Greenberg, Peter Bürger (1936-), Fredric Jameson (1934-), Jean-Francois Lyotard (1924-1998), Bryson, to Arthur C. Danto (1924-2013) and Hans Belting (1935-), probably do not consider representation merely as realistic or mimetic art. Conversely, I believe many in China still misunderstand representation as simply aligning with Marxist reflection theory or realist art styles.

Thus, representation theory differs from the Greek notion of mimesis or its subsequent revisions and developments. It is also distinct from non-Western theories, such as ancient Chinese literary theories. It represents a new development in modern art theory since the Enlightenment. Modern art theories since the Enlightenment revolve around this core issue. For example, formalism, conceptual art, readymades, and the pictorial turn all potentially relate to representation.

So, what is representation? In the first chapter of this book, I define representation in one sentence: Representation is the foundation of Western art epistemology, positing that "the essence of art is the replication of the correspondence between the mind's consciousness and external objects." The keyword here is "correspondence." In other words, if art represents something, it is the order imposed on the external world by consciousness. Hence, in artworks and art history narratives, the structure of the artwork must completely and perfectly substitute for the order of consciousness it expresses. This is the philosophical principle of representation established by Enlightenment thinkers. As Friedrich Hegel (1770-1831) stated, "Art only represents those things that align with the absolute idea." Although Hegel's assertion might seem absolute and outdated, careful study of modern and contemporary Western theory reveals that this fundamental view has influenced many art movements, including the end-of-art theories of the past two decades and current popular theories of "contemporaneity." Whether opposing or supporting Hegel's view, one cannot avoid the representational theory established by Enlightenment thinkers (discussed in Chapter 2).

Even deconstructionism, which critiques Enlightenment metaphysical idealism, does not reject representation. Instead, it extends the explicit idea of representation to mark the unmarked, referring to the invisible discourse center within the text. This is discussed in later chapters as "boundless representation." Deconstructionism's boundless representation and Hegel's manifestation of ideas are like two extremes on a pendulum's trajectory. But however extreme, they still operate within the realm of representation.

Concepts like "correspondence," "matching," and "substitution" are crucial for representation theory. All these concepts express the same idea: representation implies "the fullest equivalent." In Western art theory, debates about "resemblance" often revolve around this ultimate value of complete equivalence. As some Western theorists state, representation is akin to buying goods with money—an exchange of equivalents. We seem to have naturally accepted this notion. However, upon deeper reflection, other non-Western cultures and art histories may not emphasize such correspondence. For example, Chinese concepts like "意在言外" ("the meaning lies beyond the words"), "超以象外" ("transcending the image"), and "大象无形" ("the great form is without shape") do not stress the correspondence and substitution functions of art. Instead, they emphasize asymmetry and non-correspondence, which I call "differentiation" relationships. Artworks suggest certain phenomena or meanings indirectly (e.g., through analogy or metaphor). This pursuit has continued in Chinese art since the 20th century, despite the profound influence of Western modern art. In a book on 20th-century Chinese art history, I particularly addressed this issue and traced Chinese art history from this asymmetrical theoretical perspective.

As mentioned earlier, Western concepts of representation do not refer to specific art forms or styles like realism. In representation theory, the modes of artistic expression based on the principle of correspondence can be realistic, conceptual, or symbolic. These manifest in Western modern art as three main forms: realism, conceptualism, and abstraction (discussed in the book's concluding section). Theories legitimizing the absolute correspondence between art images and objects, art concepts and images, and art content and form are the methodologies of representation. These methodologies can be for art creation or art historical narrative. When a methodological model no longer fits the new theoretical fashion of an era, it faces the fate of innovation or replacement.

Representation has been the foundation of Western art theory since the Enlightenment. Although the media forms and types of corresponding representation are diverse, such as realism, conceptualism, and abstraction, we cannot take any single type as the sole form of representation. Ancient Chinese art also has its classifications—principle, knowledge, form, the "Six Principles," the "Six Canons," analogy, metaphor, the relationship between words and meaning, and the poetic genres "feng (风)," "ya (雅)," and "song (颂)." However, these theories do not fiercely demand extreme independence and separation of different types like modern representation theory does. For instance, the extreme opposition between abstraction and realism, the separation of aesthetics and society, and the separation of concepts and images result from Western modernist representation theory. In contrast, Chinese traditional theories of principle, knowledge, and form and the "Six Canons" and "Six Books" are mutually referential and integrated. Even in the 20th century, under the influence of Western learning, Chinese modern scholars and artists still advocated integration. Wang Guowei's "Three Realms of Poetry" integrates the poet, the object, and the process of experience. In the early Republic of China, Cai Yuanpei advocated "aesthetic education as a substitute for religion," contrary to the Enlightenment thinkers' separation of art and religion. Hu Shi's integration of current time, current choice, and current reason into modern truth also reflects the logical continuity between Chinese culture and art in pursuing modernity. Therefore, discussing and analyzing representation theory in Western modern art history helps us understand and organize our own art history.

In conclusion, the core concept of "representationalism" proposed by Enlightenment thinkers in the 18th century is an important category in Western dualistic philosophy. It is the core and foundation of Western art epistemology, capable of integrating the development history of Western art concepts. This is because it serves as a bridging concept for frequently occurring dualistic categories in Western philosophy, linguistics, and art history theory. These categories include subject and object, spirit and matter, content and form, text and context, signifier and signified. With the philosophy of representation, the possibility of exchange and substitution within these dual categories emerges, embodying the "equivalent exchange" principle mentioned earlier.

Thus, representation is not merely about depicting the "real" objects seen by the eye onto the canvas. It involves a crucial principle across various disciplines, including theology, linguistics, and sociology—the principle of certainty. Since Western traditional theology and modern art history have focused on the meanings conveyed by artworks (divinity, zeitgeist, ideological themes) and their corresponding styles and "isms," concepts such as symmetry, absoluteness, and certainty have become the truth principles for art historians interpreting the meaning of art. Serving these "truth validations" are word-based images (or image-based words), such as symbols in classical iconography, signs in modernism, and discourses popular since postmodernism.

These concepts have spawned important sub-concept groups. However, selecting key sub-concepts related to the historical logic of representation's development is crucial. I identified three key concepts—box, grid, and frame—from the terms used by different art historians in various eras. These can be unified into a historical logic concept group, summarizing three stages in Western art history and representing three different epistemological models of art. I created an illustration to show the relationship between these three concepts (see Chapter 14, Figure 14-3).

Some Western scholars have mentioned the concepts of "box," "grid," and "frame" separately. Regarding "box," three different terms have been used: one is "self-contained," meaning a self-sufficient container. Michael Podro used this concept to define the basic method of classical art research by Riegl, Wölfflin, and Erwin Panofsky. He believed German classical art history followed the principle of a cubic box to analyze works and their symbolic meanings. Additionally, Gotthold Ephraim Lessing used the concept of "window" to discuss the principles of classical art, essentially referring to placing a narrative within a cubic box. The term "box" was directly mentioned by Panofsky, who, in his book "Perspective as Symbolic Form," drew a diagram (Figure 5) using a "space box" to discuss the principles of Renaissance art creation. Regarding "grid," Rosalind Krauss, a student of Greenberg and a prominent critic from the "October" group, wrote an article discussing the modern "grid" in painting, viewing it as a split and unity between spirit and narrative. Lastly, Immanuel Kant was the first to introduce the concept of "frame" as an aesthetic term, emphasizing the value of the artwork within the frame, with the frame itself being mere decoration. Jacques Derrida later criticized Kant's notion of internal value. Derrida argued that a work becomes a work, or the internal becomes internal, because of the existence of the "frame." The "frame" determines where the work is produced, for whom, and, where it belongs (where it is displayed).

I discovered that while these scholars discussed these concepts, they were not limited to perspective. They subtly suggested specific modes of art creation and understanding during their respective periods. However, they only focused on one concept at a time, addressing a particular style of an era, without ever discussing "box," "grid," and "frame" together. Nor did they interpret them as inseparable historical concepts within the "evolutionary" chain of Western art history. Thus, when I finally managed to use the conceptual imagery of "box," "grid," and "frame" to combine Western art historical epistemology and narrative principles into a historical logic, I felt extremely excited! Although this is just my personal view, I believe it has a self-sufficient nature, open to testing and criticism. Therefore, I eagerly share it with readers and colleagues.

About the author:

Gao Minglu is an art critic and curator from Tianjin, China. He holds a Ph.D. from Harvard University and currently teaches in the Department of Art History at the State University of New York at Buffalo.

The Modern Significance of Calligraphy

A Dialogue on Ancient Script and Calligraphy

LIU Zhengcheng & RAO Zongyi

The renowned sinologist, Rao Zongyi (饶宗颐), passed away on February 6, 2018, at the age of 101. During his lifetime, he was an honorary professor at the Chinese University of Hong Kong and Nanjing University, among other institutions, and the president of the Xiling Seal Art Society (西泠印社). His scholarship spanned virtually all areas of Chinese studies, achieving remarkable accomplishments, and he was proficient in Sanskrit. He was often mentioned alongside Ji Xianlin (季羡林), with the academic community referring to them as "Southern Rao and Northern Ji."

To commemorate Rao Zongyi, today we present a dialogue between Liu Zhengcheng (刘正成) and Rao Zongyi from 1999 on "Ancient Script and Calligraphy." As Liu Zhengcheng stated in the preface of his book "Dialogues on Calligraphy Art: Liu Zhengcheng's Calligraphy Dialogues" (《晤对书艺:刘正成书法对话录》): "In the modest study-cum-living room of Rao Zongyi's apartment on the Mid-Levels in Hong Kong, our conversation suddenly brought Chinese calligraphy into a broad historical and cultural perspective. I felt as though I had entered a dazzling treasury. At that time, Rao Zongyi wanted to show me a photograph of the Rosetta Stone (《罗塞塔》) he mentioned during our talk. Although he couldn't find it then, I found it after returning to Beijing. His comparisons between ancient Egyptian and Babylonian cultures and the issues of script and calligraphy opened my eyes to the common features of human artistic origins and allowed me to gather many 'fruits' from the 'tree of Chinese characters.'"

Time: May 1999

Place: Rao Zongyi's residence on the Mid-Levels, Hong Kong

Participants:

Rao Zongyi (Chair Professor at the Chinese University of Hong Kong, Director of the Institute of Chinese Culture)

Liu Zhengcheng: (then Deputy Secretary-General of the China Calligraphers Association, Editor-in-Chief of *Chinese Calligraphy* (《中国书法》), now Editor-in-Chief of *Complete Works of Chinese Calligraphy* (《中国书法全集》), President of the International Calligraphy Association)

I. The Chinese Character Tree—The Successful Development of Chinese Pictographs

Liu: Have all the pictographic symbols in Western writing systems been phased out?

Rao: The strength of Chinese characters lies in their one-character, one-sound structure, whereas Western systems often involve five or six sounds for a single symbol, along with other constraints. Overly complicated systems inevitably perish. Eventually, they adopted the current alphabet, which greatly simplified things—using letters to represent sounds and relying on language to manage everything. In contrast, the Chinese place greater emphasis on the written word. If our ancestors had followed the West and switched to an alphabet, you calligraphers would have been out of a job long ago! (Laughs)

Liu: If that happened, Chinese tradition would've been destroyed.

Rao: Western letters are entirely phonetic systems. Even in ancient Greek civilization, they abandoned cumbersome pictographic letters.

Liu: Do you think the long-lasting pictographic nature of Chinese script is inseparable from its abstract beauty?

Rao: Firstly, each character has one sound, with pictophonetic construction being predominant. This combination preserves the pictorial beauty while maintaining a connection with language, forming a literary system that integrates form and sound. Chinese script thus doesn't chase linguistic changes. Secondly, Chinese political life has always emphasized applying script to decrees and rites, rather than language. Therefore, language development is relatively distant from script. Hence, Chinese script controls language, keeping "script and language separate" (书同文). The notion of "unifying script" ostensibly standardizes character forms, but it actually prevents script from changing with language. Letters are entirely phonetic, while Chinese characters are only partially phonetic, keeping script non-phonetic. This integration of art, literature, and the beautiful combination of form and sound has created a flourishing "Chinese Character Tree" (汉字树), with rich branches and leaves. The intertwined relationship of script, literature, and art (calligraphy) constitutes the greatest charm and distinctive feature of Chinese culture.

Liu: The New Culture Movement separated script and language. Did the vernacular movement have any negative effects?

Rao: The vernacular movement narrowed the gap between script and language, which was progress. However, if traditional excellence is seen as a burden and completely negated, that's entirely wrong.

Liu: Can modern prose compare aesthetically to the prose of the Tang and Song masters?

Rao: It depends on the perspective. The perspectives of today and ancient times differ, and they shouldn't be confused. One cannot use modern standards to judge the ancients, and vice versa.

Liu: Modern calligraphers rarely write in vernacular; most write classical poetry and prose. Does this indicate that classical texts have greater capacity within the same number of characters? Classical texts may have richer connotations and extrinsic meanings, while vernacular texts are more limited.

Rao: Not necessarily! But ancient works are inexhaustible!

Liu: Today's conversation seems to focus on two main points: the mystery of Chinese script's pictorial nature and its advantages in integrating form, sound, and meaning.

Rao: Another advantage is that character evolution is closely related to calligraphy. Each era's calligraphy has its own characteristics. Our works express the author's feelings and may resonate with viewers.

Liu: The Han dynasty summarized the "Six Principles" (六书) as the ancient rules for character creation.

Rao: The "Six Principles" were already applied in early oracle bone inscriptions. By the Yin (Shang) dynasty (殷代), Chinese script was mature, which enabled its inheritance and development. If it were as complex as foreign scripts, it might have switched to letters long ago.

Liu: Some say the "Six Principles" were the Han people's speculation. Is that correct?

Rao: The Han people didn't speculate; they summarized the principles, though not comprehensively. Calling it speculation is due to partial understanding. We shouldn't underestimate our ancestors!

Liu: You mean skepticism about ancient texts should be cautious?

Rao: Being too clever is harmful!

Liu: Li Xueqin (李学勤) said this century is an era of skepticism about ancient texts. We need to move beyond it.

Rao: I've long said skepticism is acceptable but shouldn't lead to outright denial. That's the scientific attitude.

Liu: You believe the "Six Principles" were applied in the Yin dynasty and are a key reason for Chinese script's vitality.

Rao: Exactly. That's why it flourished and remained popular.

Liu: Chinese script expresses profound meanings with simple graphics.

Rao: And its meanings grow richer over time!

Liu: You've studied Chinese and Western scripts for years. Comparatively, is Chinese calligraphy's charm mainly due to its unique script?

Rao: Calligraphy has several charms, with script being a significant aspect.

Liu: Some advocate for "modernizing calligraphy," even suggesting removing Chinese characters and replacing them with abstract forms.

Rao: What is self-created abstraction? I must loudly warn: Be cautious!

Liu: We shouldn't discard the most valuable aspects. Chinese characters have both beautiful forms and unique meanings. Completely abstract calligraphy would be the end!

Rao: Not just calligraphy, but many classical languages also stem from script.

II. The Modern Significance of Calligraphy—Expressing a Person's Spirit

Liu: Calligraphy is very popular on the mainland. People from all walks of life are involved. I've noticed many in Hong Kong are also engaged in calligraphy. What do you think is the modern significance of this traditional art?

Rao: The main significance is that calligraphy can express a person's spirit. Achieving such a level in calligraphy is challenging. Treating calligraphy merely as decoration is wrong. Calling it "visual art" is problematic because calligraphy isn't just visual; it primarily involves the mind and soul. No great calligrapher's work is just about visual appeal!

Liu: As the saying goes, "the handwriting reflects the person." In my article "The Tendency of Calligraphy to Become Artistic" (《中国书法的美术化倾向》), I mentioned the influence of art on Chinese calligraphy, but using artistic concepts to define calligraphy is problematic.

Rao: We shouldn't use purely Western concepts to discuss calligraphy. Literature and art are about the soul and personality. I read your study on Huang Daozhou (黄道周); it's excellent! His work reflects his spirit and personality. All great calligraphers are like that. Wang Duo (王铎), despite being a "second minister," was a great poet, which is why his calligraphy was so good.

Art is not just about writing a few characters. Writing a few characters alone doesn't make an artist. I don't believe it!

Liu: Su Dongpo (苏东坡) said, "Ancient scholars discussed calligraphy along with the person's life; if not an outstanding person, their skill, though excellent, wasn't valued."

Rao: Exactly! We must first discard the term "visual art" to discuss calligraphy. Calligraphy isn't just visual; otherwise, it would be no different from cartoons.

Liu: What are your impressions and views on the development and achievements of calligraphy in the mainland and Hong Kong?

Rao: This question involves too much; different starting points yield different answers. Forgive me for not answering (laughs).

Liu: Not answering is an answer (laughs).

Rao: I think calligraphy can be regarded as art and is recognized by contemporary society and internationally. I'm very satisfied with that.

Liu: At the end of 1998, at the "Paris Chinese Calligraphy Art Exhibition" ("巴黎中国书法艺术大展"), President Chirac (希拉克总统) viewed the exhibition and wrote an inscription, praising Chinese calligraphy as the art of arts. He appreciated the beauty of calligraphy, showing its influence and charm. Professor Rao's intention in not answering might be to let calligraphy develop freely. Is that correct?

Rao: Calligraphy should develop freely! Why? Because art cannot be generalized; everyone has their unique insights and limitations. Dictating how they should create is unfeasible.

Liu: You mean calligraphers should express their opinions and not adhere to fixed formats but find their own paths.

Rao: Exactly! That's the best way; everyone is happy.

Liu: Thank you.

(Professor Rao Zongyi's dialogue is included in his *Collected Works of Rao Zongyi in the Twentieth Century*(《饶宗颐二十世纪学术文集》).

Li Jieren: Old Tastes, New Life

Reassessing the Judgment of "China's Zola"

LI Yi

The label "China's Zola," coined by Guo Moruo (郭沫若, 1892-1978) in 1937 to describe Li Jieren (李劼人, 1891-1962), has been popular for over eighty years and has become an authoritative title for the writer. However, this judgment contains misinterpretations, as it emphasizes the Western origins of Li Jieren's works while neglecting his deeper spiritual qualities— innovations rooted in traditional cultural elements. Strictly speaking, Li Jieren expressed modern life through the refinement of "old tastes," a literary model that differs from many modern writers and should be considered an alternative path in the study of modern Chinese literature.

In 1937, Li Jieren's "Great Wave" trilogy (《大波》) was published by the Zhonghua Book Company in Shanghai. Guo Moruo (郭沫若), his classmate from their time in Chengdu, was so excited after reading it that he "was intoxicated for four or five days. It had been twenty or thirty years since I spent entire days engrossed in a novel." Guo Moruo wrote a lengthy article, "Awaiting China's Zola" (《中国左拉之待望》), comparing Li Jieren to the French naturalist novelist Zola (左拉), believing that "Li's creative plan intentionally emulated Zola's 'Les Rougon-Macquart' series (《鲁弓·马卡尔丛书》)." He passionately called out, "Please quickly write your new 'Les Rougon-Macquart,' one by one!" Guo Moruo's anticipation for Li Jieren, despite not elaborating on the topic in detail, was undoubtedly a great support for his old classmate. Since then, "China's Zola" has become Li Jieren's most resounding title and widely circulated in the research on Li Jieren, especially from the 1990s onward, often regarded as a classic evaluation. From 1937, when this accolade was first given, through to the 1950s when Cao Juren (曹聚仁) referred to him as the "Oriental Zola" (东方的左拉), and continuing into the 1990s and beyond, the label "China's Zola" has been popular for over eighty years. However, the misalignment and discrepancies between Li Jieren's and Zola's literatures have been intentionally or unintentionally overlooked. For example, Li Jieren's article "French Naturalism and Its Novelists" (《法兰西自然主义以后的小说及其作家》) published in 1922 in "Young China" (《少年中国》) is often cited as evidence of his foreign literary influences. But in that very article, Li Jieren discussed the failures and drawbacks of the "Zola School," noting: "The success of the Zola School is entirely due to the method of experimental science, so when writing about a merchant, one must immerse oneself in the market, blend in with the traders, and then write. However, the failure of the Zola School lies precisely in this. It focuses only on practical experience, neglecting the power of the spirit."[1] By 1935, when he was conceiving and writing "Dead Water Ripples" (《死水微澜》), he firmly stated: "I will never impose modern thoughts on ancient people."[2] This suggests that, regardless of the "French literary trends" he was involved in or the "modern China" thoughts he adhered to, he had reservations and apprehensions. Therefore, if we consistently interpret Li Jieren's literary significance through the lens of certain "progressive" trends or "era" directions, it might be a risky endeavor. I am not attempting to deny the significant connections between Li Jieren and the

Zola model or French literature, but rather to emphasize that a more thorough and detailed discussion must include the writer's hesitations and prudence. We need to further contemplate: What are the differences between Li Jieren and Zola, or the so-called "modern thought" concepts? Shouldn't we more comprehensively review, clarify, and correct the significance of Li Jieren's writings? How did the various "old tastes," which the writer preserved and respected, translate into the modern "new life" he depicted? Taking the "Great Wave" trilogy as an example, we can examine and analyze the historical narratives and character destinies emphasized in the novels, in conjunction with Li Jieren's literary ideals.

The label "China's Zola" attached a French naturalist literary tag to Li Jieren, presenting an image of him responding to Western advanced literary trends. Over the years, scholars have summarized this approach: objectively depicting reality, the continuity of the novel (the "river novel"), the conscious pursuit of historical writing, and so on. These are the fundamental characteristics of 19th-century French literature, from Flaubert to Balzac and Zola and are also key resources for Li Jieren to move from the classical vernacular novel tastes of the late Qing and early Republican periods towards "new literature," ultimately constructing the "Great Wave" trilogy. In recent years, young scholars have analyzed the details of Li Jieren's borrowing from French literature, such as literary language, chapter structure, environmental description, portrait depiction, and psychological expression, dissecting how these influences drove the writer towards maturity. However, scholars studying Li Jieren often encounter doubts: even with evidence, including the writer's own accounts, Li Jieren's literary pursuits are not easily defined by this "French influence" or the trends of the times. The perceptive writer Zhou Keqin (周克芹) once said, "For years, we didn't dare talk much about Li Jieren's works because it was hard to pinpoint their exact themes."[3] Sinologist Cheng Yi (郑怡) found that the historical writing of the "river novel" in the "Great Wave" trilogy had its own characteristics. The so-called "epic" actually involved "tediously recounting a series of mundane activities such as living room conversations, drinking and dining, strolling and shopping, meetings and speeches, marriages and funerals."[3] Some scholars have noted an interesting phenomenon: Li Jieren strove to discuss the "structure" of his novels, but the art of "structure" borrowed from Zola did not leave a deep impression on the broader audience. What resonated more with the public were some descriptive methods, especially the depiction of female characters in his novels. "The interpretation and acceptance of Li Jieren have diverged so much that it has become a confusing account."[4]

Indeed, many of Li Jieren's "borrowings" from Zola and French literature seem tenuous and dubious, but his portrayal of a series of female characters shines brightly and appears methodical. These Chinese women have all acquired a French name: Madame Bovary.

The title "China's Zola" was a French label attached to Li Jieren by critics, but Li Jieren never translated Zola's novels. Instead, the father of French naturalist literature, Flaubert, was Li Jieren's true focus. He translated Flaubert's masterpiece "Madame Bovary" three times. Hence, "China's Zola" sometimes evolved into the more appropriate "Oriental Flaubert," and the protagonist of "Dead Water Ripples", Cai Dasao (蔡大嫂, or Deng Yaogu 邓幺姑), has been interpreted as "China's Madame Bovary." Not only Cai Dasao, but other female characters in the "Great Wave" trilogy such as Wu Dasao (伍大嫂, or Wang Sigu'er 王四姑儿) and Mrs. Huang Lansheng (黄澜生太太, or Long Er 龙二小姐) also exhibit rebelliousness, courage, and indulgence in desires similar to Madame Bovary, forming a veritable "Madame Bovary" ensemble. Some have even compared Chen Lihua, the protagonist of Li Jieren's other novel "Dance of the Heavenly Devil" (《天魔舞》), to Madame Bovary, suggesting an even closer connection between Li Jieren and French naturalist literature. [5]

From the emergence of new literature, the prominence of modern female consciousness, and the depiction of women in Li Jieren's early Republican-era novels, the appearance of women in the "Great Wave" trilogy undoubtedly bears distinct French marks, demonstrating the indispensable Western origins of new literature development. However, researchers have differing views, with even the term "Madame Bovary" eliciting various opinions. Liu Zaifu (刘再复) asserted that "Deng Yaogu is China's Madame Bovary,"[6] while Gao Yuanbao (郜元宝) argued, "Mr. Zaifu's claim that Deng Yaogu in 'Dead Water Ripples' is China's Madame Bovary is somewhat inaccurate because their origins, experiences, characters, and the author's intended meanings differ. The only similarity is their insatiable longing for a fresh world beyond their reality."[7] Moreover, some scholars contend that Li Jieren's "Madame Bovarys" are essentially half-new and half-old, with incomplete determination and action in their "anti-feudal" and "anti-traditional" efforts, thus contributing to Li Jieren's "narrative dilemma"[8]

Compared to the earlier "China's Zola" judgment, the characterization of "half-new and half-old" might again remind us to pay special attention to Li Jieren's local context when identifying the "anti-traditional" gestures in his characters and life scenes.

For instance, in Li Jieren's literary world, does Cai Dasao's temperament and behavior prove her rebellion against feudalism or her conservatism in yielding to feudalism? Perhaps neither is entirely accurate. Cai Dasao's behavior logic may be entirely unrelated to the feudal system. She neither wants to be confined by traditional rules nor intends to become a new woman of the anti-traditional era. The fundamental reason driving her actions is the enormous allure of "a good life" in Chengdu:

> *What especially enchanted Deng Yaogu was the description of the life of wealthy families in Chengdu and the dazzling attire of the women. Whenever the second aunt passionately recounted these stories, she couldn't help but rub her eyes and say, "My life is over, dragging out my days in the countryside! If I want to live the old life again, I'll have to wait for the next life! Yaogu, with your good fate and cleverness, you might marry into a city family in the future, and then you'll know what it's like to live in Chengdu!"[9]*

"The taste of life in Chengdu" became the driving force of life, the lever capable of influencing life's choices. To match the "three-inch golden lotuses (foot bonding)" of the ladies in the city, young Deng Yaogu gritted her teeth and endured the pain of foot binding, even quarreling with her mother who tried to dissuade her: "Mother, you can't control me! Why shouldn't a country girl's feet be bound small? I insist on binding them, insist on binding them, insist on binding them! If it kills me, it's my business!"[10] This is also a very typical scene: foot binding is seen today as a representative of "feudal" cultural oppression of women, and demanding foot binding is certainly a feudal thought, while opposing foot binding is a sign of modern women's liberation. However, in the Deng family, it was precisely the elders who cherished their daughter and opposed foot binding, while the rebellious Deng Yaogu insisted on it! Clearly, in Li Jieren's experience, feudal/anti-feudal was not sufficient to encapsulate the social changes he perceived. To understand Li Jieren's unique Chengdu stories, we need to step out of the past theoretical assumptions of "feudal/anti-feudal" or "Chinese tradition/Western modernity," and return to the character structure and survival logic of Cai Dasao (Deng Yaogu), first restoring the facts of their thoughts and emotions, and then making judgments.

Cai Dasao, Wu Dasao, and Mrs. Huang Lansheng, this ensemble of "Madame Bovarys," differ significantly from their French petite bourgeoisie counterparts in that they never had the romantic fantasies and spiritual dreams that transcended material and carnal desires. Nor did they end up committing suicide by poison due to the shattering of their ideals. Like Madame Bovary, Cai Dasao, Wu Dasao, and Mrs. Huang Lansheng rebel against the realities of family and marriage. However, Madame Bovary is evidently more immersed in intellectual and emotional adventures; her spiritual quality surpasses the ordinary, and it is the reality that deconstructs her fantasies that drives her out of this world. Thus, the symbolist poet Baudelaire, who could explore "Les Fleurs du mal," also exclaimed, "This woman is indeed sublime. She is Caesar of Capua, she pursues ideals!"[11] On the other hand, all the rebellions of Cai Dasao, Wu Dasao, and Mrs. Huang Lansheng stem from the deficiencies of real life rather than dissatisfaction with this mundane world itself. Therefore, they indulge in new pleasures, find comfort in material gains, and easily adapt to new environments and orders after resolving temporary crises. These Chengdu stories are unrelated to sublimity or romantic tales of love. As Deng Yaogu's parents "naturally no longer consulted their children and proceeded step by step according to rural customs. By around September 20th, Deng Yaogu naturally became Cai Dasao."[12] This natural progression still reflects a life driven by material instincts rather than spiritual fantasies. Li Jieren quietly observes and re-creates this, "writing from a biased perspective without satire,"[13] and the literary form is as "natural" as the Chengdu stories themselves. There is no stance of "translating" Zola or Flaubert, nor an intentional infusion of contemporary ideals to elevate societal vanguards. Therefore, there is no risk of falling into the "narrative dilemma."

From the perspective of seeking romantic legends, Madame Bovary's emotional fantasies may have some connection with the trend of female liberation during the May Fourth Movement. The May Fourth era was indeed a time for young people to dream, including dreams of national salvation, academic achievements, and family aspirations, along with dreams of free love. However, Li Jieren's "Great Wave" trilogy intentionally deploys "what contemporary writers lack,"[14] and "never imposes modern thoughts on ancient people."[15] He aims to present a local story outside of "modern thoughts," a narrative of human changes beyond the grand narrative of the era.

This local story, to some extent, recreates the traditional towns outside China's modern central cities. It meticulously reveals the brewing and occurring human movements and changes within the seemingly calm traditional town life, thus embodying "Dead Water Ripples." Here, the "dead water" is not the grand metaphor of stagnant China devised by poet Wen Yiduo (闻一多) out of intense indignation; Li Jieren's "Dead Water Ripples" is a direct portrayal of the self-satisfied provincial capital city life. Under the commercial cultural upheaval of the Ming and Qing dynasties, similar rudimentary forms of town life appeared in southern China, and the origins of the Chengdu story lie here. Li Jieren abandoned the oft-repeated surges and currents of the "era's main currents" in central cities and instead started from China's "non-central" cities, discovering another thread of the silent evolution of Chinese society and human nature. This discovery cannot be summarized using existing theoretical frameworks—whether it is the mode of importing Western literature or the mode of expansion of the May Fourth New Culture Movement.

Compared to the direct introduction of

Western literary concepts that highlight the central themes of May Fourth anti-traditionalism, Li Jieren's restoration of traditional ecology and his reliance on local provincial experiences might be considered as an "old taste." This "old taste" is, first and foremost, a traditional concern that lingers in the mind. Such a concern, deeply rooted in the past, allows Li Jieren to perceive that the traditional Chinese living environment is also quietly brewing and accumulating a potential for self-evolution, or in other words, is giving birth to its own new life demands. Li Jieren sensitively captures the subtle traces of self-evolution within traditional Chinese society and human nature, using these as important clues to observe new changes in life.

Historians have discussed an interesting phenomenon: in ancient Chinese society, mainstream ethical constraints did not completely suppress certain freedoms in the personal sphere. "The first kind of political freedom that emphasizes human rights never formed in traditional China. However, the second kind of moral or spiritual freedom appeared very early in China."[16] This is a curious form of separation, especially after the Song and Ming dynasties, as the development of the commodity economy increased this personal enjoyment tendency, even in a society dominated by Confucian ethics. Not only the citizen class but also intellectuals could build an emotional world outside family ethics.

In the late Qing and early Republic periods, similar situations expanded and continued in some regions of China where the commodity economy was developed, such as the Chengdu Plain. This is the richest agricultural civilization area in western China, where developed handicrafts and urban commerce appeared early. The prosperous and pleasurable urban life of Chengdu had a significant impact on the surrounding agricultural areas, gradually dismantling the traditional agricultural ecology of China. Moreover, due to the impetus of foreign economic

shocks and the invasion of foreign civilizations, this deconstruction force was stronger and more rapid than in any previous era. In Li Jieren's fictional world, we can see that the pace of people's life changes could no longer be stopped. Cai Dasao moved from Banzhuyuan to Tianhuizhen and then from Tianhuizhen to greater Chengdu, continuously changing her lifestyle; Wu Dasao, in the semi-tiled, semi-thatched house society of Shanglianchi, transitioned from loving her husband to frequently associating with "boyfriends" and finally finding shelter under Hao Yousan; Mrs. Huang Lansheng, from Miss Long Er to an official's wife, grew from a naïve and pure lady to maneuvering effortlessly among multiple ambiguous relationships with men, emerging as a heroine in the men's world. Among them, the continuous progression of Deng Yaogu (邓幺姑) — Cai Dasao— Gu Dasao (顾大嫂) is the most typical. Initially, Cai Sister was determined not to adopt foreign religions, but after becoming Gu Dasao, she soon followed into the church, even adopting Western fashion:

> *Her elder sister asked her where she learned to dress like that. She shook her head and smiled, "Young lady, if I tell you, you'll laugh... Last winter, with Jinwa's father, we went to the church for the foreign winter solstice festival and saw a foreign woman dressed like this... Do you think it looks good?"*[17]

All social and human changes start from within the traditional structure, more precisely from the self-dissolution of traditional concepts. In China, the signs of moving beyond agrarian civilization appeared repeatedly as early as the Song and Ming dynasties and became irresistible by the late Qing and early Republic periods. Before the new rationality was universally established, deconstructing traditional moral concepts and reviving natural human desires became a general trend, both domestically and internationally. Before Enlightenment rationality replaced religious theology, the West also experienced a sensuous revival during the Renaissance. Jacob Burckhardt described the societal phenomenon that first appeared during the Italian Renaissance: a hedonism based on selfishness, posing a significant challenge to medieval morality: "Individuals first inwardly freed themselves from the authority of a state, which was in fact despotic and illegitimate. What they thought and did, whether right or wrong, today would be considered rebellious. Seeing the success of others' selfishness drove them to defend their own rights with their own hands. When they sought to restore their inner balance, due to the revenge they pursued, they fell into the hands of the devil. Their love was mostly for the satisfaction of desires."[18]

This is the vibrant secular life depicted in Boccaccio's "Decameron". The progression of modern European culture included not only Shakespeare's dramas and poetry, and Petrarch's elegant sonnets but also the citizen's worldly portraits discovered by Boccaccio. The dual advancement of elite creation and secular discovery powerfully propelled the transformation of spirit. China's modernization process is similar, but unfortunately, the mainstream narrative of our literary history still focuses on how writers drew on foreign influences and how individuals transcended the mundane to achieve personal spiritual creation, while the continuous dialogue with the internal resources of secular society and the recording of the self-evolution of social culture remain largely unaddressed.

In Li Jieren's depiction of Chengdu, we witness a departure from tradition and the self-propelling progression of secular changes. This process, largely, does not need to imitate the models of elite culture; it is driven by the demands to "satisfy desires." As Cai Dasao summarized, "To live a lifetime in such wild joy,

it would be worth it even to die!"[19] Wu Dasao is equally straightforward: "A husband must earn money to support the family. Otherwise, he might as well close his eyes and be a turtle, living off his wife. If he wants to leave, he should never come back—she doesn't care for such a husband. She never wanted to live by sewing; 'marrying a man means clothes and food!' If she still had to rely on her needlework after marriage, she would rather not marry and be less burdened."[20] As for Mrs. Huang Lansheng, "She firmly believed that pleasure is the ultimate purpose of life. She was born to live like this, not by chance, and she could not betray herself or the will of heaven by being overly scrupulous."[21]

Li Jieren not only perceived that the changes in modern China stemmed from traditional China itself but also revealed the unique directions and characteristics of these changes. Firstly, the initiation of the change process lies in the deconstruction of traditional agrarian civilization rather than a certain leakage of personal desires from classical times. While Cai Dasao, Wu Dasao, and Mrs. Huang Lansheng are indeed pursuers of desire, more importantly, their changing attitudes toward life are driven by the stimulation and attraction of modern urban life. It is the urban environment that opens the door to their desires and provides the space for their self-indulgence. Similarly, the changing urban lifestyle repeatedly tests their survival skills, allowing them to seize opportunities and mature intellectually amid life's upheavals. They have firmly stepped onto the ground of modern society; their experiences and behaviors are no longer akin to the courtesans who engaged in poetic exchanges with literati in ancient China, nor are they like the tragic Huo Xiaoyu or Du Shiniang who sank her treasure chest in anger, or even the virtuous Dong Xiaowan. They have bid farewell to the passivity of ancient women and begun to take control of their own lives. Cai Dasao mastered her own bound feet and welcomed a clandestine affair with Luo Waimouth, finally choosing to remarry proactively; Wu Dasao controlled her husband, conquered her in-laws, and also managed the emotions of a young student, Hao Yousan; Mrs. Huang Lansheng dominated both inside and outside the family, with her husband, cousin, brother-in-law, and a host of men including revolutionaries all bowing at her feet.

Secondly, these changes cannot be simply incorporated into the intellectuals' "anti-feudal" discourse, thus easily leaving an impression of being "half new, half old." However, if we do not confine ourselves to mainstream intellectual paradigms and self-impose these era's "central themes," we would recognize that the local customs and scenes Li Jieren unfolds are an integral part of the long-overlooked pluralistic modernization process.

Why do these deviations from mainstream intellectual "central themes" still belong to a diverse path of modernization? The core here is the development of self-awareness or the proactive agency of human existence.

The emergence of "modernity" results from humanity's farewell to the Middle Ages. The Middle Ages signify two types of constraints: one is the ideological constraint of religious ideology, and the other is the constraint of the secular feudal patriarchal system. It was only by departing from the Middle Ages that "subjectivity" could be born, and with it, subjective consciousness, which in turn led to the proactive actions of individuals to construct their own ideals. The proactive choice in life is the main manifestation of the growth of self-awareness. Therefore, the enhancement of proactive behavior in human nature is the foundation of "modernity" culture. As Giddens noted, "The more traditional controls are lost, the more everyday life, influenced by the dialectical interplay of the local and the global, is reconstructed, and the more individuals are forced to negotiate life choices among a diversity of options."[22] The proactivity of characters like Cai Dasao aligns with the development of "self-

awareness" promoted by the May Fourth New Culture Movement.

Indeed, these literary women born in remote regions did not have the opportunity to march in the streets of central cities like Beijing or Shanghai with female students to "fight feudalism," nor did they have the chance to pave a completely new future through education and employment. They were also not privileged to indulge in elite culture and create their own romantic dreams. However, their efforts to grasp their own destinies were sufficient to shape themselves, fostering new temperaments and personalities. This constitutes a substantial historical transformation beyond the modernity landscapes of Beijing and Shanghai.

Wu Dashao comfortably accepted the support of her "boyfriends" without any guilt associated with traditional morality. Yet, she was not entirely fickle or treacherous. For those benefactors who were genuinely kind, she reciprocated their sincerity. When her family was about to leave Chengdu with her husband, she showed genuine emotion for Hao Yousan's reluctance:

> *Wu Dashao's grandmother wanted him to stay for lunch, but he felt heartbroken staying there. He stood up and said to Wu Dashao, "I wish you a safe journey! I won't come to see you off the day after tomorrow. You have many things to do, and I have my own affairs. After this parting, who knows when we will meet again!" He was very emotional and couldn't continue speaking.*
>
> *Wu Dashao burst into tears, grabbed his arm desperately, and said, "Don't worry! As long as you don't forget me!"*[23]

At that moment, the relationship between the

benefactor and the courtesan transcended mere physical desire, and a faint sense of love born out of equality was visible. The humanity of the indulgent Wu Dashao and the "self" of the decadent Hao Yousan both appeared somewhat different.

Mrs. Huang Lansheng's development of character stepped beyond the traditional boundaries of a woman, advancing into an unprecedentedly unfamiliar world.

Firstly, she broke through the survival boundaries of traditional women and took control of her life. Self-taught in the art of human nature, she maneuvered gracefully among several male admirers and effortlessly entered the vortex of contemporary life. Initially within her family, and then in broader social relationships, including enjoying the benefits of the latest revolutionary forces: by funding militia leader Wu Fengwu, Mrs. Huang ensured her interests in the new regime. A woman using her adept understanding of contemporary human nature to intervene in society and achieve her interests is no longer a small story of personal feelings within the family but a "modern narrative" reconstructing interpersonal and social relationships. She had stepped out of a life centered around family networks and into the realm of modern social relationships, actively engaging in the core activity representing modern China—revolution. Cao Juren lamented, "Only the decisive Mrs. Huang truly grasped the 'revolution'."[24]

Secondly, through her rudimentary understanding of new ideas, she formed a confident perspective on womanhood, boldly and plainly criticizing societal norms, which was enough to shock the world:

I don't believe that men and women are fundamentally the same, so why should women be the ones to remain chaste? No one understands this principle. What's worse is that women, when they hear about a woman losing her chastity or having an affair, immediately adopt a disdainful attitude, as if they are the only virtuous ones and others are not respectable. In reality, I see through this; their disdain is due to jealousy. They envy others' ability to have an affair. Most virtuous women are simply cowardly and incompetent. It's like poor people seeing others eating well every meal, with whole chickens, ducks, and rich meat—they, too, would want to eat like that but can't afford it, so they claim to be virtuous and unwilling to harm animals.

We women have been bullied throughout history. When chaos strikes, our bound feet make us unable to run, neither can we die easily, being timid and afraid. But the men should be the ones to die. They panic more than women, as if a knife is already at their necks. Yesterday, if the men had been calm, not scared to the point of soiling themselves, taken a few to scout, and reassured the women and children, wouldn't everything have been fine? Yet, not one acted like a man. I'll say something bold—what's the use of having that thing between their legs?[25]

Although Mrs. Huang was justifying her indulgence, we may question her moral standards, but we cannot deny that she and women like her were starting to define themselves differently. Consequently, they were moving farther away from the traditional values of Chinese women.

The American sinologist Kristin Stapleton even regarded Cai Dashao (Deng Yaogu) as a "hero." He said, "Li Jieren's works do have heroes, perhaps the most significant being the protagonist Deng Yaogu in 'Dead Water Ripples.' Deng

Yaogu is evidently not a traditional type of female hero. She has several flaws, her greatest weakness possibly being her emptiness. But at the end of the novel, she finally gains the courage to take charge of her life. By agreeing to marry Gu Tiancheng, she protects Cai Xingshun while clearly stating the conditions under which she will live with Gu. She will not become a Christian. The agreement Deng Yaogu reaches with Gu Tiancheng in such a painful context is undoubtedly a creative act. It may not be an ideal agreement, but it might be the best choice she could make to secure her position. I believe this is all we can ask of our heroes."[26] I understand that Stapleton's praise of "heroism" is primarily an affirmation of a positive life attitude. We know that it is precisely this proactive life attitude that propelled human society from ancient times into modernity, achieving historical transformation. Cao Juren had a similar observation, noting that the women in Li Jieren's novels "are passionate, astute, and capable of grasping reality."[27]

Every cultural tradition has multiple facets: the mainstream orthodox aspect that suppresses human nature, and another that breaks through constraints and releases desires. In the process of historical transformation and value replacement, tradition continues to extend and shape the future in its own complex way, entangled with modern demands. This means that a singular modern rationality is often insufficient to explain historical evolution, especially when starting from a single mainstream ideology, as it easily falls into the trap of determinism. Mainstream ideological summaries are often based on a few central cities, unable to encompass the diverse contexts of Chinese society. Moreover, tradition and modernity are not binary opposites. As one historian put it, "From Professor Benjamin Schwartz's insightful research, we know that sharply opposing 'tradition' and 'modernity' is a significant mistake in the study of modern Chinese history. In fact, neither 'tradition' nor 'modernity' are simple, static, or homogeneous concepts. Tradition is a continuously evolving and changing existence, containing a myriad of conflicting ideas and qualities. The same is true for 'modernity.' Furthermore, ideas or things generally categorized as traditional may contain modern elements, and what is termed modern may include aspects that do not align with modern spirit."[28] The growth of female consciousness presented in Li Jieren's fictional world transcends the mainstream narrative of "negating tradition—introducing the West," offering an alternative conclusion for examining China's modern transformation.

About the author:

Li Yi is the Dean and Professor at the College of Literature and Journalism, Sichuan University. His research focuses on the history of modern and contemporary Chinese literature, trends in modern and contemporary Chinese literary thought, modern Chinese poetry, and studies on Lu Xun.

Endnotes:

[1] Lijieren. "Novels and Novelists after French Naturalism." Originally published in *Shaonian Zhongguo* (Vol. 3, Issue 10, 1922). Cited from *Complete Works of Lijieren*, Vol. 9, Sichuan Literature and Art Publishing House, 2011, p. 152.

[2] Lijieren. Letter to Shu Xincheng, June 14, 1935. *Complete Works of Lijieren*, Vol. 10, Sichuan Literature and Art Publishing House, 2011, p. 39.

[3]   Zhang Yiqi. "Zhou Keqin Discusses Lijieren's Works." In *The Character and Works of Lijieren*, Sichuan University Press, 2001, p. 165.

[4]   Zheng Yi. *Ordinary and Epic: Lijieren's 'Modern History of Novels', Modern Chinese Culture and Literature*, Vol. 15, Bashu Publishing House, 2015.

[5]   Zhang Chen. *How 'Modern' Are 'New Novelists': Lijieren's Transition and Its Limits*, Master's Thesis, Nanjing University, 2021.

[6]   Xie Jun. "Chen Lihua: The 'Madame Bovary' with Bashu Characteristics—A Case Study of *Tian Mo Wu*." *Research on Lijieren: 2016*, Sichuan Literature and Art Publishing House, 2017. Some even assert that Lijieren was borrowing from French literature to create 'Westernized' women (Tan Guanghui. "On the Western Thoughts in Lijieren's Later Works," *Research on Lijieren: 2011*, Sichuan Literature and Art Publishing House, 2011, p. 190).

[7]   Liu Zaifu. "A Century of the Nobel Prize in Literature and the Absence of Chinese Writers." *Beijing Literature*, Issue 8, 1999.

[8]   Bu Yuanbao. "Influence and Divergence: A Brief Discussion of *Dead Water Ripple* and *Madame Bovary*, among Others." *Chinese Comparative Literature*, Issue 1, 2005.

[9]   Long Yanzhu. "The Incompleteness of Female Image Writing in Lijieren and Guo Moruo's Works." *Seeking Truth*, Issue 5, 2013.

[10] Lijieren. *Dead Water Ripple. Complete Works of Lijieren*, Vol. 1, Sichuan Literature and Art Publishing House, 2011, p. 21.

[11] Lijieren. *Dead Water Ripple. Complete Works of Lijieren*, Vol. 1, Sichuan Literature and Art Publishing House, 2011, p. 20.

[12] Baudelaire (France), translated by Guo Hong'an. "On *Madame Bovary*." In *The Salon of 1846: Baudelaire's Aesthetic Essays*, Guangxi Normal University Press, 2002, pp. 52 – 53.

[13] Lijieren. *Dead Water Ripple. Complete Works of Lijieren*, Vol. 1, Sichuan Literature and Art Publishing House, 2011, p. 30.

[14] Lijieren. Letter to Shu Xincheng, June 14, 1935. *Complete Works of Lijieren*, Vol. 10, Sichuan Literature and Art Publishing House, 2011, p. 39.

[15] Lijieren. Letter to Shu Xincheng, August 6, 1935. *Complete Works of Lijieren*, Vol. 10, Sichuan Literature and Art Publishing House, 2011, p. 41.

[16] Li Xiaoti. *Yesterday's Journey to the City: Leisure and Religion in Modern China*, Linking Publishing, 2008, p. 201.

[17] Lijieren. *Dead Water Ripple. Complete Works of Lijieren*, Vol. 1, Sichuan Literature and Art Publishing House, 2011, p. 10.

[18] Jacob Burckhardt (Switzerland), translated by He Xin. *The Civilization of the Renaissance in Italy*, Commercial Press, 1979, p. 445.

[19] Lijieren. *Dead Water Ripple. Complete Works of Lijieren*, Vol. 1, Sichuan Literature and Art Publishing House, 2011, p. 184.

[20] Lijieren. *Before the Storm. Complete Works of Lijieren*, Vol. 2, Sichuan Literature and Art Publishing

House, 2011, p. 85.

[21] Lijieren. *Old Edition of The Great Wave (Part I)*. *Complete Works of Lijieren*, Vol. 3, Sichuan Literature and Art Publishing House, 2011, p. 190.

[22] Anthony Giddens (UK), translated by Zhao Xudong and Fang Wen. *Modernity and Self-Identity*, Sanlian Bookstore, 1998, p. 5.

[23] Lijieren. *Before the Storm. Complete Works of Lijieren*, Vol. 2, Sichuan Literature and Art Publishing House, 2011, pp. 226 - 227.

[24] Cao Juren. *Outline of Chinese Literature: New Novel Commentary*, Sanlian Bookstore, 2007, p. 246.

[25] Lijieren. *Old Edition of The Great Wave (Part I)*. *Complete Works of Lijieren*, Vol. 3, Sichuan Literature and Art Publishing House, 2011, pp. 95, 96, 195.

[26] Skunlun (USA). "Lijieren's Historical Perspective." In *Lijieren's Epic Literary Pursuits*, Chengdu Press, 1992, pp. 95 - 96.

[27] Cao Juren. "Lijieren's 'Great River Novels'." *Research on Lijieren: 2007*, Bashu Publishing House, 2008, p. 454.

[28] Li Xiaoti. *Yesterday's Journey to the City: Leisure and Religion in Modern China*, Linking Publishing, 2008, p. 315.

Training Birdsongs as a Chinese Art Form

GUO Shixing

I

In old Beijing, training birds to sing was an art form, particularly a melody known as the "Thirteen Tunes of the Skylarks" (百灵十三套). From the Qing Dynasty to the present, no one has definitively explained how this set of tunes came into being or what it signifies. After reading Walter Benjamin's analysis of arcades, I felt inspired and would like to discuss this topic with interested friends.

According to tradition, there are two versions of the Thirteen Tunes in old Beijing. In the 1930s, Mr. Jin Shoushen (金受申) was invited by *Liyan Huakan* to introduce Beijing customs. He interviewed former Qing Dynasty officials who mentioned the Thirteen Tunes, and he explained: "The Skylark's set consists of thirteen tunes. The first nine sections form the front set, while the last four make up the back set... The tunes are named as follows: *Sparrows' Chirping* (家雀噪林), *Mountain Magpies* (山喜鹊), *Red Bird* (红子), *Chickens Flock* (群鸡), *Hu Whistle* (胡哨), *Little Swallow* (小燕), *Cat* (猫), *Home Magpie* (家喜鹊), and *Goshawk* (鸽鹰) for the front set. The back set includes *Cyan Bird* (靛颏蕊儿), *Zhaizi* (柞子), *Yellow Bird* (黄鸟套), and *Thrush Tail* (画眉络儿), concluding with *Mating Lanannius* (胡伯劳交尾儿)." Apart from "Hu's Whistle," which is somewhat puzzling, most names are understandable. As for " *Zhaizi*," its scientific name is the Great Reed Warbler, commonly known as *Weizhaizi* (苇柞子).

The Thirteen Tunes primarily consist of bird sounds. I suspect that "Hu's Whistle" might be a mistake and should be "Kettle Whistle." When water boils in a kettle, the spout emits a whistle.

This version of the Thirteen Tunes is widely accepted, though further subdivisions exist between the northern and southern parts of the city. In southern Beijing, the Skylark includes sounds resembling a water wheel and a dog barking. Those with a directorial inclination might combine these two, resulting in the clattering of a water wheel overpowering a barking dog, creating a chaotic mixture of squeaking and howling. The northern Skylark, however, forbids such calls. This suggests that the northern version is more primitive, closer to pastoral life, reflecting the beauty of rural existence. In contrast, the southern version depicts the bustling city life of southern Beijing, complete with water carts and narrow streets where even dogs can be crushed.

If the "Thirteen Tunes of the Skylarks" were established during the Qing Dynasty, we can infer that the living environments of northern and southern Beijing were quite different at that time. In the Qing era, Han Chinese were not allowed to live in the Inner City, which was reserved for the royal families, princes, and the Eight Banners military camps. For instance, the Beiyingfang and Houyingfang areas near Xinjiekou were such camps. Most Han people lived in the Outer City—southern Beijing—where commercial districts and theaters were also located. Thus, the northern part of the city was quiet, while the southern part was bustling. The streets in the north were relatively wider, whereas in the south, shops extended onto the streets, with each shop trying to outdo the next in encroaching on the road, as seen in the area near Rou Market outside Qianmen. The roads became so narrow that when water carts came by, even the dogs had nowhere to hide.

Water carts were a mode of water transport before tap water became widespread. In the past, the imperial palace used water from Yuquan Mountain, while the city residents relied on well water. Many wells were shallow, producing bitter water, while those with sweet water were famous far and wide. The names *Big Sweet Water Well* and *Little Sweet Water Well Alley* between the Beijing Department Store and Beijing Hotel are remnants of this history. Sweet water was drawn from these wells and transported by cart to the various alleys. I remember seeing these carts when I stayed at my grandmother's house. In Niujiaowan Alley, just north of Shuimo Hutong (now the site of the Customs House), the back door of my grandmother's house opened onto Niujiaowan. The water cart would deliver water to the back door, and those buying water used water ladles to collect it. The vendor would pull the wooden plug from the large barrel on the cart, allowing water to flow into the ladle. Once full, the plug was re-inserted. I forget how much a ladle of water cost, but it was probably a penny or two. Every household had a water tank to store water.

From this perspective, the southern city sky-larks' calls can be seen as a theme of "Southern City Morning Serenade." At dawn, sparrows are the first to awaken, hence *Sparrows Chirping in the Forest*. The sparrows then rouse the magpies, followed by the chickens searching for food. Inside the house, the kettle starts boiling—old Beijingers had the habit of drinking morning tea, boiling water upon rising. This sequence of calls reflects an urban environment in the agrarian era, where the rural and urban coexisted.

Training a bird to master this set of calls was a laborious process. In those days, without re-cording devices, birds were trained using other birds, but this method easily led to inaccuracies. For those who demanded precision, birds were trained with original sound sources. It was diffi-cult to learn the sequence properly; once all the calls were learned, the bird had to be trained to produce them in order. If the sequence was incor-rect, the trainer would intervene, and after a few corrections, the bird would understand. Through this method of conditioning, after several years, a bird that mastered the Thirteen Tunes would graduate, though many failed along the way. To prevent the Skylark from hearing other sounds, it was often placed inside a water tank, with a cot-ton-padded wooden cover over the top. There were no soundproofing devices at the time, so this was the best they could do.

However, this set of tunes merely copies life, much like the "Along the River During the Qing-ming Festival" painting (《清明上河图》), and holds little artistic value. We have long been con-fined to the city, yearning to escape the noise. Yet, as cities continue to expand and nature retreats, many people have become unfamiliar with the sounds of the natural world. Nowadays, many bird enthusiasts can't even identify the birds' calls. Ancient poets, on the other hand, were well-versed in bird songs. Phrases like "Drive away the orioles, don't let them sing on the branches" (打起黄莺儿，莫教枝上啼), "Two orioles singing among the green willows" (两个黄鹂鸣翠柳), "Deep in the mountains, you can hear the call of the pheasant" (山深闻鹧鸪), and "The wild geese startled by the cold, their cries cut off at the shores of Hengyang" (雁阵惊寒，声断衡阳之浦) were all carefully distinguished. Yuan Zhen (元稹) even knew the name of the falconer's glove, call-ing it a "gou" (韝鹰暂脱羁). The gou was a leather sleeve used to hold a falcon (as noted in Wang Shixiang's "The Great Falcon" [《大鹰篇》]). To-day, we are far removed from such knowledge. We no longer aspire to the mountains and forests and even have birds imitate our daily toil. Is the wilderness superior to the marketplace? Of course, the wilderness symbolizes freedom, while the marketplace represents survival. Our people have never been particularly interested in free-dom—give them freedom, and they'll feel lost;

give them survival, and they'll find it fulfilling. What can we do?

Hegel once said in *The Philosophy of History* (《历史哲学》), "Everything spiritual is far removed from China." He was, of course, referring to the Christian concept of spiritual freedom. The Devil tempted Christ with three strategies, all of which aimed to make Christ abandon his freedom. Yet Christ saw through them and upheld his freedom.

Today, the methods we use to train birds are much like the Devil's temptations of Christ. After fasting for forty days in the wilderness, Christ was starving, and the Devil said, "If you are the Son of God, tell these stones to become bread." Christ refused, saying, "Man shall not live on bread alone, but on every word that comes from the mouth of God" ("The Gospel of Matthew" [《马太福音》]). In essence, we exchange the bird's freedom for bread, preventing it from singing of freedom, forcing it to sing of bread. This is the bird trainer's strategy.

But do birds not resist? Of course, they do. A newly captured Indigo-bird (靛颏) might batter itself against the cage until it's bloodied. The French, faced with this behavior, would at most pad the top of the cage with soft material. In Beijing and Tianjin, however, they would use a neck ring to tether the bird to their hand, then place it on a perch with a neck ring. The length of the neck ring was just enough for the bird to reach the water and food containers, leaving nothing for it to bump into. Even if the bird refused to eat or drink, there were solutions. One method was "drip-feeding," where the handler would continually drip water onto the bird's nostrils, causing the water to trickle into its throat. Once the bird had expelled the water from its crop, it would be starved, and then enticed with insects. After it ate the insects, they would be chopped up and mixed with artificial food. The bird would initially eat the insect pieces, then the artificial food, and once it was accustomed to the food, the insects would be removed. Thus, a bird that originally fed on live insects would be converted to eating artificial food. This process was called "opening the diet."

For particularly stubborn birds that refused to eat, artificial feeding was necessary. This required skill: one hand would grip the bird, with the thumb and forefinger controlling the head. The thumb would push the bird's lower jaw while the forefinger pulled on its nape, causing the bird to open its mouth automatically. Then, using tweezers, a piece of lamb soaked in water would be placed behind the bird's tongue. Care was needed, as the bird's tongue is hooked, and placing the food too far forward would result in it being immediately ejected. After inserting the meat, the handler would gently press on the bird's windpipe to induce slight asphyxiation. When the pressure was released, the bird, in its effort to breathe, would swallow the food. This process would be repeated every half hour, and after a few days, the bird would invariably start eating on its own. It's akin to a prisoner's failed hunger strike when force-fed intravenously.

II

In general, "clinging when hungry, soaring when full" is a natural characteristic of birds. However, after prolonged captivity, birds can develop a kind of Stockholm Syndrome. Some birds become "decoys," singing beautiful songs to lure others into traps. Others assist in hunting, and some, like the skylark, become imperial singers. In the past, training Indigo-birds (靛颏) was relatively easy. Their owners, who perhaps indulged in opium, would subdue the birds by making them addicted to the drug. The method was simple: the owner would blow a puff of opium smoke onto the bird while smoking. Over time, the bird would develop an addiction, mirroring its owner's moods—sometimes lethargic, sometimes excited. When the owner was deeply satisfied by the drug, the bird too would become "high," singing tirelessly like a rock star after a hit of "ice."

Westerners were no different in this regard. French mistresses were known to feed nightingales blood, cannabis, and opium because, as Jules Michelet wrote in *La Femme et l'Oiseau* ("Woman and Bird"): "The nightingale is the only creature that requires sleep and dreams to sing." And indeed, the Indigo-bird is a type of nightingale.

According to Mr. Jin Shoushen (金受申), the Blue-throated Indigo-bird (scientific name *Luscinia svecica*) could produce a sound known as the "Baoding Iron Ball." These Baoding balls are hollow, with small iron beads inside, and their inner chambers come in male and female versions, producing different tones. A set consists of five balls. These iron balls were favored by martial artists and local toughs in the past. Tattooed hands would rotate the five balls in the palm, creating strange sounds. The quiet Indigo-bird mimicking this noise seems oddly out of place, though it's unclear why this sound was admired.

The only city sound the Indigo-bird imitates that truly touches the heart is the sound of the "Ice Bowl." In the past, vendors selling sour plum soup would roam the streets, not by shouting, but by clinking two small copper bowls (known as ice bowls) together. The sound they made was a rhythmic "der—zheng, der—zheng." On unbearably hot afternoons, as students sweated over their homework, the distant sound of the ice bowls echoing through the alley would cool them down even before they tasted the drink. When the Indigo-bird mimics this sound, it can make the summer heat in a room dissipate instantly. And on cold winter nights, when the Indigo-bird occasionally sings a "dog days" tune, it can transport you back to the clear and cool autumn, where "the shallows dry up, revealing a clear pool, and the smoky light condenses into a purple twilight on the distant mountains (潦水尽而寒潭清，烟光凝而暮山紫)."

The Bluethroat (蓝靛颏), also known as *Luscinia svecica*, is a small bird similar in size to a sparrow, with brown plumage. The male's throat is sky blue, and its song is particularly melodious.

Among all birds, the one that puzzles me the most is the Red Bird. Its scientific name is the *Marsh Tit* (沼泽山雀), and its song has the strongest sense of rhythm. In Xingtai, the Red Bird can mimic drumbeats, chanting, "Start a beat, start a beat!" with a metallic tone. It's unclear whether drums imitate this bird or if the bird imitates drums. The British naturalist W.H. Hudson, praised for "successfully perceiving the true face of nature," once quoted C.A. Witchell, who said, "Our musical scales have a long history, and the intervals we use have passed from the instruments of humans to the ears of songbirds over thousands of years." However, Hudson expressed doubt: "This is far from convincing... Many of these birds live in the wild and have never heard human music, yet their songs and calls follow the same intervals as our musical scales." I agree with both viewpoints—some birds probably have indeed learned from human music, and human music must have drawn inspiration from birdsongs. Ultimately, the purest music is the sound of nature.

Humans and birds share a common understanding of perfect intervals and scales. I once experimented by using recordings of various Peking opera singers to stimulate birds to sing, and I found that the better the singer, the more effective the stimulation. Top-tier performers like Tan Xinpei (譚鑫培), Yu Shuyan (余叔岩), Jin Shaoshan (金少山), Qiu Shengrong (裘盛戎), Mei Lanfang (梅兰芳), and Cheng Yanqiu (程砚秋) all worked well. Second-tier singers were less effective, and as for those who paid to produce their own recordings, the birds simply ignored them. When I found it hard to judge the quality of the performances myself, I would leave it to the birds to decide. However, I do wonder—are the birds responding to the singers or to the erhu (胡琴) accompanying them? After all, the best singers are often paired with the best erhu players.

Unfortunately, due to overhunting, the Red Bird has lost much of its linguistic repertoire, much like how the Khitan language has disappeared. Most Red Bird in Xingtai no longer possess this distinctive call, which is a great loss. In the past, the Red Bird of Beijing's lowlands were known for their excellent voices. A popular saying, "The Red Birds of Jishuitan—carrying a watery tone" (积水潭的红子——带水音儿), serves as evidence. But as the lowlands were hunted out, bird catchers moved south, first to Hebei, then to Henan, and Shandong. Several years ago, Hebei had already lost its valiant spirits, and bird catchers from Henan had traveled as far as Shanghai to catch Red Birds. Perhaps the birds there now speak in the soft, lilting tones of the Wu dialect.

Mr. Jin Shoushen also mentioned that a certain prince from the Qing Dynasty kept twelve Red Birds, all capable of singing the same tune. When one bird was missing, another would take its place. This prince was fond of listening to the main melody in chorus, which was truly a sight to behold.

The fate of the Red Birds (红子) is particularly tragic. When they are very young, their eyes not yet fully opened, bird traders remove them entirely from their nests. These nestlings are then artificially fed minced beef and bird feed while listening to the songs of older, caged birds to learn how to sing. Those who aren't taken as nestlings but are captured a bit later, when their feathers have formed, are called *hotfeathers* (热毛子). These birds can still be trained to sing. Once they grow older and can fly, they are referred to as *branch-hoppers* (过枝子), but by then, they can only produce their natural calls. Any bird that emits a "chirp chirp" sound is deemed undesirable.

These little tits (山雀) are in constant flight throughout the year. A *branch-hopper* Red Bird must be evaluated. If it produces sounds like "chirp chirp," "hee hee," or "hoo hoo," it is considered an error. Similarly, if it simplifies a syllable—for example, turning "ji ji gun er" (鸡鸡棍儿) into "ji gun er" (鸡棍儿)—it's a mistake. If it produces triplets—such as turning "ji ji gun er" into "ji ji ji gun er"—that is also unacceptable. The rules are strict: no continuous syllables, no stuttering.

These errors are corrected using the *disrupting* method—when the bird makes a mistake, the trainer taps the cage to stop it. If repeated corrections fail, the bird is deemed unfit to join the flock, as it might influence other birds to make similar mistakes. In such cases, the bird must be released.

In the cage, birds are not allowed to perform somersaults, peck at the cage, tremble, twitch, or roll around. The correction method involves tethering the bird to a perch with a neck ring, ensuring it can eat and drink while tethered. Once it calms down, the training is considered successful.

In reality, what we call "vocal mistakes" in birds are actually cries of protest. Some people have observed that when these "errant" birds are released, they immediately sing beautifully in the trees, without any mistakes. The persistent pecking and rolling in the cage are signs that the bird has developed a form of depression. Although it is said that "everything spiritual is far from China," it seems that everything related to mental illness is quite close to us. Just as China can enhance the ideological consciousness of mentally ill patients, it can also train depressed birds to be obedient. However, in my view, a tethered bird merely transitions from manic depression to clinical depression. While manic depression in birds is suppressed, manic depression in humans is often celebrated.

In my efforts to treat the depression of birds, I consulted literature on human depression. It is said, "Manic patients, unlike typical depression sufferers who withdraw and isolate themselves, often have wide-ranging interests, enjoy socializing, and are highly engaged in activities. They are prone to impulsiveness and may act recklessly without much forethought. The most representative symptom of manic depression is that patients often appear cheerful, even elated, and might express feelings like, 'The world is truly wonderful.'" I wonder what would happen if a person with depression were to handle a bird—what would be the outcome? From my observations, many bird enthusiasts exhibit varying degrees of depression. This is also one of the motivations behind my writing the play "Birdman" (《鸟人》).

III

Do birds have spiritual aspirations? In reality, these small birds possess far more knowledge than the city dwellers who are limited by their narrow perspectives. In the spring, the Indigo-birds (靛颏) migrate from distant Southeast Asia, flying north along the coastline. Northern China serves as a crucial stopover where they replenish their energy before continuing their journey. During the day, they hide in cotton fields, vegetable patches, and reed marshes to avoid predators. At night, under the cover of darkness, they travel continuously, reaching Northeast China by morning. The Red-throated Bluethroat (红靛颏) breeds in the Greater and Lesser Khingan Mountains and the Heilongjiang region, while the Bluethroat (蓝靛颏) migrates even further to Siberia and the Arctic Circle. Along the way, they must evade countless dangers. Many, both young and old, perish on this arduous journey to propagate to the next generation.

During the Qing Dynasty, a book titled *The Indigo-bird Chronicles* (《靛颏谱》) detailed the migration routes and strategies of these birds. The clever Indigo-birds, for example, would hitch rides on boats while crossing the strait and the Yangtze River, hiding in the rigging to conserve energy. The book also included illustrations of various physical characteristics of the birds. For a bird that has undergone such complex experiences, being confined to a cage with a diameter of just one foot, unable to move or fly for years, must be profoundly depressing. It expresses its entire story through song, with some of its melodies echoing the lament of the legendary Yang Silang: "My home is in the rear hills of Cizhou County, in the Huotang Fort. My father is a noble official, and my mother, the esteemed Lady She. Fifteen years ago, during the Sand Beach Meeting, I was captured by the enemy and taken to a foreign land."

The 18th-century ornithologist Jules Michelet observed nightingales captured during their migration from Northern Europe to North Africa, passing through France. He wrote, "With touching notes, they depict the images that flash through their minds, portraying things they once loved but no longer see. Perhaps they have forgotten their failed migration and believe they have reached Africa or Syria, a place with a brighter sun... It is their love and their battle, their nightingale's tragedy. They see the forests they loved, the things that once beautified the woods; they see their agile and graceful postures, the thousands of charms of a life in flight—things that our lives can never comprehend. When their eggs hatch, their sons—the future nightingales—grow up with sweet voices. In the dark nights of their confined cages, they listen, intoxicated, to the future songs of their sons."

Birds also communicate environmental changes through their songs. In Australia, the Lyrebird can mimic the sound of chainsaws cutting down trees. It replicates everything from the chainsaw starting up to the blade smoothly slicing through the bark, then struggling as it hits the dense heartwood, and finally, the thunderous crash as the tall tree falls, breaking the smaller trees and bushes around it. The imitation is so precise that it feels disturbingly real. This signifies yet another bird habitat destroyed by humans—a song that mourns the loss of life and can move one to tears.

In the past, an Indigo-bird that could mimic the sound of a magpie was highly valued because such birds were rare. Today, however, many Indigo-birds can mimic magpies, a result of magpies thriving around human settlements, feeding on human garbage. In earlier times, food scarcity limited magpie populations, as there was little edible waste in the garbage. But now, with more food waste available, the magpie population has increased. Bluethroats are also known to mimic the calls of frogs, as they often forage near reed marshes and ditches, which are home to frogs. Bird owners used to consider frog calls as undesirable sounds. However, these days, Bluethroats rarely mimic frog calls because pesticides have driven frogs to near extinction in many areas. When a bird does mimic a frog, it becomes a rarity.

In the UK, thrushes have learned to imitate car alarms, a clear sign of noise pollution. In China, it's not just the thrushes—larks can do it too. The traditional *Thirteen Tunes of the Skylark* are becoming increasingly difficult to find. Another concerning trend is that the birds' songs are becoming less melodic and more like rap, with louder and louder sounds. Both birds and humans are experiencing noise pollution, which is interfering with their sense of hearing, leading to a postmodern shift in music. Hudson noticed this phenomenon a century ago when he said, "The dulling of hearing caused by harsh noise is also a result of getting accustomed to the high volume of musical instruments. Our civilization is a noisy one, and as noise increases, the smaller, more refined instruments that require a quiet environment to be appreciated lose their ancient charm and eventually fall out of favor. This is a trend toward louder instruments and denser sound; the piano is universally loved, and nowadays, the louder it roars, the more people seem to enjoy it." He seemed to have foreseen the rise of heavy metal music fifty years later.

Wouldn't a captured bird simply go silent, like Xu Shu in Cao Ying, refusing to utter a word? Unfortunately, it cannot. Humans have learned to exploit the nature of birds. When several male birds are placed together, they compete for dominance in their songs, striving to assert their vocal authority. People take advantage of this by hanging several birds in close proximity, triggering a competitive singing match. Moreover, during the mating season, birds will naturally call for mates, much like the "chirping" of crickets when they engage in courtship with their melodic serenades. If neither of these conditions is met, humans can still control the bird's singing through the manipulation of light. This is where the use of *cage covers*, commonly known as *cage veils*, comes into play. For birds like the Red Birds, which are kept under cover year-round, a translucent white veil is used. Other songbirds like larks, thrushes, and indigo-birds are kept under opaque blue covers. When a bird is kept in darkness for an extended period, the sudden exposure to bright light after the cover is removed excites it, prompting it to sing joyfully. Westerners have discovered this as well, although they tend to use green blankets to cover their birdcages.

Birds love the light and fear the darkness, which is why many of their songs are odes to the sun. However, as the saying goes, extremes lead to reversals. A bird's intense longing for sunlight, when unfulfilled, can also lead to abnormal singing. They sing of a sun they can no longer see. While people in our country treat birds relatively well, in 18th and 19th-century England and France, people would exploit the finches' natural tendencies by blinding them. These birds, blinded and filled with despair, would then "desperately and pathologically create a harmony of light through their voices, forging a sun from within that belonged only to them." This, perhaps, was the birds' spiritual yearning.

It sounds quite cruel, but when you consider

that people would castrate young boys to preserve their singing voices, you begin to understand the depths of human perversity.

In contrast, people here don't go to such extremes. When capturing falcons, they might sew shut the eyelids of pigeons used as bait and tether them with strings. This prevents the pigeons from seeing the falcons and fleeing, thereby keeping the falcon's target in sight.

IV

Singing for love is also one of the primary spiritual supports for birds. Love, as we understand it, didn't always exist. It was only during the Renaissance that poets like Shakespeare elevated the concept of love to its highest form. As for the Greeks who fought for Helen, I believe it was more about possessiveness; even Zeus's understanding of love was nothing more than a crude instinct. Birds, however, are different. For thousands of years, they have been faithful to love.

The European tradition of capturing nightingales as cage birds dates back to the Elizabethan era. Their observations were quite detailed. Hudson noted, "If a nightingale is captured after finding a mate—meaning after the female appears, which is usually a week to ten days later than the male—it will quickly die in captivity out of sorrow. Those captured before the female arrives can survive until the molting period, but it is certain that the blow is fatal. Of those who survive a year in captivity, barely one in ten makes it through." In this regard, the older generation of bird enthusiasts in our country followed a commendable tradition: they did not keep older birds. Birds that have experienced pairing and mating can sometimes die tragically during the breeding season, especially Red Birds (红子) that have laid eggs. How can you tell if a bird hasn't mated? Birds in their first year will molt into breeding plumage after reproduction, akin to humans wearing a wedding ring. For Indigo-birds (靛颏), you check their wing markings; for thrushes, you check their

original feathers; and for Red Birds, you examine their chest feathers.

Another admirable tradition among the older bird enthusiasts was the release of birds perched on poles—species like orioles, old Xi'er, red-capped robins, finches, goldfinches, crossbills, and raptors like eagles and falcons. They were released in the spring. This practice was partly due to the cost of feeding them; after a winter of heavy labor, the birds would reach their breeding season and could no longer be kept, so it was better to release them for reproduction—like how state-owned enterprises buy out workers' service years. However, caged birds cannot be released. Long-term captivity causes them to lose their ability to fly and forage, and releasing them would be akin to sentencing them to death.

Some raptors, when released, would circle their former owners for a long time before flying away. This is a manifestation of the *Stockholm syndrome*—a bond formed through prolonged training or working together, or perhaps even through shared performances. Mr. Jin Shoushen once described a dramatic falconry scene: "At dawn the next day, the preparations were complete—meals cooked, everything ready. The order to depart was given: herding sheep, riding horses, carrying falcons, and leading monkeys. Like stars surrounding the moon, they escorted the master straight into the wilderness. Suddenly, in the pale grass, they spotted a wild cat (or a hare). The large eagle on the arm was ready to fly but was still hooded and couldn't chase the prey. In an instant, the small falcon—the kestrel—was released, swiftly pulling off the large eagle's hood. The kestrel's task completed, the eagle, now with clear vision, pursued the wild cat. Once the wild cat was taken care of (killed), the eagle's job was done. At this moment, the monkey riding the sheep would catch up and place the wild cat on the sheep, and they would return triumphantly." Animals, too, love games, and no one invents more variations of games than humans. How could the eagle have anticipated such activities? Once it gets involved, it becomes addicted, losing much of the joy it once found in hunting purely for survival. This is why it's reluctant to leave.

Drama is something birds also pursue. In ancient Greece, Aristophanes wrote *The Birds*, where a flock of birds, attempting to sow discord between humans and the gods, decided to build a city in the clouds—*Nephelokokkygia*—to block the smoke from human sacrifices from reaching the heavens, thus provoking the gods' wrath. In Belgium, Maurice Maeterlinck wrote the play *The Blue Bird*, featuring over a hundred characters, where the bluebird, symbolizing happiness, is found and lost repeatedly, suggesting that true happiness is fleeting, or perhaps even unattainable.

But birds are also masters of mischief. Hudson recounted a chilling tale: One spring, a pair of house martins built a nest on the lintel of a country house in England. "Just as the nest was completed, a pair of sparrows intruded and took it over, laying their eggs inside. The house martins didn't fight back but didn't leave either. They started building another nest as close to the old one as possible, clinging to the original structure. The new nest was quickly built, completely blocking the entrance to the old one. The sparrows disappeared. At the end of the season, after the house martins had flown away, the homeowner opened the sealed nest and was shocked to find the female sparrow still inside, reduced to a skeleton, crouched over four eggs." This is practically the bird equivalent of *A Rose for Emily* by Faulkner. The house martins' intelligence rivals

that of novelists, or perhaps Faulkner's intelligence doesn't surpass that of the house martins.

Comparing humans to birds isn't my invention. In *The Decameron*, a woman compares a certain part of her lover's anatomy to a nightingale. Gorky likened revolutionaries to stormy petrels, and Li Kui simply insulted people by calling them "birdmen." My own play, *Birdman* (《鸟人》), explores the metaphorical relationship between humans and birds. Humans imprison birds, but in caring for them, they become the birds' slaves. By stripping birds of their freedom, humans also lose their own. This is what I realized from visiting bird markets—the best gift birds have given me.

Birds have countless stories, and even days and nights wouldn't suffice to tell them all. Birds are the most tenacious creatures on earth. An albatross, for example, once it spreads its wings, does not land again. It flies over the ocean for seven years, feeding and sleeping in the air, only to return to its birthplace after seven years to reproduce. So who has evolved more, humans or birds? Who has become better? It's hard to say. The Bible contains this proverb: "Do not worry about tomorrow, for tomorrow will worry about itself. Look at the birds of the air; they neither sow nor reap, yet your heavenly Father feeds them." This isn't an excuse for laziness but a warning against greedily hoarding excess wealth. Birds never overeat, as the saying goes, "Birds won't die from overeating, and fish won't die from hunger." Have we humans managed that? On one side, we produce more than enough, while on the other, people are starving. In truth, we are not as wise as the birds.

About the author:

Guo Shixing, is a Chinese playwright, director, and writer. He wrote his first play, "The Fishman" in 1989, followed by "The Birdman" in 1991 and "The Chessman" in 1994. Guo also wrote scripts for the TV series "The Old Master" and the film "The Sun Also Rises", which won the Best Adapted Screenplay at the 44th Golden Horse Awards. He directed his first play, "The Memorandum," in

2008 and has since written and directed several plays, including "The Blizzard and Marriage Situation."

Random Musings on Square Dancing

HUANG Jisu

Overview

China has experienced tremendous changes over the past decades, and the future of the world remains uncertain with countless variables emerging constantly. Observing such a society is paramount, and conclusions should be kept in check to avoid rash assumptions. This article primarily presents my direct experiences from participating in square dancing over the past ten years, while also incorporating insights from my broader life experiences. I consider square dancing as an observatory of contemporary life, focusing on aspects such as space, community, meaning, and aesthetics. I also position myself within this context as a reference point.

The Origin

Recently, due to the resurgence of the pandemic in Beijing triggered by the Paradise Bar, restrictions have tightened once again, and square dancing has been banned along with indoor dining. One evening, after dinner, as I stood at the intersection near the Art Museum, contemplating where to wander, I noticed two people dancing the *ghost step* (also known as "shuffling") near the subway station. I quickly joined them. After two days of practice, I had just about managed to keep up with the new dance "Shuffling Frenzy" (《曳路狂奔》) when the next day, the dancers were gone. I spent a long time looking for them, and finally found a person who knew everything happening on the streets. As expected, the city management had cleared out the dancers as part of the pandemic prevention measures, "even the diabolo players on the west side were driven away." Looking at the empty streets, my heart felt empty too. Just then, Zhao Tingyang (赵汀阳)

urged me to submit an article, so I thought, since I can't dance, why not write about square dancing?

I've always prioritized fitness due to my poor health when I was young. I started walking in the 1970s and never stopped. In 2002, I got a swimming card and swam until the pool underwent major renovations in 2009. Then I swam in Houhai in Shichahai (什刹海后海). The first year was amazing—clear water, beautiful willows, and white clouds above. It felt like living in a painting. But in the second year, water plants grew, and my skin got scratched. In the third year, I heard that two migrant workers drowned because they got entangled in the water plants, so I stopped going. In 2012, I switched to square dancing, and it's been ten years now.

In 2013, when I was just getting familiar with the dance but not with the dancers, I authored an article titled "Singing and Dancing Under the Cross" (《十字架下，载歌载舞》) about my experiences dancing near the Bamian Cao Church (八面槽教堂). However, I haven't written about it since—not because there was nothing to write about, but because I was concerned about interpersonal relationships. I value the friendships I have with my dance companions, and I didn't want to betray their trust by writing about them. They never treated me as an outsider, and I didn't want to become a special member of the group by wearing a mask. Additionally, the dance group I was part of, which was the longest-lasting in Beijing, disbanded due to the pandemic and other reasons. Looking at old photos and videos feels like wandering through a beautiful yet melancholic "Secret Garden" (《神秘园》). Unconsciously, my mindset changed, and I felt an urge to write about square dancing again, perhaps to preserve those beautiful memories. Moreover, having observed society for so long, I was curious about what else I could learn from the widespread phenomenon of square dancing, which has swept across the nation and includes people from various social strata.

In Ancient Times

Instead of defining square dancing outright, I believe it's better to understand it through its history. Once the history is explained, the definition will naturally follow.

The history of square dancing can be traced back to the dance patterns on pottery from the Majiayao culture (马家窑文化, BC 3300-2100) five thousand years ago. If we extend this globally, it goes even further. However, ancient history is not the focus of this article. Interested readers can refer to dance history books. Here are a few key points:

1. Primitive Dance: The earliest human dances were square dances. In ancient times, limited space in caves and huts meant that people had to move to open areas to dance. These dances were communal, with everyone participating. Some individuals stood out, dancing more flamboyantly and drawing attention, but they were not yet professional dancers. They were like hot peppers in a dish, both ingredients and spices. People danced out of spontaneous joy, as described in ancient texts: "Emotions move within and manifest in words. When words are insufficient, they sigh. When sighs are insufficient, they sing. When singing is insufficient, they dance without knowing it."[1] The best term to describe this would be "wild dancing," where "wild" indicates an overwhelming excitement.

2. Historical Constraints: For an extended period, mainstream Chinese society (comprising scholars, farmers, artisans, and merchants) was bound by ritual music culture, hierarchical relations, and strict gender segregation. Dance was almost an otherworldly concept for them. Historically renowned dancers were often slaves or concubines, and being promoted to a concubine or even an empress was their path to happiness. Dance became a professional performance by dancers in luxurious mansions and palaces, watched by the elite, while commoners enjoyed dance through theater. The elite, sometimes intoxicated, would join in, but it wasn't always clear whether it was still dance. For the authorities, mixed-gender gatherings at folk theaters were akin to public indecency and were often suppressed.

3. Cultural Remnants: It's not entirely accurate to say that the Chinese have been disconnected from dance for millennia. Traditional dances like the dragon and lion dances have persisted. The Yangko dance (秧歌舞) is particularly noteworthy as it retains the spontaneity, mass participation, and communal spirit of primitive dances, which are the fundamental characteristics of modern square dancing. Ancient scholars only appreciated solitary dances like "dancing at the sound of a rooster" (闻鸡起舞) or "dancing with a sword under the moon" (月下舞剑). Their disdain for Yangko dance revealed a contempt for its vibrant life force, which they described as "vulgar and obscene." The life force is the core or soul of all art.

In Modern Times

The period before 2000 can be considered the prehistory of square dancing. The last forty years of that period coincided with the first half of my life, during which I encountered two types of dances with some external or internal connections to square dancing.

The "Loyalty Dance": About fifty years ago, we practiced the "Loyalty Dance" (忠字舞) on our elementary school playground. I still remember the lyrics: "The Yangtze River flows eastward, sunflowers turn towards the sun, with great enthusiasm we welcome the Ninth Congress, we sing loudly and joyfully." The song wasn't good even then. The individual dance movements are not much different from those in other dances, but when put together, they seem awkwardly funny. Despite my family's political persecution during the Cultural Revolution (文革), I didn't dislike the dance due to politics; I just found it unappealing. In contrast, I was deeply enamored with the song "The People of Yanbian Love You" (《延边人民热爱您》), although I don't recall the dance. The singer, a member of our school's propaganda team, was stunning in a yellow military uniform that would be comparable to Louis Vuitton today.

The Loyalty Dance was undoubtedly a square dance. We danced it not only on the school playground but also along Wangfujing Street (王府大街) and East Chang'an Avenue (东长安街) all the way to Tiananmen Square (天安门广场). Participation was mandatory; the teachers wouldn't allow anyone to stand by and watch. The scale was massive, with millions of people dancing. However, it was not spontaneous: a government directive would mobilize the nation, and once the directive passed, the dance vanished without a trace. Unlike today's square dancing, which persists regardless of restrictions, people find ways to dance. I recall one rainy day at the Bamian Cao Church square, where dancers with umbrellas moved like ice skaters on the wet ground. Spontaneous dances require social self-organization, which was limited and unstable in the all-encompassing government system of the first thirty years. People could gather to practice Tai Chi or do radio calisthenics, but dancing was risky, as it could be labeled as a "bourgeois lifestyle" or "new class struggle trend."

It's essential to clarify the relationship between the "Loyalty Dance" (忠字舞) and the "Red Guard Dance" (红卫兵舞). Some people see them as one, as the Red Guard Dance is also called the Loyalty Dance. They are similar, but I prefer to see the Red Guard Dance as an elder or cousin of the Loyalty Dance for the following reasons: First, the Red Guard Dance included not only loyalist dances for the Great Leader but also rebellious dances against class enemies, which were different in form. Second, the Red Guards emerged in 1966 and were essentially dissolved by military control in 1968. Third, during the peak years of 1966 and 1967, the Loyalty and rebellious dances were mainly performed by young Red Guards. By 1968-69, the Loyalty Dance was performed by the masses, as the Red Guards had been sent to the countryside and became known as "educated youth." Lastly, the Red Guards danced out of their own volition during the chaos of the Cultural Revolution when no one could command them. However, once order was restored, the Loyalty Dance was organized and led by revolutionary committees at all levels, performed to celebrate the Ninth Congress (九大). After the Congress ended, the dancing ceased.

Today's red-themed restaurants using the Red Guard Dance and Loyalty Dance to attract business are essentially the same as performing monkeys or nude services. Many people in society panic because one or two out of a million square dance groups play red songs and dress like Red Guards, loudly claiming a Cultural Revolution revival. Such exaggerated and reckless accusations are remnants of the Cultural Revolution mentality.

Ballroom Dance: The introduction of ballroom dancing in modern times was a revolutionary event in the history of Chinese dance. For ordinary people, dance was no longer just something to watch but something to participate in. I first saw ballroom dancing in the late 1970s. The first thirty years of revolutionary culture and asceticism reached their peak during the Cultural Revolution. Those ten years were not about "educating through entertainment" but hiding entertainment in education. Young people read the "Rural Medical Handbook" (《农村医疗手册》) as romantic literature, and the promotional windows with photos of Red Detachment of Women (红色娘子军) warriors kicking their legs attracted long gazes from men. When the Cultural Revolution ended and history's pendulum swung back, on one side were Teresa Teng (邓丽君) and velvet flowers, and on the other were repressed human nature and material desires rushing towards each other like star-crossed lovers. Over the forty years of reform and opening up, the ballroom dance craze may not have led, but it certainly outpaced the qigong craze, the business craze, and the political craze.

Square dancing's key elements are all present in ballroom dancing, except for the "square." Ballroom dance, also called "dance hall dance," was mostly held indoors because outdoor sound equipment wasn't convenient. However, in the late 1970s and early 1980s, the widespread use of tape recorders opened up new spaces for ballroom dancing. I first encountered ballroom dancing near a pavilion in Beihai Park (北海公园) on a small open space where five or six beginner men and one or two beginner women were awkwardly holding, guiding, and stumbling over each other. It looked like they were practicing wrestling. By the 1990s, pairs of men and women were commonly seen dancing the quickstep and waltz in squares and parks. Nowadays, ballroom dancing is almost exclusively outdoors. This shift signifies two things: First, ballroom dancing moved from the workplace (or state units) to society (parks and squares), becoming an activity organized by the community and calling on the state only when conflicts arose. Second, as it moved from workplace activities to community spaces, ballroom dancing evolved from occasional events to daily entertainment and fitness activities for residents.[2] Its function and meaning have changed.

Ballroom dance and square dance have many overlaps. Some ballroom dances, like the cha-cha and rumba, have elements incorporated into square dance. A square dance might consist entirely of simple three-step, four-step, or sailor's steps. Despite this, ballroom dance retains distinctive and relatively stable characteristics. In terms of form, dances like the waltz and Latin dances are instantly recognizable. Functionally, the terms "ballroom" or "social dance" are sufficiently clear. After the ten years of the Cultural Revolution, ballroom dance provided the masses with a legitimate opportunity for extramarital physical contact, causing a nationwide frenzy and frequent bloodshed in and around dance halls. Even in recent years, despite the many modern avenues for romantic interaction, ballroom dance remains a charming path for romantic encounters. Sometimes, passing by their groups, I see women dressed like brides, leaning back ninety degrees, spinning like whirlwinds with their partners. It's a dreamlike moment everyone yearns for. Around the ballroom dance groups, single men often linger, their eager eyes glinting like lights on water. This envelops the dance floor in a warm, hormonal atmosphere. A few years ago, during severe air pollution in Beijing, we would discuss on WeChat whether to "freely move" when pollution levels hit "blue." Meanwhile, the ballroom dance group in the south wouldn't even consider stopping. Yellow, orange, red—they treated them all as green. That group had several incidents. Once, hearing a commotion, I saw a man dart past me so fast it seemed he had wings. The reason? Either his wife was confronting him, or his partner's husband was attacking. While the male-female pairing gives ballroom dance its core appeal, removing the moral constraints significantly diminishes its energy. Although ballroom dance has a considerable reach, it is no longer the largest.

Tracing the prehistory of square dancing should include gymnastics, qigong, and tai chi, but that would be endless. So, let's talk about the present state of square dancing.

The Space

From my memory and understanding, the Yangko dance around the year 2000 opened the curtain for square dancing. I mentioned the origins of the Yangko dance earlier, so no need to repeat, but it's important to emphasize: the Yangko dance used to be grassroots, and it still is; it used to be confined to the countryside, but not anymore.

The first time I saw Yangko dancing was in the square in front of the China Art Museum (中国美术馆). Twenty years ago, a not-too-high iron fence divided the square into two parts, with the inside belonging to the museum and the outside to the public. In the late 1970s or early 1980s, during a particularly hot summer, a childhood friend and I brought our army cots and slept next to that fence under the starry sky, which still lingers in my memory. Back then, many open spaces in Beijing were accessible to the public. In the 1990s, one of my greatest joys was flying kites in Tiananmen Square (天安门广场), imagining them soaring into the lonely depths of space like the Voyager. Squares are the natural habitat for square dancing; without them, it's like fish without rivers or lakes.

So far, urban planning in China hasn't designated specific areas for square dancing, but some public spaces are indeed suitable. However, the square in front of the Art Museum is no longer available because they added another fence outside the original one, leaving no room for dancing. In recent years, as state power has strengthened, even slightly significant places, including the Beijing People's Art Theatre (北京人艺) where we used to climb steps and play badminton as kids, and the square in front of the Shenwu Gate (神武门), have become like military zones. A magazine office near my home even installed modern iron spikes, and I can't imagine why armed assailants would target a publication that no one would read even if they paid you.

Recently, there's been a campaign to "offer suggestions for the 20th National Congress." I don't know the proper channels, so I'll just submit my suggestion here:

To implement General Secretary Xi Jinping's instruction that "the country is its people," and to strengthen the bond between the Party and the masses, I propose that all relevant departments[3] at various levels of government, party, education, science, and culture consider opening the currently restricted squares or open spaces in front of their offices, without affecting their normal functions, to serve as daily leisure and entertainment venues for citizens.

Ideally, parks—like Beihai (北海) and Jingshan (景山) Parks—should be paradises for square dancing, but reality differs. First, parks are far from home, and the commute takes time. Second, the timing is off; square dancing usually happens after dinner, while parks close early. Third, in recent years, many parks have adopted stringent stability measures akin to those of the police, imposing numerous restrictions. Some have even banned larger gatherings like choirs and square dancing. In fact, parks are far enough from residential areas to avoid disturbing residents, and their large spaces and many trees mean different groups wouldn't necessarily disturb each other. Couples seeking quiet spots have plenty of secluded areas. The key lies in how park managers perceive the park's function and their power. Absolute tranquility may be the ideal state for some managers.

Compared to the solemnity of government offices, many commercial areas are bustling. At the Tongzhou North Yuan Wanda Plaza (通州北苑万达广场), there are eight or nine square dance groups lined up, along with people kicking shuttlecocks, skateboarding, playing with diabolos, and socializing with dogs. It's like a big food market where you can sample various activities. I learned to play the diabolo there, once even making it whistle. Small open spaces in roadside green areas also serve as dance spots. Near my home, the Imperial City Ruins Park (皇城根遗址公园), a narrow strip about two kilometers long and twenty meters wide, has several small open spaces housing various square dance groups like fitness dance, ghost step dance, ethnic dance, sailor dance, and zombie dance.[4] Each group ranges from two or three people to twenty or thirty. You can also find square dancers near subway stations, under overpasses, and beneath elevated highways.

Square dancing occupies public spaces, but it's not the only occupant. Conflicts arise: dancers are obstructed by pedestrians, brass ensembles, or skateboarders. I was once knocked over by a skateboard while dancing, and my friends worried about me when I didn't show up the next day. The main "enemies" of square dance are twofold. First, nearby residents. Since square dancing is a daily activity, it can't be far from residential areas, inevitably causing noise complaints. Some residents don't mind and might even join someday, while others are disturbed, whether due to children claiming they can't do homework, genuine health issues, or just general annoyance. Early Yangko dances were loud with real drums and suonas, comparable to construction noise. Though modern sound systems allow for volume control, conflicts remain sharp. Square dance, as the main cause of the disturbance, involves large groups needing high volume, but even small groups or individuals can be heard from a distance. Some dances are mild and use soft music, but others prefer intense, energetic tunes, like those fit for a heist scene.

The other "enemy" is within the square dance community itself. Different groups often have territorial disputes or boundary conflicts, which can be physical or auditory. Physical boundaries are easier to establish—just mark a specific brick or tree. The challenge lies in the auditory boundaries, i.e., volume. Due to limited space, especially in the old eastern and western city districts, two dance groups sometimes end up close to each other, and their music overlaps, causing confusion. To avoid competing leadership, one group raises its volume to drown out the other, leading to an arms race of sound that annoys nearby residents, resulting in thrown objects or other acts of hostility. Once, while dancing in the Imperial City Ruins Park (皇城根遗址公园), a man angrily interrupted, shouting colorful language, though only "I" and "you" were printable.

While these conflicts can't be completely eradicated, achieving general harmony isn't too difficult with mutual understanding and compromise. Over the years, through pleasant adjustments and unpleasant frictions, a sort of truce has emerged. Dancing typically starts around 7 PM and ends around 9 PM, almost a standard. Unlike the disruptive behavior of rich kids speeding through the night, square dancers won't disturb your sleep. As for volume, the reckless, anything-goes approach is fading. Since the volume of dance tracks varies, continuous play can be problematic, but group members often adjust it promptly to avoid upsetting neighboring groups and residents. The principle that you can't be happy if you make others unhappy is simple yet elusive in many areas, including politics and international relations. Surprisingly, it's almost instinctive in the public space of square dancing, making me proud as a participant.

At this point, I must commend and caution the government. In the process of square dance communities forming, the government has played a generally reasonable and appropriate role, worth referencing or learning from in other fields. Relevant departments follow regulations, intervening when necessary and stepping back when appropriate, neither overstepping nor shirking responsibility. Imagine if the government issued a directive putting square dance under the Central Civilization Office, working with the Ministry of Culture and Tourism, General Administration of Sport, Armed Police Force, China Dance Association, and China Musicians Association, to approve songs and dances[5], set organizational guidelines and rules, then appoint street committees to register dancers, form dance groups, and "establish party branches on the toes." If such a plan were implemented, square dancing would either disperse immediately or fizzle out within a month. Conversely, if the state were entirely hands-off, "gatherings" would indeed turn into "disturbances," and some dance floors could become arenas for martial arts. Currently, the state's role is primarily to mediate major conflicts and maintain basic order. When residents complain, the police come to warn: "Keep disturbing, and we'll confiscate your sound system." If two dance groups clash, the police stand between them, and the tension drops. In fact, just having the police occasionally patrol resolves most noise and conflict issues.

However, I sometimes worry that some police officers, wielding significant enforcement power, lack a proper understanding of their roles. Their rough style and lack of meticulous work habits can lead to both overreach and negligence. Abuse of power and laziness are two sides of the same coin, common among many social managers. Once, the police aggressively arrived, claiming we were disturbing residents, threatening to confiscate our sound system and take the group leader. Initially just an observer, I couldn't help but argue: "Disturbance is about volume, and volume can be adjusted. I've specifically gone to nearby residential buildings several times, and the sound isn't that loud. You can check yourself. We can agree on a volume with residents; we'll follow it, and you supervise. How about that?" He said some people are very sensitive and can hear even a little noise. I replied, "Some people can read letters with their ears, but you can't use special abilities as a standard!" The officer then

claimed square dance often involves illicit relationships. I retorted, "That's not your business; if a fight breaks out, then you intervene. Your duty is maintaining order, not moral policing."

During the pandemic, many open public spaces, including the square in front of Bamian Cao Church, were "legally" closed—not just prohibiting gatherings, but entirely banning people. This is overkill. For social managers, closures are the easiest form of management. China's national system, with its 2,000-year-old grand tradition and 70-year-old minor tradition since the Qin and Han dynasties, has evident institutional advantages but also undeniable shortcomings. The historical achievement of the reform and opening-up lies in overcoming and correcting this system by rebuilding the market and recreating society, thus liberating the enthusiasm and creativity of hundreds of millions of people. China's future healthy development depends on a complementary, competitive, and mutually beneficial relationship between the state, market, and society. Achieving this requires collective effort, especially the strongest state supporting rather than suppressing the weakest society. For square dancing, the state should reduce large, rarely used squares in urban planning and use the saved resources to build more small squares for daily use by residents. In terms of management, it's sufficient for police to act appropriately and maintain order without overstepping.

The People

Beijing's earliest square dances were Yangko dances. From their appearance and attire, participants were likely retired corporate or commercial employees, belonging to the lower income and cultural strata, aged between 50 to 70, and predominantly female. The Yangko teams occasionally had some elderly men, but they were mainly responsible for playing instruments like the suona and drums, clearly showing their background in physical labor. For a long time thereafter, square dance remained dominated by middle-aged and elderly women, hence the term "square dance aunties" (广场舞大妈). This term, like "hutong grandpas" (胡同大爷) and "Chaoyang residents" (朝阳群众), carries certain class connotations, reminiscent of Beijing's old Tianqiao with its "Crippled Tian," "Bald Head Pan," and "Crazy Chang," or snacks like mung bean juice, pig's liver, and mustard tuber.

Behind the people are identity and values. It's hard to guess what others are thinking, but I can share my own journey into the world of square dancing. As mentioned earlier, I started paying attention to square dancing around 2009 when I needed a new way to exercise daily, preferably something enjoyable—I had tried long-distance running, but it felt like a chore. My upbringing was influenced by the traditional masculine ideals in "Water Margin" (《水浒传》), and the word "dance" was almost non-existent in my life dictionary. Watching dance performances in art shows was my least favorite part, whether it was "Swan Lake" or "The Silk Road." Seeing young boys dancing as backup for female singers felt particularly awkward; I'd rather my son work in sanitation than do that. Watching was already a chore, let alone participating. The Loyalty Dance left such a bad impression that I'd rather kneel three times and kowtow nine times. Ballroom dancing, mimicking gentlemen and ladies, felt pretentious, and the unclear relationships between men and women seemed risky—who knows when you'd get stabbed. And as for the gaudy red and green Yangko dance, reminiscent of rural weddings, I knew I wasn't cut out for that.

I carried all these thoughts as I looked for a new fitness routine. Several square dance groups were active in my area, and during my walks, I would stop to watch. Gradually, I noticed some changes compared to before. First, it wasn't just Yangko anymore; the new dance styles were simple but not outdated. Second, the dancers looked younger, with more middle-aged participants.

Third, the proportion of men increased, no longer just elderly men with saggy vests. Fourth, there were fewer feminine arm movements like "soft hands" and "lotus fingers"; the dances focused more on legwork, resembling sports, so there was no fear of dancing like a sissy. These changes, like four hands pulling and pushing me, finally led me to join a square dance group at Bamiancao Church in 2012. Hundreds of people were dancing the "sixteen steps," a simple routine anyone could learn. Amidst the chaos of my first dance, I discovered I had a knack for it! On my way home, I decided to continue dancing with newfound confidence.

In China, music has an unspoken hierarchy corresponding roughly to social classes. At the top are Mozart and Verdi.[6] Cultural elites might also listen to Errenzhuan (二人转) or Lianhualuo (莲花落), but not as true fans—more like a casual visit or a weekend at a farm stay. Dance has a similar hierarchy, with ballet at the pinnacle. I indirectly know two ladies, each weighing about 160-170 pounds, who signed up for ballet classes at a steep cost, supposedly to "cultivate their temperament." Square dance, unsurprisingly, ranks lowest. At a dinner party, I once praised the benefits of square dance to some ladies who, with an air of foreign aristocracy, said, "That sounds wonderful! I'll definitely join when I'm old." (They were already old enough.) Once, a lady honestly remarked, "Isn't that music a bit too low-class?" Indeed, the core participants of square dance belong to society's lower tier.

There's an obvious reason why the lower class chooses square dancing: it's free. The middle and upper classes go to gyms, clubs, or bars (where they might also dance ballroom or disco). Cost is likely a factor: if it's free and accessible to everyone, is it even worth going? The upper class doesn't mind donating clothes or giving out red envelopes to the lower class, but mingling with them isn't part of their life goals. The media and online criticism of square dance groups often cite noise complaints, but there's also a palpable disdain from the middle and upper classes towards the lower class—think of how they frequently lament about "populism" these days. It's said that China's lower class resents officials and the wealthy, always hoping for Jack Ma to fall from grace. The upper class isn't any better; they want the lower class to stay in their corners, despising them for standing up, let alone dancing in public. I once asked a woman, "If elderly foreigners dance like this, you'd probably think it's all democratic and free, like they've never been oppressed. But when Chinese elders dance, why does it annoy you so much?"

For years, I've hardly heard of intellectuals joining square dance. Some might dabble for a project or research, but that's it. Intellectuals, economically speaking, aren't far removed from the lower class—they're like neighbors. Given all the books they've read, they should be more culturally and identity-wise free. Yet, decades of bureaucratization and marketization have profoundly affected them, mentally placing them in the elite and wealthy class. Frankly, people like me who have danced for years are rare. Like a barber who can't cut his own hair, I can only try to analyze my own class. Despite being labeled a "scholar" or "cultural figure," I never felt that way. Perhaps because I've always been on the periphery of my field, never nurturing respect for the center. Over time, I prefer standing in the back or near the door, allowing for late arrivals and early departures, coming and going freely. This mindset didn't necessarily push me towards square dancing but at least didn't hinder it. I've never felt out of place in square dance, and I find it far more engaging to stretch and chat with fishmongers and ticket sellers than to sit at round tables discussing "subjectivity," "post-colonial knowledge production systems," and other academic jargon with top experts and lead scholars.

When I say that the primary participants of square dance belong to the lower social class, I feel conflicted, because in my experience, they differ somewhat from what many, including myself, originally understood as the "lower class."

First, let's talk about moral standards. This includes two aspects: nature and cultivation. The distribution of good and evil should be fairly even across the population, as the saying goes, "there are good and bad people everywhere." Given China's rapid development over the past few decades and the "bold get rich, timid starve" mentality, one could argue that the upper class has more opportunities to commit misdeeds. Just browsing WeChat, I saw a video of a guy bragging about scamming people, saying, "Isn't it because I'm smarter than you?" Most square dancers I meet are kind-hearted. I remember a woman showing us an ultrasound photo of her six-to-seven-month-old granddaughter and tearing up with emotion. Such genuine affection may have vanished among the more refined egoists. This dancer takes care of her elderly mother, watches her grandchild, looks after her sick husband, and manages the group's sound system and music—truly a life of toil. According to the materialist view that prosperity leads to civility, the upper class should be well-mannered. Perhaps development isn't there yet. Despite many calls for "nobility" and etiquette schools, upper-class manners seem limited to superficial "sorrys" and "excuse mes." Dig a bit deeper, and you'll find unscrupulous merchants, corrupt officials, and mob bosses. While some square dancers speak roughly, most are polite, know their limits, and follow the rules. Sometimes I even think they're too timid.

Next, let's talk about education levels. There's a disconnect between official credentials and actual capabilities. In late Qing China, the gap between a scholar and a peasant was immense. Ah Q was illiterate, unable to sign his name on a death sentence. Modern society's widespread primary and secondary education, along with accessible reading materials, means formal schooling isn't the only way to improve literacy. The spread of the internet, Weibo, and WeChat since the late 1990s has significantly boosted the reading and writing skills of ordinary Chinese people. The value of academic degrees—bachelor's, master's, Ph.D.—is not what it used to be. One of our group members, a retired factory worker, writes WeChat posts that are more eloquent than some scholarly articles I've read. Earlier, I mentioned a refined lady who found square dance music too "low." When I asked her to elaborate, she couldn't. In contrast, several of our group members can describe the melody, emotion, rhythm, and style of music with remarkable precision in just a few words. One of our former members, known as Sister Wang, learned dances quickly and was very composed. She and her husband used to sell vegetables at the Dongsi morning market until it was shut down.[7] Her husband not only excelled in ballroom dancing but also enjoyed calligraphy and painting. Broadening the scope, I've noticed many ordinary housewives, who have nothing to do with art, have honed their aesthetic skills by matching clothes, choosing curtains, and selecting tablecloths. Their sense of color, shape, texture, tone, and composition is often as keen as that of master artist Fan Zeng (范曾).

Moreover, the demographic of square dancers has significantly changed over the years. The proportion of young people and outsiders (the so-called "new Beijingers") has noticeably increased. In an era of rapid technological advancements, new media, platforms, and templates, innovation is valuable, and youth is capital. The influx of young people undoubtedly elevates the social status of square dancing, countering public prejudice. The ghost step dance (鬼步舞), which has swept the nation in recent years, features prominent figures like Helen (海伦) and Han Chun (寒春), with many group leaders being fashionable young women. Spectators often watch with the same interest as a fashion show. The involvement of outsiders can be understood similarly. Today's primary square dancers, many from rural areas, are significantly younger than the mostly retired Beijing locals, ranging from their thirties to fifties. My current group leader, whom I thought was in her thirties, turned out to be over forty with grown children. When I commented on her fair skin and asked if she'd ever done farm work, she replied that she'd done it all, and her mother-in-law still urges her and her husband to return to their twenty acres. Their lifetime of physical labor means their physical age is often younger than their chronological age.[8] This provides the necessary physical conditions for square dance to evolve into more intense, challenging, and youthful forms. Young people and outsiders bring fresh blood to square dancing, preventing it from aging into a "zombie dance" for septuagenarians. Robust, agile rural workers not only boost China's economic development but also revitalize the urban spirit through square dancing, a noteworthy contribution to contemporary cultural history. Of course, there's a bittersweet side. A man from rural Hebei, in his fifties but as agile as a fifteen-year-old Beijinger, danced the ghost step with impressive vigor. During a chat about rural marriage prospects, he angrily noted, "As long as city boys can stand and walk, they can get a wife. Our rural boys, no matter how handsome or fit, struggle unless they own a house in town."

Sometimes, watching square dancing reminds me of the Qigong craze of the past. Both had comparable numbers of participants, but they reached different social strata. Qigong began among the urban middle class, initially promoted for health and fitness, but by the late 1980s, it had morphed into the dubious realm of "special powers." It swept through the upper echelons, infiltrating many grand and iron gates, but fizzled out once it approached quasi-religion status. In contrast, square dance has consistently adhered to its original purpose of fitness and entertainment, never straying from dance, with the lower class as its foundation, gradually and steadily expanding. This is probably what we call resilience. I can't understand how the elite, once manipulated like dough by the likes of Zhang Hongbao (张洪宝) and Li Hongzhi (李洪志), can now look down on square dancing.[9]

About the author:

Huang Jisu, is a sociologist and playwright. He is currently a research fellow at the Chinese Academy of Social Sciences and the deputy editor-in-chief of *the International Social Science Journal*. His notable screenplays include "Accidental Death of an Anarchist, Intentional Death of a Leftist Artist," "Che Guevara," "We Walk on the Broad Road," and "The Story of the Cat and the Mouse."

Endnotes:

[1] The analysis of the process of emotional externalization by the ancients is considered classic: emotions that cannot be contained within the heart seek someone to share them with; there are those incessantly babbling beside wine bottles and at courtyard gates. If talking isn't enough, they shout—no need for me to give examples from adult movies; when the shouting reaches a climax, it transforms into singing—it's not uncommon to find tourists singing on mountain peaks or riverbanks. When the excitement peaks, the limbs cannot contain themselves, and thus, they begin to dance.

[2] In the Republican era, there were commercial dance halls, and social dancing could become part of daily life, but it was limited to a small number of Westernized elites in places like the "Oriental Paris." In the first 30 years of New China, there were no commercial dance halls. Social dances were typically hosted in canteens or auditoriums of various work units, with participants and order managed by the units. Given the socio-political environment at the time, dancing was not a daily occurrence, although certain memoirs suggest there was a period when there were daily dance events in Zhongnanhai. See Li Jinping, *The Days I Danced with Central Leaders in Zhongnanhai*, https://net.blogchina.com/blog/article/210581.

[3] Military and police personnel are temporarily irrelevant, and as for hospitals, the general public won't go there either.

[4] At this point, we can define "square dance": it can be understood in broad and narrow senses. In the broad sense, it refers to all kinds of dances spontaneously performed by people in public squares, including yangge, sailor dances, ethnic dances, line dancing, social dancing, and more. In the narrow sense, it refers to group dances, line dances, or partner dances that are less complex than the aforementioned types but incorporate elements of each.

[5] It seems that some government departments have indeed introduced sample square dances. For example, the square dance *The East is Red*, choreographed by dancer Xia Bing, won the championship in the seventh national fitness dance competition. During the Wuhan epidemic, she also created the square dance *The Most Beautiful Rescuers*. It is likely that these dances have never been seen in public squares, and square dance enthusiasts have probably never heard of them.

[6] The "nouveau riche" among the economic elites certainly cannot accomplish this, but they will mold their children in that direction.

[7] I used to frequently visit the morning market at Dongsi to photograph the colorful fruits and vegetables.

When it was shut down, Sister Wang told me that the vendors took many photos as souvenirs. The richness and softness of their emotions were no less than those of the middle-class bourgeoisie.

[8] In the past, rural people appeared young when they were little, then suddenly aged, as if they went from eighteen or nineteen straight to fifty. In recent years, with the mechanization of agriculture, labor has become less strenuous—less strenuous work is actually a form of exercise. Additionally, rural people who migrate for work, especially women, generally place more importance on skincare and appearance. They apply lotions and wear sun protection, and their skin age is significantly younger than it was in the past.

[9] When I was a child, there was a cafeteria near my home where the chefs would knead dough with their feet.

Account of Returning to China in the Year of Wuxu: Encounters in Taiwan

WANG Yafa

While I am still not too old and can move around freely, every time I return to the motherland and Taiwan, I always seek to visit some remnants of the former dynasty, conduct some fieldwork and interviews, view the remaining relics, and leave some verifiable evidence to help restore the intentionally forgotten history.

This time, during my trip back, I focused on Taiwan, Japan, and mainland China. Here is a brief account of what I encountered along the way:

In recent years, whenever I return, I spend more time in Taiwan than on the mainland for three reasons:

In Taiwan, taking the metro (locally called "MRT" or 捷运) requires no checkpoint security inspections, no fear of various heavily armed police officers (nowadays, mainland police are divided into: civilian police, armed police, special police, traffic police, internet police, train police, forest police, fire police, sea police, railway police, air police, auxiliary police, and others. Recently, there's even a new "volunteer police" or 义警). You just swipe your card and pass through the gate easily.

On the metro, young people do not occupy seats reserved for the elderly and disabled. They actively offer their seats, with polite attitudes and a relaxed atmosphere.

In Taiwan, there is no internet censorship, so you can browse freely—VOA, BBC, Google, YouTube, Facebook—anything you want. These three points alone make me exclaim, "Amazing, my Republic of China!" The fortunate thing is,

the CCP has always considered Taiwan an inseparable part of China, so my love for Taiwan spares me from being called a traitor by the "Fifty Cent Party" (五毛党).

During my stay in Taiwan this time, besides sightseeing, visiting bookstores, and seeking out local snacks at markets, two notable visits were to two friends—one an old acquaintance and the other a new one.

I

Mr. Huang Tiancai (黄天才) and I are old friends. He served as the president of the Central Daily News (中央日报), the ROC's special envoy to Japan, and the chairman of the Central News Agency (中央通讯社). He is a veteran member of the KMT (国民党) with over seventy years of party membership, a staunch supporter of Chiang Kai-shek (蒋介石) and his son Chiang Ching-kuo (蒋经国). We became friends due to his friendship with Zhang Daqian (张大千), which I interviewed him about a decade ago, and we have kept in touch since. Every time I visit Taiwan, I must see him. Last year, at the age of 92, he even wrote a heartfelt preface commemorating his old friend Zhang Daqian for the album Remnants of the Maya Mansion (《摩耶精舍遗韵》) that I published in collaboration with the National Palace Museum in Taiwan.

Conversations with these veteran KMT members invariably touch upon the decline of the KMT and the incompetence of its successors. Mr. Huang, whose hearing is somewhat impaired, often needs me to write concise messages on a small blackboard. When I wrote "The current KMT is shortsighted," he took the blackboard, glanced at it, and vehemently remarked, "Not just short-sighted, but utterly hopeless..."

When I mentioned the cessation of the Central Daily News, a newspaper with a 78-year history, he lamented, "They cut their own throat, self-destructed!" and sighed, "The KMT was ruined by Lee Teng-hui (李登辉)!"

I then asked, "How could a century-old party be ruined by just one man?"

He lowered his head and remained silent.

Knowing from Mrs. Huang that he had already entertained several guests that day, I quickly bade farewell to avoid tiring him.

On my way home, I pondered: if a century-old party could be ruined by one man, isn't that a good thing? Such a good thing should not be monopolized by the KMT alone...

II

My new friend, Mr. Jin Zuwu (金祖武), was introduced to me by Master Shiguang Yuan (释广元), the abbot of Jinglü Temple (净律寺) in Taipei.

Master Shiguang Yuan, a visionary, secured a piece of barren land on the outskirts of Taipei from Chiang Wei-kuo (蒋纬国) in the 1950s to build Jinglü Temple. Adjacent to the temple, he established a cemetery that became the resting place for many cultural elites of the Republic of China, including Wang Yunwu (王云五), the inventor of the four-corner method of indexing Chinese characters for the Commercial Press (商务印书馆); Cheng Cangbei (程沧被), deputy director of the KMT Central Propaganda Department and first president of the Central Daily News (《中央日报》); Lang Jingshan (郎静山), founder of the China Photographic Association and master photographer; Peking opera star Meng Xiaodong (孟小冬); and KMT military and political figure Wang Xinheng (王新衡). Among

them lies Jin Jiyuan (金吉元), whose tomb is beside that of Meng Xiaodong. Although not as famous as the others, he is worth mentioning.

Jin Jiyuan's father, Jin Tingsun (金廷荪), was the financial manager for Huang Jinrong (黄金荣), later partnering with Huang Jinrong and Du Yuesheng (杜月笙) to establish the Sanxin Company (三鑫公司). His former residence at 82 Xinhua Road in Shanghai was also the headquarters of the Sanxin Company.

After 1949, Jin Jiyuan moved to Taiwan and married Du Yuesheng's daughter, Du Meixia (杜美霞).

While reading The Collected Poems and Essays of Zhang Daqian (《张大千诗文集》), I found a couplet he wrote for Meng Xiaodong: "Soul returns to heaven, fame remains in the world; the tragic song of Guangling ends; unafraid of threats or bribes, she upholds the spirit of a heroine." The postscript read: "Madame Du, Meng Linghui, ten years ago when ruffians stormed her residence in Hong Kong, attempting to abduct her to the mainland. She firmly rebuffed them. Realizing they could not coerce her, they offered a million yuan for her to record audio and video. She lamented, 'This land is no longer safe,' and moved to Taipei. Her righteous stand is admirable and rare in ancient times. Zhang Yuan, also known as Daqian, respectfully wrote this." (杜夫人孟令辉捐帏，十年前女士在香港，暴徒入其寓所，欲劫持之以往大陆，叫嚣弥日，恫吓万端，女士严词斥绝之。若辈知不可屈，忽出百万元为寿，托言允为录音录影，女士私叹曰:"是邦危，不可以居矣。"即遄来台北，大义凛然，求之远古已为不易，喜可敬也。张爰大千拜挽。) Zhang Daqian's words were not baseless, but I found no corroboration in other books about Meng Xiaodong. If there were clues, they were vague.

When I visited Master Guang Yuan at Jinglü Temple in Taipei last year, I took the opportunity to pay respects to the sages. Seeing that Meng Xiaodong's tombstone was inscribed by Zhang Daqian with "Tomb of Madame Du Meng" (杜门孟太夫人之墓), I discussed the abduction incident with Master Guang Yuan.

Master Guang Yuan mentioned that the tomb next to Meng Xiaodong's belonged to Mr. Jin Jiyuan, whose wife, Ms. Du Meixia, was Du Yuesheng's daughter from his wife Yao Yulan (姚玉兰). I knew that after moving to Taiwan, Meng Xiaodong lived on Linyi Street in Taipei, near Yao Yulan's residence. It was said that Yao Yulan and her daughter, Du Meixia, visited Meng Xiaodong almost daily, maintaining a very close relationship. Since Yao Yulan had passed away, Du Meixia might be the only one privy to the details.

I asked Master Guang Yuan to introduce me to Ms. Du Meixia. He told me that Ms. Du was currently in poor health and undergoing hospital treatment, but he would help me get in touch.

The next day, I contacted Ms. Du's son, Mr. Jin Zuwu, who agreed to meet me at a café near Cathay General Hospital (国泰医院) in Daan District (大安区).

With Mr. Luo Xuzhang (罗旭彰) guiding me, I found the café. As soon as I pushed open the glass door, Mr. Jin recognized me, stood up, and greeted me. After a few pleasantries, we conversed in Shanghainese. Although born in Taiwan, he spoke perfect Shanghainese, as Shanghai was where his grandfather and maternal grandfather rose to prominence and the homeland his parents always longed for. The family's native tongue was undoubtedly Shanghainese.

We exchanged works. He gifted me a red-covered, hardcover book titled Commemorating the 110th Birthday of Ms. Meng Xiaodong (《孟小冬女士一一〇诞辰纪念》). He told me he was currently responsible for the "Ms. Meng Xiaodong Chinese Opera Scholarship Foundation" (孟小冬女士国剧奖学基金会) and had many interactions with the Peking Opera community on the mainland.

I asked if he had any recordings of the Winter Empress (Meng Xiaodong), and he said he did, promising to give me a copy at our next meeting.

We talked about his grandfather, Du Yuesheng, his other grandfather, Jin Tingsun, and his uncles, Du Weifan (杜维藩), Du Weishan (杜维善), and Du Weiping (杜维屏), who lived overseas. We also discussed the changes to his family's residence at the corner of Xinle Road (新乐路) and Shaanxi South Road (陕西南路) in Shanghai, which is now a restaurant he recently dined at.

Finally, we talked about Mr. Shen Huichuang (沈惠窗) of Dacheng Magazine (《大成》杂志) in Hong Kong. He told me that the Taiwan-based Showwe Publishing House (秀威出版社) was about to publish a complete set of Dacheng's reprints. I mentioned that Dacheng had published my articles: one was "Tears of the Ink Lotus" (《墨荷泣诉》), about Zhang Xinming (张心铭), Zhang Daqian's nephew, who was persecuted to death during the Cultural Revolution; another was "The Stubborn Old Man Ye Qianyu" (《倔老头叶浅予》), recounting my early 1980s interview with Ye Qianyu (叶浅予). Mr. Shen told me that Ye had illustrated my manuscript with two drawings.

I never received payment for my contributions to Dacheng. Once, while discussing this at Mr. Xie Zhiliu's (谢稚柳) "Zhuang Mutang" (壮暮堂) with the presence of Wen Wei Po reporter Mr. Zheng Zhong (郑重), he asked me to convey to Mr. Shen that Dacheng had published several of his articles about Mr. Tang Yun (唐云) without any payment or notice. I told him that not getting paid was one thing, but I also lost a painting. When I sent Mr. Shen the manuscript of "Tears of the Ink Lotus," I included a photo of an ink lotus painting by Zhang Xinming. Mr. Shen said the photo was unclear and asked for the original. After receiving the original, he didn't return it promptly, saying he would hand it back to me personally when I visited Hong Kong. Not long after, Mr. Shen suddenly passed away, and the painting's whereabouts remain unknown. The painting, inscribed by Mr. Xie Zhiliu, is very precious, and I regret its loss to this day. However, publishing Dacheng in Hong Kong was not easy for Mr. Shen. Each issue relied on a monthly subsidy of 50,000 Hong Kong dollars from Mr. Xu Jiliang (徐季良), president of the Suzhou and Zhejiang Association (苏浙同乡会), and donations of paintings from Mr. Zhang Daqian to barely sustain it. It was tough for him.

Mr. Jin told me the complete set of Dacheng reprints was being printed, and he would ask the publisher to reserve a set for me.

Finally, he apologized for meeting near the hospital, explaining that he had hoped to bring me to see his mother if she felt well enough today. Unfortunately, she was still weak, so he was very sorry. Understanding his meaning, I smiled, took the flowers from Mr. Luo, and said, "I understand. Since it is not possible today, please present these flowers to her on my behalf and wish her a speedy recovery. I will visit next time I am in Taiwan."

We shook hands and parted ways, having had a very pleasant conversation.

Postscript: Just now, while flipping through Commemorating the 110th Birthday of Ms. Meng Xiaodong, I found many precious photos of her later years in Taiwan, especially those with Zhang Daqian (张大千), which I had never seen before. Delighted by these discoveries, I have noted them here.

III

Mr. Liang Jianru (梁剑如) is a friend I met in Sydney. He is a Hong Kong entrepreneur who, although based in Australia, works primarily in Hong Kong. Last year, during his vacation in Sydney, we agreed over a meal to meet in Taipei this May and visit the Academia Sinica to see the Hu Shih Memorial Hall and the Fu Sinian Library.

Early that morning, accompanied by our friend Mr. Luo Xuzhang from Taipei, four of us arrived at the Academia Sinica.

The environment there is tranquil, with towering palm trees and red-brick buildings exuding a Republican era atmosphere. Walking into it feels like stepping into the old streets of Nanjing or the Republican-era buildings of Shanghai's Jiangwan district, giving a sense of returning to the Republic of China.

I have always revered Mr. Hu Shih (胡适) as a beacon of the Chinese New Culture Movement and a model for free intellectuals.

In 1958, invited by Chiang Kai-shek, Hu Shih returned from the United States to serve as the president of the Academia Sinica. During the inauguration ceremony, Chiang praised him and tasked the Academia Sinica with the "arduous task of reviving national culture and completing the mission of anti-communism and anti-Russia." The issue of the CCP's criticism of Hu Shih was also mentioned.

When it was Hu Shih's turn to speak, he pointed at Chiang and said, "Mr. President, you are wrong." He emphasized that the Academia Sinica should focus on academic pursuits and not be a political institution. Addressing the CCP's criticism, he argued that it wasn't a personal moral issue but opposition to his advocacy for scientific methods in scholarship. This made Chiang very angry, and that night he wrote in his diary that this was "the second greatest affront in my life," calling Hu Shih "truly a madman." He was so upset that he couldn't sleep despite taking sleeping pills.

No matter how much Chiang Kai-shek was denigrated or how often Hu Shih opposed him, Chiang still personally wrote an elegiac couplet for Hu Shih after his death: "A model of old morals in new culture; a paragon of new thoughts in old ethics," and "Combining wisdom and virtue." Chiang Kai-shek was a gentleman who did not betray those who had served him and did not humiliate scholars. He is a hero who upheld Chinese cultural heritage in modern history.

Let me add a few side notes here.

In the spring of 2000, I visited Hu Shih's former residence in Shangzhuang Town, Jixi County, Anhui Province—now the Hu Shih Memorial Hall (胡适纪念馆). There, I met the curator, Mr. Hu Yukai (胡育凯), a nephew of Hu Shih. Mr. Hu complained that the memorial hall lacked funding and that the government did not care. I told him, "Your uncle was the greatest enemy of the CCP. The fact that you have this memorial plaque, thanks to fellow villager Hu Jintao, is already a big favor. To run the memorial well, you must seek support yourself. You can solicit social donations and also seek help from the Hu Shih Memorial Hall at the Academia Sinica in Taiwan." My words seemed to inspire him. He said the director of the Hu Shih Memorial Hall in Taiwan had visited and mentioned the possibility of future exchanges, but he had lost the contact information. After returning to Shanghai, I provided him with the contact address of Director Pan from the Hu Shih Memorial Hall in Taiwan.

A few years ago, I spoke with Director Pan over the phone. He told me that Mr. Hu Yukai had passed away.

Mr. Hu Yukai was only a year older than me. Due to his relationship with Hu Shih, he was deprived of educational opportunities and suffered greatly. My interactions with him are detailed in my essay, "Impressions of the Two Hu Shih Memorial Halls" (《两个胡适纪念馆的观感》).

Let's return to the main topic.

Mr. Liang Jianru is a serious person. Once

inside the memorial hall, he meticulously examined every exhibit. Understanding that this was his first visit, I had no interest in accompanying him and instead went to the Fu Sinian Library.

Every time I visit the Fu Sinian Library, I linger in front of one particular exhibit—a calligraphy piece sent by Mao Zedong to Fu Sinian, which inspires many thoughts:

"Mr. Mengzhen:

Following your instructions, I have written these numbers, though they are not perfect. Today, I heard the story of Chen Sheng and Wu Guang, which I find too modest, hence I quote a Tang poem for elaboration. Best regards and travel safely:

'Bamboo and silk burn away, the empire vanishes; the passes and rivers lock the ancestral dragon's abode. The pit ashes are not yet cold, and chaos erupts in Shandong; Liu and Xiang, after all, were not scholars.'"

Why did Mao Zedong copy this poem for Fu Sinian?

After much pondering, I finally found the answer.

In his youth, Mao Zedong worked as an assistant in the library at Peking University, earning eight yuan a month. His job was to find books for readers among the shelves, enduring the condescension of professors. No wonder that after becoming the "emperor," he told American journalist Edgar Snow in the Forbidden City that they did not treat him as a person; carpenters earned ten yuan a month while he earned only eight.

There's also a small anecdote according to Mr. Zhang Lifang (章立凡). It's been recorded in some Taiwanese books that Mao Zedong was not very diligent in his library work, especially with his illegible handwriting. The library director, Li Dazhao (李大钊), had criticized him. Once, when Mao misplaced a book that Fu Sinian wanted to borrow, Fu pointed it out. Mao denied it and argued, leading to a heated exchange where Fu slapped him.

Alas, this slap created a rift with China's intellectual community. Later, many innocent scholars paid the price for Fu's actions, which was truly unfair, unfortunate, and pitiable.

Fu Sinian was recognized as a principled intellectual of the Republican era. He lived a life of poverty, integrity, and candor. One small incident illustrates this: After the outbreak of the Pacific War, the U.S. provided the Nationalist government with a loan of $500 million. The then Finance Minister, Kong Xiangxi (孔祥熙), embezzled one billion yuan using the exchange rate difference, causing public outrage. At a political meeting, Fu Sinian questioned this, and under public pressure, Chiang Kai-shek had to intervene. He hosted a banquet for Fu Sinian, pleading on Kong's behalf. During the meal, Chiang asked, "Mr. Fu, do you trust me?"

Fu Sinian straightforwardly replied, "Absolutely!"

Chiang then asked, "Since you trust me, you should trust the people I employ."

Fu Sinian resolutely responded, "I trust you, Generalissimo. But to say that I should trust everyone you employ, you might as well chop off my head, for I cannot agree with that!"

Due to Fu Sinian's relentless pursuit, Chiang Kai-shek eventually had to dismiss Kong Xiangxi from his position.

Fu Sinian saw through Mao Zedong's character from the start. In July 1945, Fu visited Yan'an with a delegation. He observed that Yan'an's practices were purely despotic and anti-democratic. He had a long conversation with Mao and found that Mao was very familiar with popular novels, analyzing that Mao studied these books to understand and exploit the weaknesses of the people's psychology, much like Song Jiang.

After Mao published "Snow" (《沁园春·雪》) in the Xinhua Daily in September 1945, Fu immediately wrote to Chiang Kai-shek, asserting, "This man harbors imperial ambitions!"

Returning to the matter of Mao sending the Tang poem to Fu Sinian:

Records show that Fu Sinian and Mao Zedong had a long conversation in a cave. During this, Mao mentioned Fu's prominence during the May Fourth Movement. Fu replied: "At that time, we were just like Chen Sheng and Wu Guang; you are now like Xiang Yu and Liu Bang." Before parting, Fu asked Mao for some calligraphy. Whether Fu did this out of concern for Mao's progress in calligraphy is unknown.

Mao used the Tang poem to express his defiance: I am no longer the same young man who could be slapped around; now I am a king, wielding power like Liu and Xiang, unlettered but commanding the world. His pride and confidence are evident.

After we each finished touring the exhibits, Mr. Liang and I agreed to lay flowers at Hu Shih's grave.

Hu Shih's grave is just opposite the main entrance of the Academia Sinica.

After laying the flowers and paying our respects, Mr. Liang quietly read the vernacular epitaph for Hu Shih written by Mr. Mao Zishui (毛子水). Meanwhile, I searched for an elegiac couplet. If my memory serves me correctly, I had seen it before—it was a famous couplet personally inscribed by Chiang Kai-shek: "A model of old morals in new culture; a paragon of new thoughts in old ethics." It should have been on either side of the tombstone. However, I couldn't find it. I asked Mr. Luo Xuzhang, who had visited with me a few years ago. He vaguely remembered seeing it too, but perhaps it was removed during the Democratic Progressive Party's de-Chiang campaign. I suddenly recalled the statue of

Chiang Kai-shek in Cihu, Taoyuan, which was smashed into pieces during Chen Shui-bian's era.

At this moment, my stream of consciousness was triggered, and I wanted to say a few words to President Tsai Ing-wen. The Republic of China has not perished; it simply resides in Taiwan. Even if the Democratic Progressive Party (DPP) has gained temporary power, they do not have the authority to discard the name "Republic of China." It is the vessel for the future revival of China. Just as the Soviet Union could return to the form of Russia, China can do the same. To quote Mr. Huang Tiancai, "The KMT has lost its way, but you cannot afford to. You must look beyond the present—the future of the Republic of China lies in the vast lands of the mainland, not just on this small island."

Settling in one corner without ambition has no future. The historical lessons from the Southern Tang and Southern Song dynasties are proof enough!

As we left Hu Shih's cemetery at dusk, Mr. Liang and I discussed the teacher-student relationship between Hu Shih and Fu Sinian:

In 1949, as Hu Shih prepared to go to the United States, he worried about the safety of his family and considered sending them to his ancestral home in Jixi for protection. Fu Sinian thought this was unwise and suggested that Hu Shih's wife should go to Taiwan with him, where she could stay at National Taiwan University temporarily. He assured, "No matter how the situation evolves, I will take care of Mrs. Hu. If food is scarce, we will share porridge." Hu Shih entrusted his wife, Jiang Dongxiu, to Fu Sinian, and she stayed in the principal's residence at National Taiwan University along with Fu's nephew and a friend's family, making about ten people who shared a modest life.

After the victory in the War of Resistance, Fu Sinian came to Beiping as an official responsible for receiving the city on behalf of the Nationalist government. Many recommended him for the presidency of Peking University. He repeatedly declined, saying Hu Shih was a more suitable candidate. He agreed to act as the interim president until Hu Shih (then serving as the Republic of China's ambassador to the United States) returned. He fulfilled this promise, stepping down upon Hu Shih's return.

We talked about Fu Sinian's upright, unyielding character, his tenderness towards students, his modest lifestyle, and the traditional Chinese scholar's integrity. When we mentioned that Fu Sinian lived a frugal life, even asking his wife, Yu Dazai, to sew him a pair of cotton trousers when he received his last manuscript payment because his legs were cold and his suit pants were too thin to keep him warm, we both choked up.

After Fu Sinian's death, he left almost no inheritance. His only legacy was a room full of books. He had instructed his wife to keep this collection for their son. He also asked his old friend, Dong Zuobin, to carve a seal with the inscription "Books inherited from Mengzhen" (孟真遗子之书). "A home with books can educate a child," he hoped, encouraging his son to become an independent scholar. The truth is, despite holding multiple prestigious positions and having a widespread reputation, Fu Sinian chose to live a life of poverty and simplicity, refusing to bend to societal pressures. He once told his wife, "In my lifetime, the ones I owe the most are you and our son. My salary is meager, and our life is difficult. We have to rely on manuscript fees to make ends meet."

In 1945, during a student protest at Southwest Associated University, there was a violent clash with the police. Students were arrested, and Fu Sinian, acting as interim president, confronted the responsible KMT official, Guan Linzheng, saying, "We were friends, but now we are enemies. Students are like my children. You harm them, how can I remain silent?"

On April 6, 1949, during student protests at National Taiwan University, the military stormed the campus and arrested students. Fu Sinian personally went to the highest authorities, arguing that entering the campus without legal procedures to arrest students was illegal. He told Peng Mengji, the commander of the Taiwan Garrison Command, "If any student sheds blood, I will fight you to the death!"

Fu Sinian was gentle with his students but never obsequious to the powerful. When talking to Chiang Kai-shek, he would hold a pipe, cross his legs, and gesticulate freely. Chiang, knowing his character, never minded. Fu Sinian repeatedly refused to take official positions in the KMT government, choosing instead to remain an independent scholar and participate in politics without becoming a politician. He self-deprecatingly called his efforts "a scholar serving the country, that's all!" His integrity and uprightness command deep respect.

On December 20, 1950, after giving a speech at the Provincial Senate, Fu Sinian suddenly clutched his head and exclaimed, "Something's wrong!" before collapsing. He was diagnosed with a brain hemorrhage and, despite all efforts to save him, passed away at the age of 54.

Alas, to die on the podium, a talent snatched by the heavens. Fu Sinian's death caused a great stir in Taiwan. Students took to the streets to mourn their mentor. Even Chiang Kai-shek personally attended the funeral. On the day of the memorial service, more than five thousand people attended, and there were over 270 elegiac couplets.

As we talked, we soon arrived at the hotel. Before parting, we decided to visit Fu Sinian's tomb at National Taiwan University the next morning.

Fu Sinian's tomb, also known as "Fu Garden" (傅园), is located to the right of the main gate of National Taiwan University, behind a grove of royal palm trees. Sixteen Doric marble columns support a Greek temple-like roof. Under the roof stands a stone sarcophagus with the inscription "Tomb of Principal Fu Sinian" (傅校长斯年之墓) in small seal script, with "December, 1951" (中华民国四十年十二月) and "Erected by National Taiwan University" (国立台湾大学敬立) in running script on either side.

Entering the cemetery, we solemnly laid a bouquet of yellow and white calla lilies and performed three deep bows.

Standing in front of Fu Sinian's tomb, my thoughts surged:

In 1948, as the defeat of the Nationalist government became inevitable and plans were made to retreat to Taiwan, Chiang Kai-shek decided to move the national treasury's gold, the artifacts from the National Palace Museum, the collections of the Central Research Institute, and the books from the Beijing Library to Taiwan. At the same time, a "Plan to Rescue Mainland Scholars" was devised. Fu Sinian was tasked with drafting a detailed "Rescue List for Scholars," which included almost all the essential intellectuals to be saved. However, when Hu Shih waited at Nanjing Airport, ready to evacuate to Taiwan with his colleagues, he saw only a few old friends alight from the plane from Beijing. Shocked and dismayed that most of the people on the list did not appear, Hu Shih covered his face and wept, while Fu Sinian sighed deeply beside him.

Alas, an eternal cry and a timeless sigh, lamenting the countless future sorrows and the many debts of blood and tears that would follow!

Standing in front of Fu Sinian's tomb, I thought of the Hu Shih Memorial Park I had visited the previous day; I thought of Wang Yunwu (王云五), buried on the hillside of Jinglü Temple (净律寺); I thought of Lin Yutang (林语堂), who rests in his own backyard by the Yangming Mountains; I thought of Zhang Daqian, who lies among the plum blossoms at the Maya Mansion⋯ I thought of their descendants, who have studied abroad and achieved great success in their careers.

Suddenly, I heard a stream of consciousness crying in my ears, a mourning voice reading eulogies for those who, in their hopefulness, stayed on the mainland at key moments—Chu Anping (储安平), Ye Qisun (叶企荪), Fu Lei (傅雷), Zhang Boju (张伯驹), Chen Yinke (陈寅恪), Zhang Dongsun (张东荪)⋯

Spending three days in Taipei with Mr. Liang Jianru, we had the chance to pay respects to two great figures we both admired, fulfilling a long-cherished wish. Despite his Cantonese being worse than my Shanghainese, our hearts communicated, and whenever there were language misunderstandings, we often laughed, enjoying the "chicken talking to ducks" moments.

The Unforgettable Lizhuang

After parting with Mr. Liang, I returned to the mainland and went to Sichuan to continue tracing the historical sites associated with Mr. Fu Sinian and other scholars in Lizhuang.

When discussing the Academia Sinica and Mr. Fu Sinian, one must mention Lizhuang during the War of Resistance against Japan and the historic contributions of several local gentry in Lizhuang who, at a critical moment of national survival, advocated for accommodating a generation of cultural elites. One must also not forget the truth of the tragic deaths they suffered during the suppression campaigns of the new regime.

In 1940, Japanese aircraft launched frequent bombings across Yunnan with the aim of cutting off the Burma Road, thereby blocking supplies from entering China.

At this time, Tongji University, which had experienced nearly seven relocations, found it increasingly untenable to remain in Kunming and began seeking a new location. After careful consideration, they set their sights on southern Sichuan. Meanwhile, the National Central Research Institute and the Central Museum, which had also temporarily relocated to Yunnan, were contemplating new sites. Mr. Fu Sinian, then head of the Institute of History and Philology, sought a place that could not be easily found on a map.

During these turbulent times, news reached the small county town of Lizhuang in southern Sichuan, where it was learned by a man named Luo Nangai (罗南陔).

Luo Nangai was the Party Secretary of the Nationalist Party in Lizhuang District. Well-read and courteous, he was a highly respected local gentleman. He immediately contacted the district chief Zhang Guanzhou (张官周), Yang Junhui (杨君惠), Wan Yuting (宛玉亭), Fan Bokai (范伯楷), Yang Mingwu (杨明武), Deng Yungai (邓云陔), Li Qingquan (李清泉), Jiang Xuhui (江绪恢), and other town gentlemen and notables to discuss the possibility of accommodating Tongji University in Lizhuang.

Despite some concerns raised during the meeting about Lizhuang's small size and population of just over three thousand, which might make it difficult to host a southward migration team of more than twenty thousand people, Luo Nangai persuaded everyone by stressing that the nation's crisis was everyone's responsibility. They reached a unanimous agreement to invite Tongji University to Lizhuang as a place of refuge.

They immediately sent a telegram to the Ministry of the Interior, the Ministry of Education, Tongji University, and other relevant units in the name of the Lizhuang local government. The telegram, drafted by Luo Nangai, read: "Tongji moving to Sichuan, Lizhuang welcomes, all needs, local supply."

After the telegram was sent, Tongji University dispatched experts to investigate and soon finalized the decision.

The relocation route for Tongji University involved entering Sichuan via the Sichuan-Yunnan and Yunnan-Guizhou highways, then transferring to boats at Luzhou to reach Lizhuang. The journey was fraught with mountains and rivers, presenting extreme challenges. Notably, the cultural relics now housed in the National Palace Museum in Taiwan were transported to Lizhuang along this route and stored in the Zhang Family Ancestral Hall.

Along with Tongji University, other institutions that moved to Lizhuang included the Institute of History and Philology, the Institute of Social Sciences, the Institute of Physical Anthropology of the Academia Sinica, the National Central Museum, the China Architecture Society, the Institute of Arts and Letters of National Central University, and more. Renowned scholars such as Fu Sinian, Dong Zuobin (董作宾), Wu Dingliang (吴定良), Tong Dizhou (童第周), Tao Menghe (陶孟和), Li Ji (李济), Liang Sicheng (梁思成), Lin Huiyin (林徽因), Jin Yuelin (金岳霖), John Fairbank (费正清), Wu Wenzao (吴文藻), Bing Xin (冰心), Wang Shixiang (王世襄), Luo Zhewen (罗哲文), Luo Ergang (罗尔纲), Wu Mengchao (吴孟超), and others made Lizhuang a renowned place. International mail and packages simply addressed to "Lizhuang, Sichuan" could reliably reach their recipients.

We must thank Lizhuang, thank Luo Nangai and the local gentry, and thank the people of Lizhuang for protecting the lifeblood of our nation at a critical moment of national survival.

At this point, I couldn't help but stand and bow deeply to the screen, showing my respect for Lizhuang.

After the victory in the War of Resistance in 1945, Tongji University and all the central institutions relocated back, bidding farewell to Lizhuang.

Recalling the difficult five years spent there, one cannot but mention Fu Sinian borrowing grain from the military, Liang Sicheng completing his History of Chinese Architecture (《中国建筑史》) under harsh conditions, or Lin Huiyin's "Lady's Salon" anecdotes and her struggles with illness while studying.

During their six years in Lizhuang, countless touching stories unfolded among these national elites, far beyond what this short essay can cover. However, one story must be told and remembered:

In 1950, during the suppression campaigns of the new regime, it was stipulated that all Nationalist Party officials above the district chief level were to be executed.

Luo Nangai, the former Party Secretary of the Nationalist Party in Lizhuang, along with Zhang Guanzhou, the district chief, and Yang Junhui, the town chief, were the primary targets for the new regime's executions to establish their authority.

On the day of the execution, the suppression work team gathered 300 poor peasants, armed with wooden sticks, forming two lines. Several revolutionaries, tied up, were escorted through the lines, beaten to death before even reaching the execution site.

Although the men were dead, the new regime was not done with them. Executioners dragged the bodies to the execution ground, shot them to complete the procedure, and prepared to display their bodies on bamboo stakes, intending to exhibit them as a deterrent. However, as they pried open their skulls, a sudden torrential rainstorm began, forcing them to hastily bury the bodies and abandon their gruesome plans.

Readers, one cannot dismiss tales of divine intervention. As a young man educated under Communist materialism, I did not believe in such things. But after witnessing two strange events in

Australia, I can no longer deny the existence of such phenomena.

In the 1990s, those who came to Australia might remember the murder of cardiologist Dr. Zhang Renqian. On the day of his funeral at St. James Church, as the priest called for the casket to be lifted, the sky suddenly darkened with clouds, and rain poured down. As soon as the casket was carried out, the rain stopped, and the sun shone again. Another incident involved my friend Zhao Yansheng's mother. During her funeral, as the master of ceremonies called for the casket to be lifted, the sky instantly filled with dark clouds and torrential rain began to pour. If such coincidences happen at the command "lift the casket," how can one not believe in divine response?

Returning to the unjust execution of Luo Nangai and others, such cruel methods surpass ancient Chinese punishments like death by a thousand cuts. It is a pity that the people at that time were so isolated from the world that they didn't know about the "Guinness World Records"; otherwise, it would surely have made the list.

In 2010, someone proposed that Luo Nangai, a scholar who had contributed to the relocation of central institutions, and who had no blood debts, should be posthumously exonerated. The higher authorities replied that the "suppression campaigns" were decreed by the founding father and were an unshakable case. After much discussion, they finally referred to him ambiguously as an "enlightened gentleman." Such ancient wrongful cases, which number in the millions from remote areas to Tiananmen Square, from the shores of the East China Sea to the inside and outside of the Red Walls, cannot be redressed unless the sky falls.

In my old age, despite my frailty and poor eyesight, I continue to write, hoping to inspire my peers to follow the scholarly spirit of Hu Shih in exploring our national history. I encourage everyone to use the internet, visit libraries, go to the Taipei National Historical Museum, delve into old magazines like Biographical Literature (《传记文学》), and search through old documents and the remaining elderly to recover the true history of our nation.

Don't forget, restoring intentionally forgotten history and correcting intentionally altered history is our generation's responsibility!

About the Author:

Wang Yafa, a writer residing in Australia, has frequently written articles in recent years introducing mainland Chinese artists to readers in Australia, Hong Kong, and Taiwan.

ECHOES OF TIME

The Bitter Reality behind Beijing's Aid to Vietnam

CHEN Tushou

I

In the early 1950s, as the Indochina Peninsula was engulfed in conflict, China provided extensive material support to the Vietnamese Communist Party in its struggle against French colonial forces. This period saw the gradual development of China's foreign aid strategies and methods, which reached a legendary peak in the 1960s and 70s. Aid to Korea and Vietnam set the highest standards and practices for China's foreign assistance, influencing aid policies and methods for the next two to three decades. The primary emphasis was on ensuring aid personnel adhered strictly to the spirit of internationalism, performing only good deeds and avoiding any wrongdoing.

In the "Code of Conduct for Technical Personnel Aiding Vietnam" issued internally by the Ministry of Foreign Trade on July 23, 1955, Chinese personnel involved in foreign aid were required to "unreservedly pass on scientific and technical knowledge to the Vietnamese comrades" while "avoiding any form of great-power chauvinism and maintaining a humble and amiable attitude towards the Vietnamese people." They were repeatedly reminded to "follow the reporting system, oppose all undisciplined and unorganized speech and actions," and to ensure that "all technical materials and documents were exchanged through official channels, not handed over privately to any individuals or organizations." Discretion and confidentiality were paramount in foreign aid work.

At the end of 1956, the Military Commission's General Finance Department and General Logistics Department discovered that taxing aid materials to Vietnam increased settlement prices, reducing the actual quantity of aid materials and complicating explanations to the Vietnamese Party and state. After discussions with the Ministry of Foreign Trade, high-level military officials decided that aid materials produced by military system industrial enterprises, except for cigarettes, alcohol, vegetable oil, and soap, would be exempt from commodity circulation tax or goods tax. (See the Beijing Municipal Tax Bureau's notice on December 28, 1956, regarding the tax exemption for aid materials to Vietnam produced by the military system.) This set a precedent for tax exemption on aid products.

In June 1960, the Central Ministry of State Farms directly instructed the Beijing Municipal State Farms Bureau to send 100 Holstein cows to Vietnam. Due to a severe milk shortage in Beijing at the time, city leaders discussed with the Ministry of State Farms the possibility of not drawing cows from Beijing. However, under the banner of "internationalist duty," the Ministry enforced the selection standards: "Holstein cows, bulls aged 2-4 years, weighing over 450 kg, with a lactation period yield of over 5,000 kg; cows aged 4-8 years, weighing over 350 kg, with a lactation period yield of over 3,500 kg. Hooves should be straight, strong, udders and teats healthy and well-developed, and coat color black and white." (See the Beijing Municipal Agricultural and Forestry Bureau's notice on August 25, 1960, to the Red Star, Shahe, and Peace Communes regarding the assistance of livestock and poultry to Vietnam.) These communes had to provide 100 Holstein cows, 2,000 duck eggs, 30,000 chicken eggs, 400 quail eggs, and 10 nutrias, leaving Beijing's leaders in a difficult position due to the city's own food shortages.

The plan also required selecting a dozen politically reliable and responsible veterinarians and livestock handlers to accompany the shipment to the Pingxiang station in Guangxi, ensuring they prepared the necessary feed for the journey and the first three days in Vietnam. The transport procedure included providing a large and small water bucket, a bridle for every six cows, a trough for every three cows, and a set of large and small brooms, shovels, and brushes for every six cows. This mode of transport became standard in the 1960s and 70s, with a well-established procedure for quarantine, securing train cars, and handover.

The aid program went through several years of adjustment, with the Vietnamese frequently providing feedback and minor complaints after receiving materials. For example, the Vietnamese reported that packing lists or technical documents were often incomplete, some equipment lacked parts, and fragile equipment was not marked with "Handle with Care," resulting in damage or loss during transport and rendering the equipment unusable upon arrival. (See the Beijing Municipal Bureau of Mechanical and Electrical Industry's notice in August 1961 on ensuring proper packaging and shipment of aid equipment.) The Vietnamese dissatisfaction sometimes led them to seek compensation and reparations from Beijing's State Planning Commission, prompting repeated directives emphasizing that only politically reliable personnel should handle the final packaging of goods.

Between 1963 and 1964, frequent incidents of steel materials being found defective and unusable led the Ministry of Metallurgy to order that all unusable materials be returned to China, with the original supplier bearing all transportation costs. The cost of these returns was added to the compensation fund managed by the China Foreign Metallurgical Construction Corporation.

II

After 1965, the volume of aid requested by Vietnam grew significantly, sometimes to what could be considered astronomical figures at the time. In early summer, Vietnam suddenly asked China to lend it 200 million jin of grain. After deliberation, China's top leadership decided to provide the aid in full, deeming it an urgent political task and requiring local authorities to deliver it on time, in full, and with the right quality.

At this juncture, China had just emerged from the "Three Years of Difficulties," and the grain reserves had only just begun to show some surplus. This newfound abundance gave the authorities the confidence to allocate 200 million jin of grain. According to a State Council notice, in addition to the 118.5 million jin arranged by the Ministry of Grain, an additional 81.5 million jin was to be drawn from the supplies earmarked for Beijing, Tianjin, Shanghai, and major cities in Liaoning Province. "The supply and marketing cooperatives are to procure the grain at negotiated prices and hand it over to local grain processing plants or warehouses, which will manage the distribution under unified coordination by the Ministry of Grain. The difference between the procurement price and the uniform purchase price, along with costs and expenses, should be reported step-by-step for reimbursement by the Ministry of Finance." (See State Council telegram on May 18, 1965, "Notice on Urgently Supporting Vietnam with 200 Million Jin of Grain"). This large-scale grain mobilization was carried out quietly on the surface, but in the main grain-producing areas, it involved massive mobilization under a series of smaller directives. Such large-scale grain allocations became common during the Cultural Revolution, and officials at all levels were well-practiced in the operational procedures and motivational tactics.

Between 1965 and 1966, several national commendation ceremonies were held in the industrial and technological fields, recognizing units and individuals for their unique contributions to supporting Vietnam. These often became exemplary models receiving special favor from the government. For instance, the Tangshan Locomotive and Rolling Stock Plant manufactured a narrow-gauge steam locomotive ordered by Vietnam within fifty days. After rigorous testing on various Vietnamese rail lines, it met all quality requirements and received high praise at the national conference on mechanical product design. Initially, this factory was only a repair shop with no experience in manufacturing locomotives. Taking on the task was sudden and daunting.

During that year, educational campaigns about the situation in Vietnam and the fight against American aggression were widely conducted in major cities. Reports on the situation in Vietnam were disseminated at all levels, films about Vietnam's struggle were shown, and exhibitions of photographs from Vietnam were organized. Vietnam's resistance naturally became the focus of public concern and excitement, fostering a nationwide atmosphere of solidarity against a common enemy. Coincidentally, a Vietnamese delegation visited the Tangshan factory. The factory organized two mass meetings, inviting the representatives to share stories of Vietnam's heroic sons and daughters bravely fighting the enemy, which further ignited the enthusiasm of the cadres and workers involved in designing and manufacturing the locomotives. Some designers declared that designing locomotives to aid Vietnam with their pens was equivalent to fighting the American imperialists on the Vietnamese battlefield with guns; each drawing was a bullet aimed at the American imperialists. (See "Document 14 of the 1965 National Mechanical Product Design Work Conference," "Relying on the Three-in-One Design Team to Quickly and Effectively Design and Manufacture Locomotives to Aid Vietnam").

A group of people with no prior experience in locomotive design managed, driven by political fervor and determination, to produce a steam locomotive meeting Vietnam's battlefield requirements in a short period. The process involved extensive coordination, collective problem-solving, and overcoming numerous challenges. For example, the original rear coupler of the Vietnamese locomotive was rigid and lacked buffering, frequently causing problems on the hilly Vietnamese railways. The Vietnamese requested improvements. Engineer Deng Jiugong, a former worker, consulted his colleagues and drew a sketch based on their suggestions, resulting in a simple yet effective modification. The Vietnamese boiler was riveted, but it needed to be welded. Young technician Zhao Xishou brought his sketch to his team for discussion, where workers offered many useful ideas. The driver's cab, for which the Vietnamese provided an incomplete overall plan, needed modifications to make it larger and cooler. Meng Xiangrong, a newly appointed quota officer, worked with his mentors to make the cab both beautiful and functional, adding an extra layer of wood for insulation. Originally, ash had to be manually removed from the fire grate, but the Vietnamese requested a pneumatic shaking grate. The narrow locomotive frame could not accommodate a pneumatic shaking grate, and splitting it into two parts risked breaking the shaft due to boiler expansion. Despite eye problems, 73-year-old engineer An Baoshu, with help from 80-year-old engineer Tang Zhongqian, ingeniously installed the pneumatic shaking grate within the frame.

Everyone was astonished to find that, while an average locomotive required 5,000 drawings, this aid-to-Vietnam locomotive was completed with only 907 drawings. Typically, the technical conditions for a boiler would require about 200 specifications, but this time only eight were set, yet the resulting boiler was excellent. The cadres and workers attributed these achievements to the collective wisdom and miracles inspired by the nationwide fervor for aiding Vietnam.

III

During 1965 and 1966, the fervor for supporting Vietnam against American aggression reached its peak. Enthusiastic citizens across the country, either spontaneously or through their work units, sent cash and goods to the Vietnamese Embassy in China and the permanent representative office of the National Liberation Front of South Vietnam. Some even sent gold, silver, and jewelry.

Given the growing volume of such donations, the State Council's Foreign Affairs Office had to intervene. On July 22, 1965, it issued a "Supplementary Notice on People's Donations to Support Vietnam," stating: "From now on, all regions and government agencies shall not accept donations of money or goods from the public for supporting Vietnam. Any received donations should be returned (if the address or name is unknown and it cannot be returned, it can be handed over to the Ministry of Internal Affairs for handling). When returning, a letter should be included to encourage the donors' enthusiasm. At the same time, explain that our government has already given significant support to the Vietnamese people and that personal donations are not currently being accepted." For cash and goods already sent, if it was not specified whether they were for the North or South, they should be handed over to the permanent representative office of the National Liberation Front of South Vietnam, with the names and addresses of the donors included. The receiving unit should then send a reply to the donor explaining the handling situation.

The most troublesome issue was that citizens were also sending various domestic vouchers to the Vietnamese side, causing headaches for the handling personnel. The Foreign Affairs Office issued a specific directive: "All domestic vouchers should be returned to the sender and not handed over to the Vietnamese side. If the sender's name or address is unknown and the vouchers cannot be returned, they should be handed over to the issuing agency for handling. Grain and oil vouchers should be sent to the Ministry of Grain, cloth vouchers to the Ministry of Commerce, and public bonds and overseas remittance coupons to the People's Bank of China." Post offices nationwide were instructed not to accept any vouchers for mailing and to explain this to the senders.

By the end of the year, the Foreign Affairs Office issued a more "strict" yet politely worded notice stating that "the public should not be mobilized to donate to Vietnam," "the public should not be organized to write support or condolence letters to Vietnam," and "individuals should not be encouraged to go to Vietnam to participate in the anti-American struggle." (See the December 31, 1965, notice "Handling Methods for Public Donations to Support Vietnam"). However, given the situation at the time, a hard rejection was not feasible, and there needed to be a transition period to calm the public's emotions. The notice also included an internal provision: "For support or condolence letters to Vietnam written voluntarily by the public, if handed over to the organization for forwarding, the content should be reviewed, and if there are no major issues, it can be sent out. If not sent through the organization, the local post offices should still mail them."

Many people at the time were volunteering to go to Vietnam to fight. Local governments were unsure how to handle this properly, and the Foreign Affairs Office provided a uniform response: "If someone volunteers to go to Vietnam to participate in the anti-American struggle, their enthusiasm should be encouraged. At the same time, explain that if the situation develops to the point where it is necessary, the state will organize it uniformly. The primary task at present is to do a good job in production, work, and study at their posts to support the struggle of the Vietnamese people with practical actions." This directive effectively curbed the impulse to join the war among young people until Vietnam's final victory in 1975.

Local governments also faced political dilemmas, such as occasionally discovering suspicious individuals among the donors. For instance, the Beijing Municipal People's Committee Office reported on August 12, 1965, that seven citizens had donated a total of 295 yuan to support Vietnam. Upon review, they found that Chen Qiyuan, an employee at the Tian Tang River Farm, was a dismissed teacher whose father had died in prison for a crime. The office reported this to higher authorities, questioning whether to return the 5 yuan donated by Chen Qiyuan. The other six donors were anonymous, only signing as "a worker," "a soldier," or "a young worker," except for Ma Zhi from the Eastern Suburb Component Factory Union, who signed and donated 50 yuan.

Ultimately, the Beijing Municipal People's Committee Office did not return Chen Qiyuan's donation and rounded the total to 300 yuan, which was sent to the permanent representative office of the National Liberation Front of South Vietnam with a standard letter: "We have received many letters from workers, peasants, students, and cadres supporting the Vietnamese people's just struggle against American aggression. Seven individuals have sent a total of 300 yuan, requesting us to forward it to the Vietnamese people. The donation is now being sent with this letter for your verification."

During that time, the government also had to manage political vetting and logistical support for various personnel assisting Vietnam, investing considerable manpower and effort to ensure there were no political risks involved. For example, in June 1965, the Central Organization Department issued a notice to select and dispatch road testing personnel to assist Vietnam, including 17 cooks to be selected by the Beijing Municipal Labor Bureau, with a deadline of June 25. (See the June 1, 1965, notice "Selecting Personnel for Road Testing Assistance to Vietnam" by the Municipal Organization Department). The Central Organization Department emphasized that this task was top secret, and the notice was to be returned after use. The Municipal Labor Bureau urgently selected 17 cooks from various construction companies and factories, with the list handed over to the Municipal Organization Department and the Municipal Public Security Bureau for political vetting. After passing the vetting, they were to depart from Beijing on July 7. The authorities instructed that the overseas period would be approximately one to two years, during which their household registration would be retained, and their supply suspended, with living allowances provided by the Surveying and Mapping Bureau. The individuals were responsible for their own clothing, receiving 403 feet of cloth vouchers from the commercial department. This was essentially the standard living arrangement for personnel assisting Vietnam at the time—selected hastily but considered an honor, and quickly dispatched to the battlefield.

To address the living issues of personnel and their families assisting Vietnam, the government had to consider and resolve various challenges they encountered. For example, the survey and design personnel for road construction assistance in Vietnam were mostly dispatched by the Ministry of Transportation and came from all over the country. Due to differences in wage categories and grain price adjustments across regions, there were significant disparities in grain price subsidies for each individual, affecting their work morale and family stability. As a result, on November 16, 1966, the Ministry of Transportation issued a special letter requesting that local authorities provide subsidies according to the local grain price difference subsidy methods to avoid affecting their families' livelihoods.

Throughout the entire process of assisting Vietnam against American aggression, demands for grain price subsidies and wage supplements were constant, dictated by the rigid grain and wage systems of the time. The appropriate care and preferential treatment for personnel assisting Vietnam were the results of coordination by relevant central departments, considering the harsh and challenging conditions of the Vietnamese battlefield.

IV

During the Cultural Revolution, as the scale of the war on the Indochina Peninsula expanded, China significantly increased its aid to Vietnam, encompassing not only military supplies but also a wide range of essential industrial and everyday products, including vegetable seeds transported over great distances.

On July 1, 1967, the Ministry of Foreign Trade, the Ministry of Commerce, and the Ministry of Agriculture issued a notice for the gratuitous assistance of ten thousand tons of potato seeds to Vietnam. Of this, Tianjin was to supply five thousand five hundred tons, Liaoning two thousand five hundred tons, and Beijing two thousand tons. The notice specified that white-skinned, white-fleshed seeds were to be selected, and the packaging could be in bamboo baskets or wooden boxes, with each piece weighing about thirty to forty kilograms. The shipments were to be completed in batches by September 15. This request from Vietnam was initially made at the beginning of the year to meet the vegetable needs of the Vietnamese people. China responded positively, stating that it would actively help the Vietnamese people achieve self-sufficiency in agricultural production.

Two months later, following mutual agreements, China again provided Vietnam with 34 tons of water spinach seeds, 3 tons of Chinese Spinach seeds, 1 ton of winter melon seeds, 10 tons of bitter vegetable seeds, and 5 tons of spinach seeds. Vietnam specifically requested 4 tons of Zhanjiang cabbage seeds and 3 tons of Beijing small white cabbage seeds. The Ministry of Foreign Trade, the Ministry of Agriculture, the Ministry of Commerce, and the All China Federation of Supply and Marketing Cooperatives emphasized in their notification: "To further strengthen the fraternal combat friendship between the people of China and Vietnam and jointly defeat the aggression of American imperialism, we must ensure the completion of this political task." (See the September 7, 1967, notice "On the Gratuitous Assistance of Vegetable Seeds to Vietnam"). The joint notice from the four departments also instructed all regions to use moisture-proof materials for packaging, keep the net weight of each piece below 25 kilograms, and deliver the goods preferably as requested by the Vietnamese side or slightly earlier to avoid missing the planting season.

The notice originally required the seal of the Ministry of Agriculture, but due to the ministry's seal being kept by the acting minister Jiang Yizhen, who was labeled a "counter-revolutionary and a rogue" by the Revolutionary Headquarters of the Ministry of Agriculture, the seal could not be retrieved. Hence, the Ministry of Agriculture's Office seal was temporarily used instead. This "seal usage explanation" from the Ministry of Agriculture revealed the factional strife and turmoil at the early stage of the Cultural Revolution.

By 1968, the volume and variety of food requested by the Vietnamese had increased sharply. Consequently, the State Planning Commission, the Ministry of Commerce, the First Ministry of Light Industry, the Ministry of Fisheries, the Ministry of Materials Management, the Ministry of Foreign Trade, and the General Logistics Department held a "Food Production Symposium for Aiding Vietnam" in Shanghai. During the meeting, participants studied Chairman Mao's latest instructions on assisting Vietnam: "Whatever South Vietnam needs and we can provide, we must meet their demands. There are some items that we have and can supply, which the Vietnamese have not thought of. We should proactively offer them..." The attendees unanimously expressed their determination to follow Chairman Mao's instructions to the letter, ensuring the production and supply tasks were completed efficiently and economically. During the meeting, Premier Zhou Enlai's directive was also relayed: supplies provided to Vietnam must be "convenient for transportation, easy to carry, suitable for use, and easy to conceal." This prompted the seven organizing departments to expedite the resolution of various issues related to aiding Vietnam, ensuring that the required food supplies were promptly delivered to the Vietnamese brothers.

In the aid mission notification issued by the seven departments on January 25, 1968, it was first emphasized that the urgently needed national allocated and department-managed materials (such as grain and oil, wood, tinplate, polyethylene, burlap, and solder) would be requested from the relevant departments by the managing departments, which would then allocate quotas. Local departments would organize the supply according to actual needs. The Ministry of Materials had allocated tinplate quotas specifically to the First Ministry of Light Industry, the Ministry of Commerce, and the Ministry of Fisheries, with the managing departments organizing the supply within their systems. Polyethylene film was to be produced by the Second Ministry of Light Industry and supplied accordingly. Materials such as round nails, iron wire, packing steel strips, and packing paper, which were locally supplied, were to be organized by local managing departments and given priority. The original materials allocated by the state were to be used exclusively for their intended purpose

and not diverted elsewhere. The seven departments reiterated that costs should be calculated on the principle of actual production costs plus minimal profit. This meant that there was little room for profit, making it a purely non-profit national endeavor, with many supplies being paid for by China's foreign trade department and given away for free.

Given the previously lax packaging quality, regulations became stricter after 1968. For example, plastic bags were to be made of polyethylene with a film thickness of 0.06 millimeters, ensuring uniform thickness, consistent bag sizes, and no pinholes or leaks. When making tinplate barrels, the tin coating had to be uniform and rust-free, ensuring no air leaks. The carrying handles were to be made of No. 8 wire, and the barrels were to be sprayed with a layer of green paint. When packing in wooden crates, grass board paper was to be used as a liner between the barrels, with moisture-proof paper as an additional lining. The packaging could be made from red pine, white pine, or fir, using unplaned rough boards with a moisture content not exceeding 18%. The board thickness was to be 1.2 centimeters, with an allowable variance of 0.1 centimeters. The number of boards making up each side of the crate should not exceed three, with gaps between the boards being less than 3 millimeters.

Interestingly, detailed production guidelines for processed meat products were provided, demonstrating a high level of standardization and precision. For example, the preparation of shredded pork required 100 kilograms of lean pork, 7.5 kilograms of soy sauce, 0.5 kilograms of sugar, 0.5 kilograms of wine, and appropriate amounts of salt, green onions, and ginger. The color should be normal, the meat fibers loose, with no sinews, inner membranes, or other impurities, and as moisture-free as possible. The taste should be normal, without burnt or off flavors. Each 0.1-gram sample should contain no coliform bacteria or pathogens and have a shelf life of two years.

Tofu powder was required to have the typical flavor of regular tofu, with no noticeable powdery texture and an acidity of less than 3 milliliters per gram.

Such technically detailed descriptions were rare in official Cultural Revolution documents, giving them an unusual and alien feel. The political significance and high standards of the food aid to Vietnam prompted the production factories to adhere to strict self-discipline and quality controls, ensuring that the quality was fundamentally guaranteed.

V

In early summer 1968, following discussions between the Ministry of Commerce and the General Logistics Department, the responsibility for storing aid food for Vietnam was entirely handed over to the military, who promptly managed the handover and settlement procedures. During this transfer, the Beijing Military Region Logistics Department received 25 tons of pork floss, 100 tons of tofu powder, and 100 tons of milk powder from Beijing, while also taking on 150 tons of dehydrated vegetables from Shanghai, 100 tons of lard from Hubei, 120 tons of egg powder, 200 tons of solid soy sauce from Guangdong, 30 tons of monosodium glutamate from Liaoning, and 300 tons of fermented black beans from Hunan (See Ministry of Commerce and General Logistics Department's October 16, 1968, document "On Utilizing 1968 Aid Food Reserves for Vietnam and Arranging 1969 Aid Food Reserve Tasks"). This variety and volume of aid indicate that the types of aid food had become quite extensive, with some quantities measured in hundreds of tons.

At the local level, emphasis was placed on inspecting reserve products before storage. Only qualified products were allowed into storage. Regarding reception, settlement, and storage, the Beijing Municipal Vice Food and Beverage Bureau issued a notice on August 27, 1968, detailing the aid food storage: the Sugar, Tobacco, and Alcohol Company was responsible for handling the milk powder, the Food Company for meat floss, and the Chongwen Vice Food Management Office for tofu powder, each with specific reception channels.

It seemed that the Vietnamese war front particularly favored Beijing's tofu powder and pork floss. In the aid plan laid out by the Beijing Revolutionary Committee's Planning Group on November 19, 1968, for the following year, the allocation was set at 30 tons of pork floss and a high 220 tons of tofu powder. Additionally, 360,000 backpacks, 50,000 inner waistband cords, and 50,000 outer waistband cords were added, with the Textile Bureau and Second Light Industry Bureau tasked to complete these items. Even the import of waistband cords shows the Vietnamese dependence on China for daily necessities was becoming increasingly extensive.

Relying on the importance of the aid to Vietnam, the Beijing Vice Food and Beverage Bureau repeatedly applied to the Revolutionary Committee's Planning Group in 1968 for material and construction allocations. For instance, in a report on February 23, it stated that the current equipment could not meet the aid tasks' requirements and needed to expand some equipment while producing. For dehydrated vegetable production, two drying houses needed to be constructed, 300 square meters of factory space was required for meat floss, and a new workshop with four main machines was necessary for tofu powder production. These required urgent allocations of timber, steel, cement, water pumps, gearboxes, blowers, motors, and industrial bearings.

In 1969, the demand for medical equipment from the Vietnamese side surged, with the list for the first half of the year including 100 air anesthesia machines, 200 sets of various surgical instruments, 11,000 surgical scissors, 3,000 hemostats, 22,000 glass syringes, ten 7121 ECG machines, 3,000 indirect transfusion devices, 1,000 blood pressure monitors, 8,000 boxes of human injection needles, 60,000 rolls of medical adhesive tape, 30,000 acupuncture needles, and 40,000 packs of sutures. The task was detailed and extensive. All packaging was required to use wooden crates, with board seams between 1-2 millimeters. Heavy machinery needed crate boards at least 2 centimeters thick, reinforced with wooden strips, and bottom supports to prevent collapse and facilitate mechanical loading and unloading. In the 1969 aid production plan notice, the Ministry of Health specifically pointed out that, according to higher instructions, neither the inner nor outer packaging should bear Chairman Mao's quotations, and no printed paper edges, newspapers, books, or magazines should be used as filler materials, nor should rice husks or straw be used.

In the 1970s, the pattern of aid to Vietnam largely remained the same each year, with the content and format of official documents being similar. The consistent theme was Vietnam's urgent needs and China's unwavering support to help Vietnam win the anti-American war of national salvation, with only the managing departments differing. The Ministry of Commerce and Ministry of Foreign Trade typically handled potato seeds, instructing, "To catch Vietnam's early September planting season, please complete this aid task by August." The State Construction Commission managed roofing felt materials, reallocating 400,000 rolls of roofing felt from various provinces within a year despite domestic construction needs. The Ministry of Light Industry, Ministry of Foreign Trade, Planning Commission Material Bureau, and General Logistics Department mainly oversaw military food aid, repeatedly urging the timely completion of deliveries to facilitate front-line transportation. They frequently reminded that fish sauce in canned meat should be replaced with soy sauce.

In 1973, as the war situation improved, Vietnam began focusing on modernizing its construction projects, with the North Giang Nitrogen Fertilizer Plant being a highly prioritized project, personally supervised by party and government leaders who demanded its completion and production by June 1974. Consequently, the Chinese leadership had to reallocate a complete set of fertilizer equipment initially intended for Yunnan to support Vietnam. Within three months, nearly 100 train carriages transported 3,000 tons of materials and equipment to North Giang, and the construction workforce on-site grew to around 3,000 people.

Vietnamese leaders demanded the completion of the entire nitrogen fertilizer plant within fifteen months, which increased the difficulty for the Chinese units responsible for key equipment construction. The Ministry of Foreign Economic Relations and Trade and the Ministry of Chemical Industry frequently dispatched personnel to oversee the key construction units, urging them to fulfill China's glorious internationalist duty and support Vietnam's socialist construction. They also highlighted the risk of not completing the tasks due to tight schedules, warning, "If not expedited, it will still be impossible to deliver on time, affecting the completion and production schedule." In the official notification, they stipulated, "Please seize the opportunity, provide significant assistance, and mobilize the masses to take effective measures to ensure all undelivered equipment and main components are handed over by the end of this year." They set a final deadline, stating, "Those factories with genuine difficulties must complete delivery by the first quarter of 1974." (See Ministry of Foreign Economic Relations and Trade, First Ministry of Machine-Building Industry, Ministry of Chemical Industry's October 27, 1973, document "On Urging the Production of Equipment Needed for Vietnam's North Giang Nitrogen Fertilizer Plant").

In Beijing, several factories, including the

Factory Bridge Fan Factory (responsible for axial flow fans), Beijing Analytical Instrument Factory (manufacturing infrared micro-analysis and gas chromatography instruments), Beijing Valve Factory (handling globe valves and traps), and Chemical Machinery Factory (producing hydraulic chimney valves and gas three-way valves), were assigned these tasks. These factories were repeatedly urged by the Ministry of Foreign Economic Relations and Trade and the Ministry of Chemical Industry to report progress and were reminded frequently not to delay. In the face of limited technical conditions and tight deadlines, manufacturing modern chemical equipment inevitably revealed some constraints and helplessness.

One of the most challenging tasks was assigned to the Beijing Dairy Company in early 1973. They were notified to produce 100 tons of condensed milk for Vietnam by the end of June. Beijing had never produced condensed milk before, only having produced a simplified version with a three-month shelf life for domestic sale, which did not meet export standards. The foreign trade department had overestimated the local factories' capabilities, not specifying quality requirements or packaging forms. The dairy company and the Agricultural and Forestry Bureau reported to the Revolutionary Committee's Agricultural and Forestry Group, but there was no response or production arrangement. Eventually, the 100 tons of condensed milk could not be produced on time due to time and technical constraints, making it one of the rare uncompleted aid projects to Vietnam.

In early summer 1973, the Beijing Construction Machinery Factory of the Municipal Construction Bureau received an order to manufacture 1,050 oil tanks for the Vietnamese front, each nearly 2 tons, with the first batch of 520 tanks to be completed by August 20 and promptly shipped to Vietnam. Typically, tanks were not produced in the hot summer because the workers had to work inside the tanks, enduring extreme heat and fumes, requiring a shift every ten minutes, leaving them visibly affected after each shift. However, to "support the front against American imperialism," the workers broke convention, showing great enthusiasm and enduring extreme physical limits. By working hard inside and outside the tanks, producing twenty tanks a day, they managed to complete the extremely challenging task by the end of September.

The anti-American aid to Vietnam spanned over ten or twenty years, completed with nationwide effort, immense hardship, and high costs, especially during the Cultural Revolution, when the difficulties were more pronounced, but the determination was unwavering. In retrospect, this period encapsulates an era's glory and desolation, tinged with bitterness and reflection, weaving through those tumultuous times.

About the Author:

Chen Tushou is a contemporary Chinese history writer and currently an editor for the supplement of *Beijing Youth Daily*. His notable works include *Whether Heaven Knows People Are Sick: A Chronicle of China's Literary Scene in 1949* (《人有病，天知否——1949 年中国文坛纪学》) and *Thoughts of the People in the Homeland: Glimpses of Intellectual Thought Reform after 1949* (《故国人民有所思：1949 年后知识分子思想改造侧影》).

The Cultural Cold War: The Hidden Currents of Drama in Taiwan's Age of Censorship

ZHONG Qiao

I

In 1997, the sudden passing of Yao Yiwei (姚一苇) left a profound sense of loss and respect in Taiwan's theater community. Mainly, if it weren't for Yao Yiwei's pioneering approach to drama creation during the high-pressure cultural cold war of the 1960s, integrating both Eastern and Western aesthetic theories, we would have remained mired in the anti-Communist plays of the 1950s, with the theater serving as a state propaganda machine, from which escape would have been long and arduous.

In the memorial anthology "Lamp in the Dark" (《暗夜中的掌灯者》), writer Chen Yingzhen (陈映真) penned a reflective article on Yao Yiwei, offering profound insights. The article mentions the dramatic shifts in international circumstances following the collapse of the Soviet Union and Eastern Europe in 1989, which saw socialist countries retreating to increasingly difficult positions. Based on his early interactions with Yao Yiwei and his understanding of Yao's creative and academic thoughts, Chen expressed that Yao must have been deeply concerned. However, this concern took a pivotal turn, as he noted:

"Yet, in his dramatic works and academic theories, there was never the slightest trace of the Marxist influence from China's 1930s, even in the most diluted form. Instead, there was a rigorous, rational, academic, and orthodox tone."

This highlights a crucial point: on the continuum of the Cold War, Yao Yiwei, a youth once influenced by Lu Xun (鲁迅) and involved in the progressive student movement during the Chinese Civil War, came to Taiwan and, in the theater, consistently drew from traditional Chinese classical opera aesthetics. He critically examined the intervention of Western cultural colonialism and developed scripts blending classical and contemporary drama. He also sought in Aristotle's "Poetics" the ultimate model of drama as an expression of human "virtuous action." Using traditional Chinese storytelling forms, he innovated his narratives through song and performance, while philosophically adhering to the normative social/political order defined in "Poetics" as a guiding principle of humanistic spirit. Even without Aristotle's demonstration of the "cathartic effect" of Greek tragedies in promoting Athenian oligarchy, Yao adhered to the universal values of humanity in defining "virtuous action." Such humanitarianism naturally excluded class liberation consciousness, leaning more toward the cultivation of human nature. As Chen Yingzhen put it:

"For ideals, love, nobility, tolerance, and justice... unwavering beliefs; yet never a trace of the Marxism from China's 1930s."

From this perspective, one can discern in many of Yao's scripts, whether deliberately or inadvertently, symbolic references buried within characters and plots. These references may not be directly related to the drama's themes or axes but, upon careful thought and contrast with the overall socio-political structure of the island at the time, they spark associative meanings for posterity. In what is widely regarded as Yao's most outstanding work, "Sun Feihu's Wedding Heist" (《孙飞

虎抢亲》), one can find such traces. It is not difficult to see why Yao's scripts, often praised for their classical elements, might appear disconnected from contemporary issues. This, of course, is closely related to the frequent historical or allegorical starting points shaping the overall dramatic context. Without linking the works to society and the era, it is easy to judge their aesthetic value solely on the texts. At least in Yao's intention to convey Lu Xun's sentiment of "not being an empty-talking literati," this might be overlooked or misinterpreted.

In "Sun Feihu's Wedding Heist", the traditional Chinese opera structure allows the character Sun Feihu to evolve from a notorious bandit to someone described through exaggerated hearsay: "This fellow says Sun Feihu is a rough, big, ugly, bald, and hunched-back guy." If we were to revert to the pervasive Cold War cultural context of the 1960s, this association indeed seems targeted and familiar, precisely alluding to the "Communist spy" narrative. Here, the drama uses sophisticated irony to reflect on how nationalistic doctrines during the Cold War would ultimately alienate opposition.

The drama ingeniously embeds numerous codes in its character costume changes. For example, the use of traditional opera's rhyme schemes within the narrative poetry drama, allowing characters to freely enter and exit their roles: they are themselves yet also critics of the current state. For instance, after Sun Feihu's line, "We are all the same," the four protagonists start repeatedly reflecting or blaming their situations: "We have no choices, nor are we chosen," "We cannot discern, cannot think, cannot understand," "We are just hiding behind a high wall," and finally, "We are just hiding in our clothes."

Through traditional opera's repetitive rhymes, a certain dramatic effect appealing to both refined and popular tastes is achieved. Each line of this continuous repetition subtly hints at the desolation and repression of that era, reflecting the inner struggles of people seeking an escape from confinement.

The dialogue in the play suggests metaphorically:

Zhang Junrui: ... It's a pity there is no mirror; I want to see what I truly look like. Sun Feihu: We are each other's mirror; we don't need to find a mirror.

What kind of situation renders everyone the same, where one does not need a mirror to know they are identical? This "parody" appearing in the plot development implies that a playwright like Yao Yiwei is referring to an unspeakable reality in which people appear to have different names and identities but are molded into the same person. If heretical thoughts arise, the internalized mechanisms of the Cold War will swiftly suppress them.

By seriously examining the term "cultural cold war," first raised in the early 1970s, it was taboo in the United States because the state needed to counter the Soviet Union and the socialist camp under intelligence control while maintaining its image as the champion of democracy. The substantial effect of the cultural cold war was the extensive influence and control exerted over surrounding nations aligned with the empire, creating an internalized value system that subtly penetrated societies more effectively than military, political, economic, or other forms of national or social subjugation. This was a core consensus achieved during the early 1950s McCarthyism.

Re-reading Yao's scripts reveals his skillful integration of traditional opera's context and rhyme into modern theater techniques, a key reason for his high regard. Today, the dialogue between tradition and modernity in his works offers an alternative paradigm against the Euro-American theater mainstream. The hybridization of traditional and contemporary in a restrictive and barren 1960s Taiwan poses a significant cultural question: where does such cultural context stand today? It seems lost in the waves of national modernization, discarded and eagerly eradicated. Thus, it is essential to revisit the representation of tradition and modernity in Yao's works, exploring their dialectical unity in form and content. For example, in "Sun Feihu's Wedding Heist", the pivotal dialogue after numerous role and context reversals: "We all once had hopes / In the end, they all changed," "Hope was so illusory," "We drew strength from hope," "We passed time with hope" is thought-provoking. Closing one's eyes and listening to these lines, transformed from traditional opera recitations, feels like hearing endless echoes in a bottomless dry well, resonating within the isolated self. Unconsciously, the metaphor is integrated into the contemporary reality through drama.

In 1964, at the Tamsui seashore, often fervently advocating his liberation, Chen Yingzhen submitted a novel titled "The Mute and Pitiful Mouth" to the "Modern Literature" (《现代文学》) edited by Yao Yiwei. The novel's last section depicts the protagonist recounting a dream to his doctor treating his mental exhaustion. Earlier, he witnessed a girl, who attempted to escape, being killed by her seller beside a warehouse by the railway. He says, "A woman lay before me, her body covered in mouths..." The doctor, with a habitual slight frown, asked, "And then?" He replied, "Those mouths spoke, saying: Open the skylight, let the sunlight in!" The novel ends with a quote attributed to Goethe on his deathbed. Before the novel ends, a poem from the Roman era after Antony murdered his political enemy Caesar is cited:

"Each is a mute and pitiful mouth. I let these mouths speak for me..."

Why "open the skylight, let the sunlight in"? And why the "mute and pitiful mouth" after the murder? Undoubtedly, this reflects the suffocating and repressive era under the long shadow of the Cold War in East Asia. The novel, with its realistic yet metaphorical approach, mirrors the era's atmosphere, much like Yao Yiwei's symbolic and coded dramas. Reflecting on the isolated, oppressive 1960s Taiwan, when the world was undergoing significant transformations—anti-Vietnam War movements in the US advocating civil rights and women's rights, the student revolution in Paris spreading globally, Che Guevara's messianic guerrilla warfare in Bolivia after establishing socialism in Cuba—one finds Taiwan seemingly detached. The regulated cultural inspection system operated routinely under authoritarian policies, where memories of the bloody purges of the 1950s, remaining in silent terror, seemed like an inescapable nightmare.

Could this resonate with Yao's aesthetic discourse, citing Kant's concept of "purposive without purpose"? In Kant's framework, the two "purposes" differ in meaning. Briefly, objectively, "beauty" does not exist for utilitarian purposes; aesthetic appreciation is disinterested. Yet, "purposiveness" lies in the sublimation of the pleasure of beauty. Thus, while drama aims for "purposeless" beauty, it also achieves an "extra-aesthetic" purpose: engaging with contemporary society and history, even if subtly embedded within the narrative. This humanistic spirit is the root and ultimate virtue of Yao's lifelong work in drama and academia. This perspective helps us understand why he revered Aristotle's "Poetics" as a dramatic canon.

In the preface to his play "Fu Qingzhu" (《傅青主》), Yao wrote, "Mentioning narrative poetry in theater, some might think I'm influenced by Bertolt Brecht, which I can't deny. But remember, narrative poetry is a characteristic of our drama." This was a unique theatrical expression under the Cold War's cultural context: decolonizing theater aesthetics through classical elements without claiming direct influence from narrative poetry dramas.

Narrative poetry drama inherently involves

the theater as a venue for transformative energy. In the 1960s, this was perilous—one misstep could lead to death or imprisonment.

II

In 1981-82, after completing my English literature studies at Chung Hsing University in Taichung, I continued my Bohemian lifestyle in Taipei, entering the Master of Arts program in theater. It was then that I became a student of Yao Yiwei. Looking back, as a student under a rigorous teacher, my graduate life was characterized by the tremors of writing and reading.

Now, reflecting on my initial encounters with Yao, I recall navigating several profound junctures in a long journey, each leaving an indelible impression of a solitary figure during calm moments.

In class, Yao discussed Kantian aesthetics and dialectics of tragedy and heroism under the pervasive Westernization in the theater scene. These discussions profoundly influenced me. His teachings kindled my understanding of theatrical principles. However, in the 1980s, the tranquility of academic discussions under the lamplight could not permanently anchor a restless soul. The memory of riding a motorcycle or taking a bus through the twilight-lit streets of Taipei to attend his classes remains vivid. Yet, the thrill of daytime protests often overshadowed the pursuit of academic advancement.

One memorable occasion, Yao turned the conversation to Bertolt Brecht, urging me to explore the concept of "Verfremdungseffekt" (alienation effect). It was much later that I realized Yao was using this topic to subtly convey his insights on world transformation. After reading Brecht's theoretical analyses, I naively asked Yao at his large teaching desk, "Brecht was a socialist... what's the connection to theater?" Typically smiling when discussing intellectual mysteries, Yao suddenly became serious, returning to the core topics of drama and aesthetics.

I vaguely understood but also realized I might not fully grasp his point. I noticed a calligraphy piece on Yao's living room wall quoting Lu Xun: "Fiercely facing a thousand pointing fingers, bowing as a willing ox for children." Yao often referred to Zhou Shuren, Lu Xun's real name, when discussing Chinese modern literature, but never mentioned "Lu Xun." I occasionally heard that he had faced political problems before teaching, but his cautious lifestyle and intellectual stance prevented deeper probing. Thus, I bought his works, read his assigned readings, and, with a restless mind, eventually bid him farewell.

In 1997, Yao passed away. I read a memorial piece by Chen Yingzhen that included the following dialogue:

"Yao spoke of Lu Xun's fate of turning to practical matters in his later years. 'Even when turning works into weapons, creation remains the most powerful and long-lasting weapon,' he said. I was moved but remained silent. In those desolate years, this dialogue was the safest limit."

In this context, "I" refers to Chen Yingzhen; "Yao" refers to Yao Yiwei. Gradually, I began to understand why Yao meticulously discussed Brecht's dramas with me while avoiding Brecht's socialist beliefs. This is likely related to Yao's early involvement in student movements in Xiamen, his brief exile to Green Island in the 1950s' oppressive atmosphere, and his later cautious and disciplined academic approach. Having been influenced by Marxism and Lu Xun's literary heritage in mainland China, he was swept into the radical tides of the White Terror upon arriving in Taiwan. After the tides receded, his scholarly rigor and aesthetic theories in drama became his way of containing the red waves.

The image of a calm figure at a serene ferry port stirs up waves in hindsight, yet this figure remained tranquil, turning his peace into a constant smile until the 1960s' cultural cold war. Among his many notable works written during this period, "Red Nose" (《红鼻子》) stands out.

I always believed "Red Nose" drew inspiration from Brecht's "The Good Person of Szechwan" (《四川好人》), treating allegory as a reflection of reality and contemplating human nature. However, their dramatic expressions diverge significantly. In "The Good Person of Szechwan," Brecht surrounds a divinely chosen good person with pervasive evil, highlighting human wickedness as an inevitable result of capitalist society. In contrast, "Red Nose" simplifies matters: a man accustomed to a comfortable life achieves his ideal by wearing a red-nosed mask, symbolizing divinity and displaying humanitarian spirit through sacrificial conduct.

Both "The Good Person of Szechwan" and "Red Nose" explore virtuous conduct as a means of transforming reality through drama. However, their methods and approaches differ fundamentally. Comparing their dramatic techniques, one might lose sight of how theater reflects cultural forms and actions in dialectical social development. This is particularly pertinent to 1960s Taiwan, under the Cold War's international framework. Ignoring this context misses the objective circumstances Yao faced while writing "Red Nose."

Some might question the extent to which a playwright's era influences their work. Generally, one might say, "The era influences creative thought to some extent..." However, in the 1960s, under the pervasive cultural Cold War, it went beyond influence to include political repression. The silent memory of the 1950s' anti-Communist environment became a political stranglehold, internalized in writers' self-regulation and editing, posing a significant challenge for a humanitarian playwright attempting to break free from anti-Communist "pseudo-realistic" drama.

Given these constraints, Chen Yingzhen's reflections upon reading "Red Nose" in prison in 1969 are particularly poignant: "Who better understands the world depicted in Yao's works, severed from external life by irresistible forces, than someone who has been suddenly arrested, interrogated, imprisoned, and isolated from all normal life? Reading the script word by word, I felt as if Yao's comforting and encouraging presence transcended the prison walls, like in his living room, causing me to hold back tears."

This classic passage reveals not just one writer's understanding of another's work, but why Chen felt Yao's "Red Nose" resonated so deeply. It suggests that "Red Nose" conveyed Yao's humanistic theatrical spirit. Despite the oversimplified human or societal perspectives, the divine mask enabled the portrayal of transcendent virtue.

"Poetics" as Aristotle's dramatic theory of catharsis and empathy underwent fundamental changes. Although "Poetics" was Yao's foundational theatrical theory, the "alienation effect" in his works constantly aimed to achieve this through various questions. This paradox became a driving force, making his works' aesthetic value worthy of continual exploration.

In 2022, the centennial of Yao Yiwei's birth, I dedicate this article to commemorate a teacher whose influence stirred endless waves within my soul.

About the Author:

Zhong Qiao is a multifaceted figure who is a poet, novelist, playwright, and social activist. He is currently the head of the "Chashi Theatre Group." Since the mid-1980s, he has been involved in Taiwan's "Nativist Literature Debate" and left-wing thought. He has participated in *Summer Tide* magazine and *Care* magazine and previously served as editor-in-chief of *Renjian* magazine.

Return, Hu Bugui?

WU Mengmei

Many years ago, my family lived in a small courtyard house on the south bank of Houhai, Beijing. In the yard was a large yellow lilac tree, a century-old tree that, every spring, would bloom with lilac flowers. The fragrance would overflow from the courtyard, noticeable even from a hundred meters away. Because the blooming period was long and the scent fresh and elegant, strangers passing by would often ask, "Where is this flower scent coming from?" As for the surrounding residents, they probably enjoyed the lilac blooming season as much as I did.

In those years, whenever the flowers bloomed, I would set up a table under the tree, and friends would gather from all over. Amidst the fragrance of wine, tea, and flowers, we would sometimes engage in passionate discussions and at other times in soft singing, while the lilac flowers would often fall gently in the breeze.

Hu Bugui（胡不归，the literal meaning is 'why not return'）started coming to my courtyard when the lilacs were in bloom. A friend from the Ministry of Foreign Affairs intended to introduce Hu Bugui to my younger sister as a potential boyfriend. At that time, my sister had just arrived in Beijing and was living with us in the courtyard by Houhai.

When Hu Bugui first came, I remember telling him: "Once you reach the south bank of Houhai, just follow the scent of the flowers, and you'll find myhome." He arrived covered in dust, beads of sweat on his forehead, having come by bicycle. When asked where he lived and if it was far, he nonchalantly smiled and said, "I live in Shuangqiao, not far." Every subsequent visit, he came by bicycle. It was only later, when I visited his place, that I realized it was quite a distance.

In those years of gatherings, whenever Hu Bugui was present, the whole group would naturally quiet down, listening to him like students to a mentor. The only drawback was that the more passionate he became, the thicker his Shandong accent grew. For someone like me, with limited knowledge, his extensive references to ancient and modern, Chinese and foreign sources would quickly become confusing. Often, I had to interrupt, asking him to repeat or for friends who understood to explain, before we could continue.

After getting to know Hu Bugui, my sister went on a few dates with him, but soon decided it would not work because she could barely understand what he was saying. She often found it puzzling and was too embarrassed to keep asking for clarification. Although their romantic relationship did not work out, it did not affect Hu Bugui becoming a close friend of our family, a frequent and cherished guest. Over time, and through more interactions, we gradually got used to his persistent Shandong accent, and I could understand most of what he said.

During the years we lived in Houhai, Hu Bugui frequently visited us, sometimes even staying overnight. But most of the time, he came and went alone by bicycle.

In 2005, we bought a house in Changying Wanxiang, moving in early 2006. Our new home was close to Shuangqiao, making it convenient for Hu Bugui to visit, just a half-hour bike ride away. Whenever I cooked something nice, I would call and invite him over for a meal. To us, he felt more like a family member than a friend, someone we trusted and relied on. His character and personality made him one of those rare "talented and virtuous" individuals. In an era of chaos and noise, he embodied the calm and detachment of an ancient sage.

Hu Bugui lived alone and did not pay much attention to personal comfort. In winter, bathing was inconvenient for him. When he came over, it was common for him to have a layer of dandruff on his shoulders and a noticeable odor. Treating him like family, I would unceremoniously tell him to take a shower, change into my husband's clean clothes (fortunately, they were about the same size), and wash his dirty clothes in the washing machine.

In 2007, I visited Guiyang and met a friend near there who had returned home after graduating from China Agricultural University. This friend introduced me to a female friend working at the local cultural station, who accompanied me on my tour. She was unmarried and envied the cultural life in Beijing. I immediately thought of Hu Bugui and proposed introducing them, hoping they could pursue a relationship with marriage in mind. Believing that many women value talent and character as the core of love, I wished for a beautiful love story for Hu Bugui.

After returning to Beijing, I promptly visited Hu Bugui, giving him the woman's contact details. He was delighted and soon began corresponding with her. A few months later, a friend studying for an in-service graduate course in Beijing brought me a letter and some cash from the woman, asking me to invite Hu Bugui to dine with the friend from Guizhou. Seeing the effort and kindness, I arranged for the meeting, reminding Hu Bugui to clean up and make a good impression.

However, when we picked him up, he had not cleaned up as I requested, still covered in dandruff, and smelling unpleasant. During the meal, I praised his works, emphasizing his unique and carefree lifestyle, hoping to leave a positive impression. The friend from Guizhou seemed to take it well, and their communication continued, with Hu Bugui even visiting her in Guizhou.

Yet, I never inquired too much about the details of his visit. Soon after, the woman called several times, expressing disappointment and frustration that Hu Bugui was not the cultured man she imagined and questioning why his friends, who admired his talent, did not help him gain recognition and success. Her tone grew increasingly resentful, feeling misled by my introduction. I felt deeply sorry for her shattered expectations and my misjudgment, making it difficult to ask Hu Bugui about his trip out of sympathy and guilt. The woman from Guizhou never contacted me again.

Since 2008, with the birth of my youngest daughter, our lives became busier, and the frequency of inviting Hu Bugui over decreased significantly. During this time, he fell seriously ill, nearly dying from a high fever and dehydration. Thankfully, his close friend Zeng Zhaohua, who had provided him with free housing for over twenty years, found him and took him to the hospital. After recovering, Hu Bugui changed drastically, becoming quiet and reserved, unlike his previous eloquent self. Despite occasional visits, where I'd see him brewing Chinese medicine in his cluttered room, he continued his simple lifestyle, reading, writing, and occasionally meeting friends, but never having a romantic relationship.

In 2013, we moved to Songzhuang. During the house renovations, Hu Bugui supervised the work, living and eating with the workers. Later, I engaged him in my initial exhibitions in Songzhuang, hoping he could earn some extra money and expand his social circle, especially meeting more women. I even helped him rent a small room in an art district near my home, convincing him to move to Songzhuang. Introducing him to my trusted friend, the calligrapher Zhang Shouze, he soon made many new friends. I also recommended him to Mr. Zhang Yehong at the Songzhuang Honeybee Bookstore, hoping he could find a job there to cover his living expenses. Although Mr. Zhang appreciated Hu Bugui's talent, Hu Bugui's strong accent made communication difficult with his colleagues, limiting his job prospects to occasional editorial work.

My ideal of providing Hu Bugui with "a job, a place to live, and like-minded friends" was not fully realized, but his short stay in Songzhuang was quite pleasant. He found a sense of belonging among the free-spirited intellectuals and artists there. I firmly believed that if he could settle down in Songzhuang, he would thrive. I even fantasized that a discerning female artist might fall for him, leading to a romantic relationship. However, he eventually moved back to Shuangqiao, preferring his familiar environment and avoiding the financial burden of rent in Songzhuang.

Hu Bugui's residence in Shuangqiao was provided for free by his Beijing friend, Mr. Zeng Zhaohua. In this chaotic world, Mr. Zeng stands out as a rare righteous man in my eyes. The house belonged to Mr. Zeng's parents' workplace and had been Hu Bugui's home for over twenty years. Being earmarked for demolition, the area around the house exhibited a unique sense of decay, harmonizing with Hu Bugui's leisurely and hermit-like lifestyle. For a drifter, housing is always a top priority. Mr. Zeng's support for Hu Bugui's survival in Beijing was nothing short of miraculous and kind. The rent from the subdivided old houses often supplemented Hu Bugui's living expenses. Their bond, reportedly dating back to the early 1990s when they worked at the same company, had forged a deep friendship based on Hu Bugui's

talent.

In April and May of 2019, while helping with my studio renovations, Hu Bugui seemed to struggle physically. Observing his occasional chest pain and slower movements, I urged him to get a check-up. By late May, with friends' help, he underwent tests at Peking University Hospital. The diagnosis was devastating: advanced-stage cancer with no surgical options. We kept the severity from him, creating a group to discuss how to help.

When Hu Bugui last visited my studio, we talked about life and death. He said he was not afraid of dying, having completed his 1.7-million-word manuscript, *The Original Analects* (《论语原始》), leaving him with no regrets. We agreed that knowing one's approximate time of death allows for a well-planned life closure. I shared my belief that death is not an end but the beginning of another journey, a joyful event in this context. I blessed him, saying, "In the next part of your journey, God will greatly compensate you."

I knew his health deteriorated due to his neglect and lack of self-care. With a loving wife to care for him, his life could have been different. From a Christian perspective, our bodies are temples of God, and neglecting them is an offense. Ideally, I should have shared the gospel with Hu Bugui, believing baptism would bring him peace and joy in his final days. However, I recognized the challenge of converting a lifelong rationalist intellectual without God's guidance. So, I prayed for him, shared my testimony of living with cancer, and described my joyful anticipation of the afterlife, hoping God would give him more time to know His love.

By mid-June, Hu Bugui's condition worsened, making it hard for him to leave home. On July 1st, a friend called and noticed his unusual behavior, prompting immediate concern. That night, my husband and I rushed to his place, finding him nearly naked, covered in mosquito bites, and barely coherent, with signs suggesting he had not eaten or drunk in days. Recognizing the urgency, we decided to contact his immediate family and friends, and arrange for his care.

Returning home that night, we could not sleep, reminiscing about our two-decade friendship with Hu Bugui. On July 2nd, my husband spent the day with him, awaiting visits from friends. It was decided that his close friend, Mr. Lü Xuechen, would accompany him back to his hometown in Shandong the next day.

On the morning of July 3rd, we gathered at Shuangqiao: my husband, Professor Yang Shushan from Renmin University, Mr. Zeng Zhaohua, Mr. Lü Xuechen, and I. Though Hu Bugui's condition had slightly improved, he remained mostly silent. My husband cleaned him up and changed his clothes. Packing his belongings, we found little of value beyond some books and a computer. It reminded me of Oscar Wilde's famous quote when entering America: "I have nothing to declare except my genius." Hu Bugui arrived with little and left the same, his greatest asset being his talent.

As we took final photos together, knowing he might never return, the gravity of the moment was palpable. Beijing's morning was bustling as usual, the world moving in its set path. Real life is rare; most people merely exist. Hu Bugui, an exception, came alone and left alone.

Professor Yang Shushan drove him and Mr. Lü to Beijing South Station for the high-speed train. Upon arrival in Shandong's Wulian, Yang's classmate picked him up and took him to his village. Having hidden in the bustling city for decades, Hu Bugui's life had been like a "stroll on a field of thorns." Now, returning like Tao Yuanming, I hoped his home was a peach blossom paradise.

On July 3rd, as Hu Bugui journeyed home, I read his book, *Notes on Reading Tao Yuanming's Collected Works* (《读陶渊明集札记》), in my Songzhuang studio. Knowing his homecoming lacked a welcoming entourage, with only his 80-year-old mother, I prayed the scenery he returned to could offer him some solace. May his remaining days be filled with familial warmth and the joy of books and music.

On the evening of July 4th, Mr. Lü Xuechen returned from Wulian, recounting Hu Bugui's circumstances. We decided to raise funds for his medical expenses. In my profound sadness, I wrote the following appeal (excerpted):

"Hu Bugui, a free writer, originally named Hu Shande on his ID card . A native of Wulian, Shandong, he lived incognito in Beijing for over twenty years, publishing works such as A Stroll on the Field of Thorns *(《荆棘场上的散步》),* Notes on Reading Tao Yuanming's Collected Works *(《读陶渊明集札记》), and* Miscellaneous Poems *(《辍耕微吟集》). Mr. Hu is indifferent to fame and fortune, living freely among literary friends and scholars.*

Despite enduring hardships over two decades, he always managed with the help of admiring friends, surviving several bouts of poverty and illness. Recently, after three years of dedicated work, he completed his 1.7 million-word manuscript, The Original Analects, and is seeking a publisher.

However, in April, his pain worsened. On May 24th, with friends' help, he was diagnosed with advanced cancer at Peking University Hospital. The cancer had spread, causing a rib fracture, leaving no surgical options. A recluse with no family in Beijing, he faced death alone.

On the afternoon of July 3rd, with friends' support, Mr. Hu returned to his hometown, Wulian County, Shandong.

Despite his talent and literary achievements, Hu Bugui barely managed to survive, often relying on friends' support. Now, he urgently needs funds to maintain his dignity in his final days."

My plea for help quickly spread among my friends on WeChat, and I received generous assistance from many. By July 9th, concerned for Hu Bugui's life, a group of five friends—Zeng Zhaohua (曾照华), Zhang Shouze (张守泽), Huang Bo (黄勃), Lü Xuechen (吕学臣), and me—formed a delegation to visit him in Wulian, Shandong. We arrived in Chuanfang Village, Hu Bugui's hometown, a little after 3 PM that afternoon. The small village, nestled in the hills, features stone-tiled houses with a river running through it. It might have once been a grand river, bustling with boats, which explains the village's name that suggests a boatyard. Currently, there were no young and able-bodied people in sight; only elderly white-haired villagers could be seen sitting near the base of the farmhouse walls.

Earlier that day, Rizhao writers, Mr. Shangguan Nanhua (上官南华) and his friends visited Hu Bugui. They not only brought donations but also essential supplies such as adult diapers and a large bath basin.

Following Mr. Shangguan's suggestion, they took Hu Bugui to see his future resting place to prevent his family from being overwhelmed when the time came. Local officials, including the young Deputy Secretary of the town party committee, Mr. Hu, joined the group, and everyone drove up the mountain in two cars with Hu Bugui.

They stopped at a north-facing hill with a small stream in front and a platform offering a distant view. The surroundings were lush with various crops thriving, exuding a sense of vitality. Thinking that Hu Bugui would soon rest here, gazing at the distant mountains by day and the starry sky by night, filled me with sorrow and reluctance, yet also comfort.

We discussed the approaching burial of a wise soul. God's arrangement may seem cold, but who can say it isn't a form of compassion? For someone critically ill to visit their potential grave with friends requires extraordinary understanding. Hu Bugui, enduring immense pain, walked silently with a smile, supported by his friends along the mountain path. The cool summer breeze from the valley brushed his gaunt face. This path, this mountain, this water witnessed Hu Bugui's growth and would ultimately embrace him for his final rest. Only this land has shown such consistent love and compassion for him.

Given that Hu Bugui's elderly mother, over 80 years old, was clearly unable to care for her son, we decided to find a hospital for him. After some twists and turns, we finally settled him in Wulian County Hospital on the morning of July 10.

Mr. Hu Shanyi (胡善义) and his wife Zhang Shanmei (张善梅), who grew up in Chuanfang Village and run a small foreign trade business in Wulian, were instrumental. Hu Shanyi's sister was a high school classmate of Hu Bugui. On the night of July 1, I called and messaged all Wulian people with the surname Hu in Hu Bugui's phone contacts, including his sister. Upon learning of Hu Bugui's critical condition from his sister, Hu Shanyi was shocked and contacted me. With his help, we managed to get Hu Bugui into a private room in the hospital. Hu Bugui's caregiver, Hu Shanfeng (胡善风), also from the same village and experienced in caregiving, was found through Hu Shanyi and Zhang Shanmei. From then on, all of Hu Bugui's affairs in the hospital were entrusted to the kind and loving couple.

However, the mysteries of God's plan are beyond our understanding. Just a month later, on the morning of August 10, Hu Bugui left this world forever in the morning light. His departure, I believe, was joyful, albeit with some regrets. Yet, can't even those regrets be a form of blessing?

In this impoverished era, it seems certain that each of us must cross the bridge of sighs into eternity. Now, Hu Bugui has gracefully strolled away from the thorny field of his life.

Wu Mengmei (吴梦湄): A curator and art critic active in the Songzhuang art district, Beijing.

Time of Light and Shadow: Gao Yaojie in a New York Hospital

LIN Shiyu

As I entered the hospital room, I saw a nurse inserting a catheter for Grandma Gao. The nurse explained that Grandma Gao's abdomen was severely swollen, causing frequent urination, so they decided to place a catheter to drain the urine directly into a container at the bedside.

Ninety-six-year-old Grandma Gao, dressed in a blue and white hospital gown and wearing an oxygen mask, lay there with disheveled hair and sunken cheeks. When she saw me, she waved but didn't speak.

On the morning of March 24, around 7 a.m., Grandma Gao's caregiver suddenly messaged me, saying that Grandma Gao had been taken to the emergency room by ambulance the previous night. The caregiver asked me to call the hospital to see if I could send some hot water and food because Grandma Gao couldn't drink cold water or eat Western food. I quickly called the hospital, and the staff said it was possible. So, the caregiver sent hot water and a bowl of dough drop soup, which helped Grandma Gao get through the day.

Since I couldn't make it to New York on Friday, I told a doctor friend in New York, who is also a fellow Shandong native like Grandma Gao, about her illness and asked her to visit. She brought hot soy milk in the evening, and Grandma Gao cried when she saw her. American hospitals generally don't provide hot water, and due to the language barrier, Grandma Gao couldn't express her needs, so she hadn't had anything to drink for two or three hours.

The next day, my friend's mother brought more soy milk and noodles. At 11:30 a.m., I arrived at Mount Sinai Hospital in New York, where Grandma Gao was staying. Seeing me, my friend's mother went home for lunch. Before leaving, she choked up and said, "She is a great woman who has suffered too much."

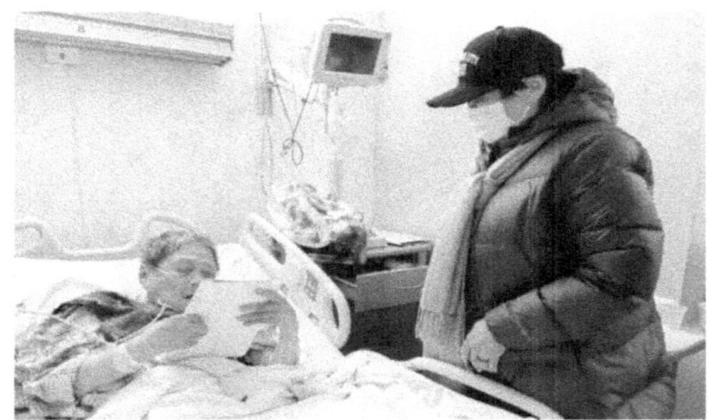

A friend corresponded in writing with Grandma Gao.

I touched Grandma Gao's emaciated arms and hands, noticing several bruises, likely from IV needle insertions. My eyes blurred with tears. One can only imagine the hardship of a 96-year-old Chinese woman, who doesn't speak English and is hard of hearing, being alone in an American hospital without any companionship.

Seeing me wipe away my tears, Grandma Gao calmly said, "I'm 96 and a half years old, almost a hundred. Being alive is meaningless; I'm a burden. Death means nothing to me."

She could have spent her twilight years in her own country, surrounded by her children and grandchildren, enjoying the happiness of family. However, her simple conscience didn't allow her to turn a blind eye to human suffering. She chose to speak the truth, resulting in a lonely end of life in a foreign land. Despite the humane care she received in this host country, the longing for her homeland kept her awake, with tears soaking her pillow on many a full moon night.

In 2019, I helped Grandma Gao edit a book titled "Two Hundred Poems: Notes on Poetry" (《诗词札记二百首》). One poem, "Sleepless Night," remains vivid in my memory:

"The moonlight, clear and bright,
illuminates my bed.
Tonight, I find no sleep,
rising to pace instead.
In this foreign land, joy's a fleeting thread.
Impatient heart yearns to return ahead.
With ailing body confined,
to whom can my sorrow be said? "

She wrote after this poem:

"The night of May 30, 2019, yet another sleepless night. The illness makes me think endlessly. At over ninety years old, wasting time, human suffering is unimaginable."

To ensure she received better care, I told the nurse Grandma Gao's story and showed her the cover of my book, "Living a Simple Life in the Rain: Oral Accounts of Gao Yaojie's Later Years" (《烟雨任平生:高耀洁晚年口述》), as well as a photo of Grandma Gao with Hillary Clinton. The nurse said she already knew her story. She held Grandma Gao's hand sincerely and said, "Thank you for everything you've done for humanity! I am honored to serve you."

When I translated this for Grandma Gao, she beamed with pride and asked the nurse, "Have you ever met Hillary? I dare not tell her about my illness; if she came to the hospital, it would be very troublesome with all the security arrangements. Last time she visited me, she brought six people! Six!" Grandma Gao held up six fingers.

"You're more famous than Hillary. Meeting you is enough for me," the nurse laughed and asked, "Can you give me, a 30-year-old woman, some life advice?"

I leaned close to Grandma Gao's ear and translated. She laughed, "I don't know what you young people think."

After the nurse left, Grandma Gao told me that on Friday, her abdominal swelling had worsened, and she suddenly couldn't speak or breathe properly. Her caregiver called 911, and the ambulance took her to the emergency room. "I've had abdominal swelling for months but didn't tell you. When you said you'd visit on Friday, I told you to come another day because my condition was severe."

So that was it. I remembered I had planned to visit her on Friday to discuss the structure of her new book. She asked me to come another day without explaining why, and I had been puzzled.

As we chatted, we suddenly heard a trickling sound from the bed. Grandma Gao sighed, "I peed again. The doctor gave me diuretics; I've been urinating all day."

A while later, a nurse came in to give Grandma Gao some glucose. Grandma Gao turned to ask what it was. I said it was glucose. She asked, "What percentage?"

I checked the bottle, "5%." "Oh, not 10%, they reduced it."

Even at 96, her early career as a doctor still showed. I imagined the scene: from the 1950s to the 1990s, Dr. Gao, with her exquisite medical skills, bustling around the gynecology ward of a hospital in Zhengzhou, deftly instructing nurses to administer 5% or 10% glucose to patients.

Decades have passed, and now she is old and frail, transformed from a doctor into a patient, lying in a hospital bed across the ocean, with no family by her side.

Aging is truly a helpless thing. No matter how strong and capable you are when young, in old age, you still face time's relentless harvest. Without the hope of eternal life, "Vanity of vanities, all is vanity."

Outside the window, spring rain drizzled, and the sky was gloomy. A fellow patient was hugging her children goodbye. The kids lovingly said, "I love you, mom," and kissed their mother's cheek. Seeing this family scene and then looking at the lonely Grandma Gao, I couldn't hold back my tears.

It was noon, and lunch was delivered. The drink was cold apple juice, a carton of milk, tomato soup, and mashed potatoes with carrot puree. Grandma Gao couldn't eat any of it. Thankfully, I brought hot soy milk and millet egg porridge in a thermos, which was still warm after two or three hours. I asked Grandma Gao what she wanted to eat, and she said soy milk. I poured her a cup, and she sipped it slowly through a straw.

After drinking the hot soy milk, she looked better. She told me that when she was first taken to the emergency room, the nurse was impatient and unfriendly. Later, a Chinese person recognized her, saying he had seen her on TV. He told the nurse Grandma Gao's story, and the nurse's attitude changed immediately. After being transferred to this regular ward, the nurses treated her much better.

Around 3 p.m., Grandma Gao's granddaughter, Xiao Lu, arrived from another state.

The young woman's mother is Grandma Gao's youngest daughter, now settled in Canada with her husband. Years ago, Grandma Gao's involvement in AIDS prevention displeased local officials, affecting her daughter, who lost her hospital job and was forced to move to Canada at over forty. Life in Canada was tough, and to make matters worse, she later fell seriously ill.

In 2019, I visited Grandma Gao and met her daughter at home. She looked unwell, with a darkened face. When I left, I ran into her again at the street corner, and we talked for over half an hour. She tearfully recounted her hardships and grievances. When we said goodbye, she expressed concern about her health and feared it might be her last visit to see her mother. She left sadly. I watched her wiping tears as she disappeared into the streets of New York.

Looking at the young woman in front of me, I felt a rush of emotions. She seemed so innocent, probably unaware of the heavy burdens her elders carried. Her grandmother and mother paid the price, but she was fortunate not to endure the same hardships. I asked about her mother's condition, and she said it wasn't good. I didn't dare to ask further.

Soon, Xiao Lu left to get the keys to Grandma Gao's apartment from the caregiver and bring some hot water. I stayed with Grandma Gao.

The rain intensified, beating against the window like a thousand galloping horses. Grandma Gao seemed tired and fell asleep. She must have been dreaming because she suddenly cried out, "Ah, ah." I rushed over and touched her hair and cheek, and she calmed down and continued sleeping. I sat across from her, gazing at this 96-year-old woman. I felt waves of sadness and reluctance.

Earlier, when Grandma Gao finished using the bedpan, the nurse didn't come for a long time. Afraid she might catch a cold, I rolled up my sleeves and cleaned her up, helping her wash. Grandma Gao said embarrassedly, "This isn't your job; my granddaughter should be doing this."

But I didn't mind. Since I met her in 2015, I've regarded her as family. I've witnessed her frail body, like a sagging bag, and touched her soul, free and noble like a bird.

Yet, time is not on her side. One day, I'll helplessly watch as the whirlpool of time sweeps her away, just as snow quietly melts off a rooftop.

Even knowing that "death is the end for all," I still dread that day. After all, I won't be able to hold her warm hand, smell the scent of an old grandmother on her, or hear her hearty laughter.

However, looking at the bigger picture, I

firmly believe that one day we will meet again in heaven. After Grandma Gao woke up, I wrote in my notebook: "Do you want to believe in God?" She took the notebook from me and wrote: "If I die, so be it."

Then she laughed and said, "Actually, I was baptized once when I was young. One day, I went to the pastor's house, and his dog bit me. I was so scared that I never went back." Later, in the 1950s, for reasons well-known, her journey of faith couldn't continue.

Grandma Gao continued, saying that after her mother and husband passed away, she made a pact with them that they must come back and tell her where they went. "But to this day, they haven't come back to tell me. Only once, my husband appeared in a dream and told me there was an envelope in the cupboard. I went to look, and there it was."

She then wrote a line of poetry on paper: "Many have died but none have returned."

Though Grandma Gao did not have the outward form of faith, she embodied its essence. Her life bore the fruits of righteousness, kindness, and compassion, demonstrating through her actions what it means to "love thy neighbor as thyself." She earned the respect and love of many. She is an apostle of love.

A moment later, the nurse came in to check her blood oxygen level—91%, a bit low, as the normal range is 95%-100%. It was already past 5 p.m., and the staff brought dinner. Looking at it, I saw it was no different from lunch, and Grandma Gao couldn't eat any of it.

I poured a bowl of millet egg porridge I had made in the morning and fed it to her. She drank it up in a few sips. I checked her blood oxygen level again, and it had risen to 94%! I felt a rush of accomplishment and suddenly recalled my trip back to China in January 2020 to visit my mother. At that time, my mother had just undergone major surgery and had a drainage tube in her abdomen. The whole night, I didn't dare sleep, keeping a close watch on that tube to make sure it stayed clear.

Often, when our loved ones are in distress, the vast world and grand events recede into a hazy backdrop. We focus solely on the small dot before us—whether our loved ones can eat well, stay warm, and suffer a little less.

The nutritionist came in, saw the untouched hospital food, and asked if the patient's diet needed adjustment. I told her to provide hot water with every meal and, if possible, hot soy milk and porridge. She noted it down and said, "We'll do our best."

Grandma Gao's granddaughter had returned, and it was time for me to go back to my home in New Jersey. Checking the time, I saw it was already 6 p.m., and it was still raining outside.

I told Grandma Gao I had to go home. "I won't die. You go ahead; Niuniu is waiting for you," Grandma Gao said with a smile, waving me off. I hugged her and said loudly in her ear, "You better not die before I come back from China."

Grandma Gao chuckled.

Written on March 27, 2023, Included in the collection *Gao Yaojie's Years in America*

In Memoriam of Gao Yaojie

A Courageous and Compassionate Chinese Gynecologist and Obstetrician

GANG He

Photo credit: provided by author

I first met Gao Yaojie when I was a toddler. She and my aunt were classmates at Henan Medical College in China, and they both lovingly held me when my parents brought me to visit my aunt. Twenty years later – when I became a medical student at the same school – Gao Yaojie was already a renowned OB/GYN doctor and department chair at a city hospital. She frequently took care of me – both in terms of my life and my studies.

Over time, I learned that Gao Yaojie was heavily involved in the prevention and treatment of HIV/AIDS, particularly among the poor farmers in our home province. These farmers had contracted HIV from selling their blood under unsanitary conditions, with contaminated instruments, and through improper procedures. Gao Yaojie supported and helped the children of these farmers, as well as the orphans whose parents had died from AIDS. However, her actions were seen as embarrassing and a loss of face by the Chinese government, especially the Henan Provincial authorities. They placed her under house arrest, restricted her communication with the outside world, and even prevented family members from seeing her. She was also denied the opportunity to travel to the US to receive the Jonathan Mann Health Award – a humanitarian award issued by the World Health Organization and back then presented by Kofi Annan, the Secretary-General of the United Nations.

During the SARS pandemic in 2003, I obtained Gao Yaojie's phone number through a friend. I called her on many occasions. She was a lonely and retired doctor – still confined to her home by the provincial authorities – and whenever she spoke about the HIV-infected farmers in the Henan countryside, she couldn't stop. I listened to her talk about the tragic situation of these farmers and their orphans, the hardships she faced while advocating for them, and the shameless actions of the Henan government in suppressing and obstructing her efforts. She was often so upset that she couldn't help but sob during our conversations. I was speechless and silently shed tears with her. Notably, our telephone conversations were under surveillance and were cut off several times.

In March 2006, under pressure from the United Nations, the US government, and overseas social media, Gao Yaojie was finally allowed to travel to the US to receive another award – the "Voice of Life," presented by former Secretary of State Hillary Clinton.

When I picked her up at O'Hare Airport in Chicago, I was overcome with emotion and hugged her as if I were hugging my mother. She smiled and said, "Oh, boy, I thought I might not see you before I die, but here you are! You haven't changed much!"

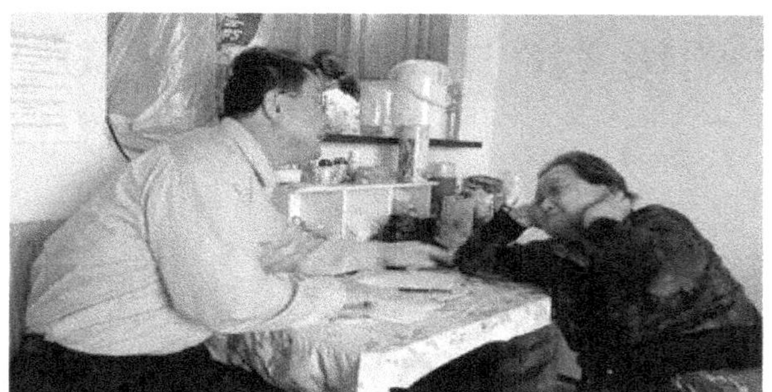

Photo credit: provided by author

I took her to her sister's house, but she showed no interest in resting. Even before she had finished greeting her sister, she took my hand and settled on the couch. She was keen to chat with me; it was as if she feared it could be her last time. She insisted on sitting next to me at the dinner table and continued to talk about the Henan AIDS endemic, ignoring her sister and daughter's attempts to interrupt her. She kept talking and talking…

I had no appetite and felt choked up. Before leaving, I hugged Gao tightly. She held my hand tightly and saw me off, repeatedly reminding me to take care of the DVDs, slides, photos, and books she had given me. "Don't worry, Gao," I said. "I may not have the courage and ability to do the work you are doing, but I can spread the truth through social media." I also handed her a $12,000 check that I raised with the help of four volunteer friends. I hoped this small amount of money could help her support a few orphans suffering from AIDS. It was raining when I left. As I got in the car, I looked back from the window and through teary eyes saw her standing by the door, waving goodbye.

In 2012, I moved to New York City, where Gao lived in a sparsely furnished apartment provided by Columbia University. Every weekend, I visited her with fresh flowers and spent hours chatting with her, mostly just listening to her talk. I hoped that, in some way, I could alleviate her inner loneliness and mental suffering. Her children were angry at her and refused to contact her because of the punishment imposed by the Chinese government. It was truly heartbreaking and shocking. And the AIDS problem remains unresolved; the Chinese government appears to cover up the endemic HIV/AIDS issue caused by contaminated blood donations and transfusions.

Photo credit: provided by author

On December 10, 2023, this brave old lady – a retired OB/GYN doctor who was recognized and respected worldwide, especially by the poor Chinese farmers – passed away at the age of 95.

Although she is no longer with us, her spirit continues to inspire hundreds of thousands of people around the world. Like the small planet bearing her name – 38980 Gaoyaojie, which orbits the Sun – I hope she will forever be remembered as she flies through this vast space.

Rest in peace, Gao Yaojie!

Brilliant Sunset: A Review of the Chinese Edition of *A Single Tear*

WANG Youqin

Describing tragic past events is no easy task, for the sorrow and pain conveyed in writing can bring oppression and sadness to the author. Describing one's own tragic experiences is especially difficult, as it is almost like reliving the horror again. It requires strong willpower, a clear mind, and a kind heart to endure the hellish experience again and use words to build a ladder of transcendence, leading both the writer and the reader to rise above. This sentiment might sound abstract, but reading Mr. Wu Ningkun's (巫宁坤) book truly evokes such feelings in me. From reading the newly released English edition over a decade ago to the current expanded Chinese edition, this impression has deepened. The new Chinese edition is a hefty 400-page book.

The story begins in the summer of 1951 when the author, upon accepting an invitation from Yenching University (燕京大学), returns from the University of Chicago to teach in China. Six weeks after arriving in Beijing, the "Thought Reform Movement" for intellectuals began, with everyone required to confess their thoughts, and activists revealing and criticizing teachers, colleagues, and even their fathers. Then came the "Campaign to Expose Hidden Counter-revolutionaries," where everyone had to "confess" their entire life from birth to the present, often under scolding and threats. Following this was the "Reorganization of Higher Education Institutions," during which he was involuntarily transferred to another university. Soon after, the "Campaign to Purge Counter-revolutionaries" began, and he was identified as a "hidden counter-revolutionary," his home was ransacked, he was publicly criticized, and one of his colleagues committed suicide. Then came the Anti-Rightist Campaign, where he was coerced into offering "opinions," which led to him being labeled as an "extreme rightist" and sent to "re-education through labor." He first went to Beidahuang (北大荒) and then to the Qinghe Labor Camp (清河劳改农场) near Beijing, enduring hard labor and starvation, watching his roommates die one by one, and losing his human form from hunger before being released after more than three years to work as a temporary English teacher in Anhui. When the Cultural Revolution began, he was put in a "cowshed," struggled against, humiliated, and witnessed his colleagues being killed. Eventually, he was expelled from the university and, along with his family, "relocated" to a rural area. After Mao Zedong's (毛泽东) death, there was a difficult and slow process of rehabilitation.

This is an individual's ordeal, but it is also a chapter of contemporary Chinese history. The persecutions he endured were commanded by the highest authorities and occurred nationwide. The great famine of the late 1950s and early 1960s affected everyone in China except for a few, including children. Yet, these tragic events, due to repeated official bans on publishing memoirs and records, and the insufficient efforts of Chinese intellectuals, have not been adequately constructed in the literary world despite their significant historical consequences. Those who experienced it could not remember or explain their experiences, and those who did not experience it firsthand knew almost nothing and could hardly believe it happened. In this context, Mr. Wu Ningkun's book is particularly important.

In the thirty years after the Cultural Revolution, a few memoirs by survivors were published, like grass growing through cracks in stone slabs. Among the influential works by authors with similar backgrounds to Mr. Wu, the most notable is "Six Chapters from My Life 'Downunder'" (《干校六记》) by Yang Jiang (杨绛), published in the 1980s. However, Yang's book is very short. While a thick book is not necessarily rich in content, a thin book certainly cannot contain the enormity of historical tragedy. I once taught American students to read a chapter from "Six Chapters from My Life 'Downunder'". Though they knew little about China, they sometimes saw things that Chinese people themselves could not. I recall one student asking, "Chinese literature rarely uses humor, but writings about the Cultural Revolution are often very humorous."

This question made me ponder for a long time. The explanation might be straightforward: the Cultural Revolution was so painful and humiliating that humor became a way to cope in post-Cultural Revolution descriptions. Yang Jiang's humor is indeed quite clever and insightful. Additionally, to gain approval for publication, direct depictions and analyses of the Cultural Revolution were not possible, so humor became a means to critique while being vague enough to avoid censorship. Despite the relative authenticity of "Six Chapters from My Life 'Downunder'", it lacks the historical texture and factual record. Some praised it as "complaining without anger, sorrow without pain," but I think this misused Confucius's (孔子) praise of the "Book of Songs," mistaking the author's self-censorship and reduction due to prohibitions as a conscious aesthetic pursuit. More than a decade after its publication, I saw news reports of Yang Jiang defending Professor Feng Youlan's (冯友兰) behavior during the Cultural Revolution and realized that the younger generation's lack of historical knowledge also points to the older generation's responsibility for not elucidating historical facts.

Mr. Wu Ningkun confronts the past head-on. In the 400-page *A Single Tear* (《一滴泪》), he uses meticulous detail rather than broad strokes to depict the various persecutions before and during the Cultural Revolution. He shows how campaign leaders spoke, how struggle sessions were organized, how colleagues were mobilized to attack the targets, the fear and timidity within the "struggle" objects, the human relationships on the brink of starvation, and the limited but resolute resistance in passivity and despair. His precise and realistic portrayal, akin to a camera lens, allows readers to understand what happened and how these atrocities occurred. This direct portrayal of reality has a unique beauty and power.

Moreover, it makes me realize that for recent history, humor, witticisms, and innuendos, while clever, are far from sufficient for constructing history. Just as one cannot rely on edge balls to win in ping-pong, building a historical record requires more substantial methods. Besides recounting his own experiences, Mr. Wu also writes about those who were persecuted to death. His compassion and empathy make it clear that this book is not just a personal complaint (though that would be entirely justified). These unnamed contemporaries are commemorated and mourned in his writing. I first learned about Jiang Nan (江楠) from the English edition of *A Single Tear* (《一滴泪》). She was a Russian teacher at Anhui University (安徽大学), whose husband was imprisoned in a "cowshed." She was raped by a powerful figure, became pregnant, and hanged herself. Her body was hastily buried and later exhumed twice, once when someone stole her sweater and once when wild dogs ate her corpse.

After the book was published, I called a writer to ask something, and he mentioned how I knew about Jiang Nan, saying she was his relative and talking about her daughter. I immediately requested they write Jiang Nan's detailed story, believing it to be more meaningful than the writer's recently published book, or let me interview them for more details. But I was refused. I understand this reaction but find it hard to accept this decision, although it is not the first time I have encountered such a situation.

Reading the new Chinese edition of *A Single Tear*, I once again encountered Jiang Nan's tragic story. I secretly hope her relatives will buy a copy, read it, and write to Mr. Wu Ningkun to commemorate Jiang Nan, who was murdered thirty-nine years ago, and to express their gratitude and respect to Mr. Wu, now nearly ninety. Age has distanced Mr. Wu from worldly fame and fortune. His record of the dead to warn the living comes from a place of pure nobility. Another deeply impressive aspect of this book is the author's description of his inner world, especially in times of great distress—his confusion, despair, and how he found inner strength to maintain dignity and self-respect. When taken for "reform through labor," he brought with him an English copy of "Hamlet" and a book of Du Fu's (杜甫) poetry. Throughout his long ordeal, he found support in Du Fu, Shakespeare, and the literature he could recite. I have never seen classic literary works so vividly combined with personal life, truly playing a crucial role at key moments. These descriptions provide a particularly interesting literary interpretation.

Mr. Wu has always been a teacher, though he did not teach long in the classroom due to severe persecution. Now, through his book, he teaches us his understanding of literature, creating a classroom without walls. He also draws strength from the love and kindness embodied by his relatives. He dedicates his book to his mother-in-law, an ordinary yet great mother who taught him the meaning of love and suffering. He does not seek to heroize himself. He writes about his suffering. Yet, through this tenacious recounting of suffering and serious discernment of right and wrong, good and evil, readers feel the "sublime spirit" he often mentions in literary figures. Thus,

during the reading process, a suffering author gradually takes on a heroic glow in the reader's heart.

In non-revolutionary times, today's young people might find it hard to imagine the suffering endured by Mr. Wu's generation. In 1952, Yenching University had five English professors, including him. During the Anti-Rightist Campaign, three male professors and the husbands of two female professors were labeled "rightists." At the start of the Cultural Revolution, two male professors, one female professor, and the husbands of two female professors were persecuted to death, and another female professor became mentally ill. Such a high density of persecution and death is scarcely known, despite their considerable reputation. I do not mean that the death of professors is more important than that of workers but that when the deaths of professors are obscure, the deaths of others are even less likely to be known. To write "63 Victims of the Cultural Revolution and Peking University" (《63 名受难者和北京大学文革》), I needed to know when Professor Hu Jiatai (胡稼胎), one of the five, died. Despite asking many Peking University (北京大学) teachers (where he taught after Yenching University was dissolved), no one knew where he went after being labeled a "rightist." I had to ask Mr. Wu for help. He gave me the phone numbers of people who might know, but even they had no results. I felt I had fallen into an absurd situation because I had printed materials "for criticism" containing Professor Hu Jiatai's "rightist remarks," but I could not find out where he was. Mr. Wu promised to help. Two days later, he called to say he had found someone who knew Professor Hu's post-1957 whereabouts. I was deeply moved by his kindness in helping a junior and his diligent work ethic. Professor Yu Ying-shih's (余英时) use of the Qing dynasty poet and historian Zhao Yi's (赵翼) poem "The country's misfortune is the poet's fortune" as the title of the book's preface is fitting. The misfortune of the country has already become a fact, but the poet's fortune will not automatically appear; it requires the poet's efforts to form. Without such poets who record history and discern good and evil, all that remains is double misfortune and more prolonged darkness. For this reason, we must thank and support poets who write about "misfortune." In comparison to such immense misfortune, there are far too few such poets.

When Mr. Wu's daughter, Wu Yimao (巫一毛), published her autobiography "A Feather in the Storm" (《暴风雨中一羽毛》) (first in English, then in Chinese), she told me over the phone that she had taken a photo of her parents and Mrs. Zheng Nian (郑念). In the photo, one person is in their nineties, one in their eighties, and one in their seventies, all smiling brightly. She said she titled the photo "Radiant Smiles" but felt it was inadequate. I don't know how I boldly suggested, "Wouldn't 'Brilliant Sunset' be better?" I haven't seen the photo, but I've read their books. In the books, we can see their hearts and work, perhaps more revealing than a photo of who they are. It is shameful that elderly people in their seventies, eighties, and nineties bear the burden of writing history, but at least we should open our eyes and admire the brilliant glow of the sunset.

The book reviewed: Wu Ningkun, *A Single Tear: A Memoir from the Anti-Rightist Campaign to the Cultural Revolution* (Taipei: Yunchen Wenhua, 2007), 394 pages. Preface by Yu Ying-shih.

About the author:

Wang Youqin, a scholar of East Asian studies, is currently a professor at the University of Chicago's Center for East Asian Studies. She is renowned for her research on the Cultural Revolution. Wang is also the founder of the online "Cultural Revolution Victims Memorial," which compiles the stories and experiences of hundreds of victims of the Cultural Revolution.

My Classmate Tang Yuqiang

LUO Weinian

My university classmate Tang Yuqiang (汤裕强) has passed away. After contracting COVID-19 and being hospitalized for over a month, he had been discharged and was recovering at home when he suddenly passed away.

During his hospitalization, on February 14, we exchanged messages on WeChat. He had passed the critical stage but still had difficulty breathing. I said, "I am glad to hear you are recovering. I, too, have been tormented by COVID-19 but have recovered, thanks to God, and am still working. If there is anything I can help with, please do not hesitate to ask."

He replied, "I am still in the hospital, but better than before. Yesterday, I had a minimally invasive procedure to release air bubbles from my lungs, making breathing easier. I'll need to stay a few more days before I can be discharged." His response reassured me. To alleviate my concerns, he added, "I have many relatives in Longyan (龙岩) who will help if needed. You don't have to worry. Thank you for your concern!"

His hometown was in Longyan, where he had many relatives. After falling ill, he was admitted to the First Hospital of Longyan. My childhood and teenage years were spent in Longyan. I lived at No. 7 Junmin Alley, just a wall away from the First Hospital of Longyan. His connection to Longyan added another layer to our relationship. Unfortunately, during our four years at university, we never talked about Longyan. I later asked him where in Longyan his hometown was. He said it was Xia Lao Village in Yanshi (雁石夏老村). Yanshi! I knew Yanshi. One summer during middle school, I went to Yanshi to learn farming and stayed in a village there for a month.

I still remember the sons of the commune secretary, Chen Wenhai and Chen Wenhe. One was in high school, the other in middle school. Before leaving, we went to a photography studio in town to take a picture. A few years ago, when I returned to China, my cousin Ya Fei took me to Yanshi to eat river fish, saying that a type of wild fish found only in Yanshi could be found there. It was the dry season, and standing on the Yanshi Bridge, we saw a large rock in the river resembling a goose's head.

I said, "The rock under Yanshi Bridge looks like a goose, and the water exposes it, hence the name Yanshi." He replied, "Yes, I've seen that rock." This was our last conversation.

Not long after, I heard of his passing.

After graduating from university, Tang Yuqiang embraced Buddhism. The passing of a Buddhist disciple is naturally different from that of a secular person. People often say that death is like a lamp going out. However, the life lamp ignited by his faith and actions has not extinguished. A few years ago, our classmate Fei Peng (飞鹏) mentioned that he was practicing with some Buddhist disciples in the mountains of Yong'an, Fujian (福建永安). The mountain, surrounded by a river, was accessible by a footbridge, with goods transported by motorboat. There was a temple in the mountain without an abbot, incense, or the sound of morning and evening bells. Some fellow practitioners gathered at the temple, practicing in a natural state, free from Buddhist rules and regulations. Because we both had faith, I became interested in his practice method. I sent him an article by a literary friend discussing faith and asked for his thoughts on his faith.

He replied with a comment, "The true nature of the universe is singular. Those who recognize and understand it are enlightened, while those who remain ignorant are ordinary people. Throughout history, there have been many enlightened ones, such as Laozi (老子), Zhuangzi (庄子), Sakyamuni (释迦牟尼), Jesus, Heraclitus, Socrates, the Sixth Patriarch Huineng (六祖慧能), and others. They are called sages, wise men, revered ones, prophets, Christ, saints, etc. Among them, some have many disciples and founded sects, even forming religions. Regardless of how many religions or sects exist, if they originate from enlightened beings, they all teach people to understand themselves and the universe, which is the so-called seeking, asking, embodying, and realizing the Way. The enlightened convey their understanding to the public, which is the so-called preaching and spreading the Dharma."

His faith was surprisingly similar to mine. He clearly distinguished between the universal truth and the enlightened ones. This is something many who consider themselves faithful do not understand. This includes Christians who do not recognize that Christ is not God and Buddhists who do not realize that the Buddha is not the Tathagata (如来).

He further said that there is a Zen book called *The Record of Pointing to the Moon* (《指月录》). In my view, the ultimate reality of the universe (the great Dao) is singular, like the moon in the sky, but the fingers pointing to the moon can be different. The various religions and sects originating from the enlightened (those who have realized the Dao) are like different fingers (different linguistic systems and ways of understanding). Thus, all the enlightened are not creators of universal truth; they are discoverers and disseminators of it. The universal truth is the ultimate original existence. As for what to call this ultimate reality—names like Heaven (老天爷), Wusheng Laomu (无生老母), Shangdi (上帝), Dao (道), God, Brahman, Emptiness (空), Allah, the Creator, Nature··· all refer to the same ultimate reality. Call it whatever you like, as long as you don't get entangled in disputes over these terms and instead understand and realize the actual truth through human language. Unfortunately, most people and religious followers are trapped in the linguistic pit and cannot grasp the truth, sometimes even resorting to violence and wars.

I paste our WeChat conversation here not only because it may be the clearest written expression of his faith but also because it will be difficult for anyone to express his faith in words again. Our classmate Fei Peng once advised him to write about his faith—specifically, the ultimate reality of the universe he mentioned. However, he did not do so. Instead, he practiced his faith through a unique direct interaction with the natural world—sun, moon, stars, the Tathagata's first creations, and people, the Tathagata's last creations.

Regarding faith, I believe there are four levels. The enlightened who attain the universal truth, having faith in the Tathagata or God and being justified by faith, is the first level. The second level is practicing righteousness through faith, validating the Tathagata through personal practice; personal practice is self-salvation. The third level is when the enlightened gather to spread their faith, turning individual faith into collective faith. The more people who believe in the Tathagata, the greater the social force for good. If a society has more than half of its people believing in the Tathagata, their faith-driven individual behaviors can collectively promote society's progress towards goodness; this is "raising righteousness through faith."

Tang Yuqiang was working on the third level. As a Buddhist disciple who saw the shortcomings of traditional Buddhism, he chose to avoid the current splendor and incense of Chinese Buddhism. Instead, he promoted what I call "natural Buddhism" in a near-naturalistic manner. Tang Yuqiang's "natural Buddhism" differs from

Master Xingyun's (星云法师) "Humanistic Buddhism." Natural Buddhism simplifies the increasingly complex modern life driven by capitalism. It uses an extremely simple lifestyle to return to nature, and through this return, approach the Tathagata. As writer Guangmu (光目) said, the essence of practice does not depend on form; any place can be a dojo, and any profession can be a dojo. Unfortunately, his practice method was not widely spread before it abruptly ended.

The ancients said, "Life and death are great matters; how can it not be sorrowful?" For, in the eyes of the world, a person's value is measured by the length of their life, so short sorrow cannot compare to long joy. In my view, a person's value is unrelated to the length of their life; it is not determined by material possessions but by understanding where life comes from and where it is going. The physical life, subject to change, ultimately ends. Understanding the immortality of the soul, reincarnation, what is there to grieve?

After writing this eulogy, I sent it to writer Guangmu, who practices in Tibet. Guangmu said: The seeds of practice sown by Buddhist disciples in this life are planted in their own soul's wisdom, that is, the Alaya consciousness (阿赖耶识). A practiced life is no longer an ordinary life but a life of wisdom. Wisdom, like seeds, is planted in the soul and will never be lost through lifetimes. In the next life, whether in the Buddha's land, in heaven, or on earth, it will sprout and grow with the soul, bringing infinite wisdom and blessings to their life of wisdom.

Though Tang Yuqiang's physical life has turned to ashes, his spiritual life remains with the universe and its creator. Though he has passed to the Western Pure Land, he has sown the seeds of his faith in the undying wisdom of his soul and in the hearts of his fellow practitioners. Given time, the spiritual life of those baptized by his teachings will surely take root and blossom, growing into a flourishing forest of faith.

My classmate Tang Yuqiang can now rest in peace.

About the Author:

Luo Weinian, a writer and publisher, is the executive editor-in-chief of *Humanities China*.

To the Unsorrowed Winter

For Alexei and Yulia Navalny

CHEN Jianli

1

What is that sound?
Cossacks cluster at the ice's sharp edge, listening—
This time, serpent venom silently infuses a soul,
repeating a self-justifying arc.
This time, the elk raises its noble antlers,
deeming it beneath itself to utter 'no' to Odin.

Carnivorous bats flood into the editorial office,
"Surrender the spines, don't force us to violence!"

Yet, the offsprings of darkness stand by their
words,
across Gulag's vastness or by the Don's sides,
on Sundays too burdened to bear.
The tears of the be-created are scarce,
his ducts carry the salt of earth,
his companions, too troubled for their own care.

2

To intimidate a rose,
is to menace all roses alike.
Oh, the wife of the Decemberist,
they despise the fragrance your mother tongue
breathes,
Will you rest your shoulders upon the lead wolf?
With its pilfered sharpness,
vowing to soothe departed souls.
Save for those exploded into shards.

Yet the eloquent double-headed eagle
unveils a mercy, newfound.

The Decemberists' wife tread lightly.
Within distant walls and wired heights,
some scorn their own gaze.
Startled by the breeze at your passage,
they no longer blame their downfalls on sanc-
tioned harms.

3

Today, we reclaim,
the handkerchief and the ring,
the throat,
the lenses and the sight
that saw through
the frivolous hymns of praise,
Including the common sense
that discarded excuses,
the ash under his feet,
witnessed hellfire,
and the rose on his chest, greeted by electric
shocks.

His gaze unwavering,
the enumerable
reasons for death,
and the flowers in vases at parting,
all bow their heads.

Finally, we demand,
let the unashamed sun bear witness,

under a sky bristling with guns,
we reclaim him,
his unashamed
corpse.

4

Mourners,
if the square can't hide
the bloodstained respect for the bayonet's pride,
it stirs the wrath of the uniforms
and the invincible pagan lords.

Kites tumble down, wreckage left no cry,
One candle, then another, bid goodbye,
to the extorted hearth,
gather at the snow-covered conscripts.

To witness for the next city laid to waste,
Though the choir's voice is hoarse, it carries grace.
There's always those who fear have not detained,
For angels, they lift their voice, unchained.

He's always cared, through days and nights so

dense,
Finding no reason to trust in pretense,
the loyalty of spokesmen, arrogant and tight,
Or the path the pontiff cites as right.

5

In the morning, we drink,
news swallowed with the water,
Ignition - as always, missiles are torn asunder.

He transports daisies from the Winter Palace to
inferno's gate,
Each glance cast, a desperate bet against fate.
Except for the wilting at high latitudes.

Now, a kindness for the dreams of Tatars, let it be.
Capital and frontier guilty of the same spree.
Meteors speak: every mother in the funeral line
Holds a resolve as steadfast as Kolchak's prime.
Now, they sanctify the early spring.
Their sons, stars in the firmament, a celestial of-
fering.

Following Rilke: From Duino to Muzot

CAI Xiaole

I

In a letter to his wife Clara, Rilke wrote: "Aren't you like the tree on the boundless plain of my wandering? I return to this tree again and again; sometimes I look at it, and thus I know where I am and where I should go." How much of this is genuine sentiment and how much is flattery is irrelevant. What's important is the psychological truth it reveals: Rilke was seeking an anchor point to confirm his existence as an individual and as a poet.

To some extent, poetry and writing offered a possibility of existence. For Rilke, writing was not merely a job or a craft; it was an "assignment" (Auftrag) from the earth, demanding that poets sing (Gesang). Through their words and songs, the existence of the earth is affirmed, and the poet's existence gains meaning. This theme, frequently sung in Rilke's poems, was also his personal experience. This sense of mission accompanied Rilke's writing career, explaining the anxiety that often surfaced in his work.

In 1910, after completing his novel The Notebooks of Malte Laurids Brigge, Rilke was initially ambitious but soon fell into a writing crisis, feeling creatively exhausted. He had poured everything into this novel. In a letter to a friend, Rilke likened himself to "Raskolnikov after the deed" (Raskolnikov nach der Tat, the protagonist in Dostoevsky's Crime and Punishment), revealing his fatigue and helplessness. At this low point, the previously acquainted noblewoman, Marie von Thurn und Taxis, extended her help. After multiple invitations, Rilke moved into Duino Castle in October 1911. In the first few months,

he remained despondent, unable to write. According to Marie's memoirs, Rilke often complained about his lack of inspiration.

It wasn't until early 1912 that things took a turn. In late February of that year, after writing a letter, Rilke claimed to have heard a voice in the wind during a walk: "Who, if I cried out, would hear me among the angelic orders?" Rilke noted this line and soon wrote the first and second of the Duino Elegies.

Duino Castle

II

"Who, if I cried out, would hear me among the angelic orders?" The opening line of the Duino Elegies is now well-known. The anecdote comes from Marie von Thurn und Taxis's memoirs. This story is linked to the then-popular spiritualism, which Marie herself was well-versed in, often hosting s é ances that Rilke attended. In this context, attributing the poem to a mysterious voice is understandable.

By depicting such a mystical writing scene, Rilke may have intended to convey that this line was a celestial utterance, beyond human capability, to be understood from a transcendent perspective. Scholars have noted that Rilke often attributed his works to a third party to imbue them with a mystical aura and cultivate his image as a born poet (Ingeborg Schnack). At times, he would also attribute less satisfying works to others to shirk responsibility, as seen in Excerpts from the *Testament of the Count C.W.*. Overall, to transcend the real world and expand the boundaries of language, Rilke occasionally adorned his works with spiritualist elements, although he wasn't entirely convinced of them.

On another occasion, during a séance, Rilke claimed to have heard the voice of a deceased woman directing him to a place with red soil, mountains, and a church. Rilke identified this city as Toledo, Spain. Later, Marie's son dreamed of a mountainous city with castles, further solidifying Rilke's resolve to visit Spain. However, it's worth noting that Rilke had long been intrigued by Toledo, having learned about it through El Greco's paintings. The woman's voice and the son's dream were likely excuses for his desire to visit Toledo.

"Toledo" by El Greco

III

The duchess keen to cultivate talent indeed funded Rilke's trip to Spain, which proved fruitful. Upon arrival, Rilke wrote to Marie, "I wandered around and absorbed everything like a child." The change of scenery invigorated him.

The landscape, with its churches and angel statues and open valleys, evoked feelings of the sublime (das Erhabene) in him. During his travels in Spain, Rilke began writing the sixth elegy, known as the "Heroic Elegy," which celebrates a life of unending action and forward momentum. The sublime tone of the poem is indebted to the Spanish landscape. Later, when he struggled to write, Rilke lamented in his letters that nothing could surpass the intensity of the Spanish scenery, leading to his creative block.

In early 1913, Rilke returned to Paris, where he wrote the third elegy that autumn. This elegy is notably intertwined with Freud's psychoanalysis, leading some scholars to hastily claim that Rilke's third elegy merely rewrites Freud's theories in poetic language (Otto Bollnow). This view is contested and detailly refuted (Käte Hamburger). It's important to note that Rilke's relationship with psychoanalysis was ambivalent. While he appreciated Freud's analytical methods through Lou Andreas-Salomé, he emotionally resisted Freud's ideas, fearing they would undermine human existence.

Earlier, when grappling with inner turmoil, Rilke considered psychological treatment but ultimately rejected it. For him, art and life were mutually exclusive; therapy would mean a tranquil, mediocre life, and he preferred the pain of writing over such an existence.

IV

In 1914, shortly after returning to Germany from Paris, World War I broke out. Although Rilke initially idealized and poetically transformed the war, its horrors and inconveniences soon affected him personally. His belongings and books were left in Paris, which he could no longer return to. He was even conscripted, escaping only through the efforts of friends (Anton Kippenberg, Katharina Kippenberg). This period was extremely unpleasant for Rilke.

His writing came to a standstill, and anxiety and fear consumed him. During the war, he lived in Munich, anxiously awaiting its end, later describing this time as "five years of prison in Germany" (cinq ans de prison allemand). Scholars have suggested that this writing hiatus was a period of preparation for an eventual burst of creativity (Dieter Bassermann). Undoubtedly, no one can write ceaselessly; time is needed to experience life, read, and accumulate language and experiences, as was the case for Rilke (Eudo Mason). However, viewing this period merely as preparation risks falling into teleological thinking, overlooking the poet's lived experience. The reality was far less poetic: Rilke's anxiety from the war and creative exhaustion drained his energy, trapping him in a vicious cycle where he couldn't write, making his condition worse.

Unlike Val é ry's deliberate break from writing or Rimbaud's voluntary abandonment, Rilke's hiatus was not a conscious waiting but a loss of writing ability under war and anxiety.

V

The impact of the writing environment on Rilke was profound. He constantly roamed in search of experiences and inspiration, visiting Russia, Egypt, Spain, and Venice. These places invariably stimulated his creativity. This time, his destination was Switzerland, Germany's neighbor.

During World War I, neutral Switzerland was a haven for artists fleeing the conflict. Rilke had spent most of the war in Munich, surrounded by his artist friends but devoid of creative desire. Realizing he needed to leave Munich, he received an invitation to Switzerland. Encouraged by friends, Rilke embarked on his Swiss journey in 1919.

Rilke was warmly welcomed in Switzerland, where he embarked on a lecture tour, visiting major cities like Bern, Zurich, and Lugano, and spending time in the mountains. His letters to Marie von Thurn und Taxis frequently mention the "Elegy-place" (Elegie-Ort), expressing his ongoing search for an inspiring location to complete the Duino Elegies. His letters vividly convey his longing to write and the pain of being unable to do so.

The poet was like a laboring beast searching for a place to give birth. He sensed this was his last chance, putting everything aside to focus solely on completing the Duino Elegies. He needed an isolated place with sublime scenery, recalling the Valais region in Switzerland, which he had visited once and found fitting. Fate led him to Muzot Castle (Chateau de Muzot).

Muzot Castle

VI

With help from various friends, Rilke moved into Muzot Castle in 1921. Living there alone, he was very satisfied, writing in a letter: "Peace, that sweetest, purest thing." Rilke finally felt he could continue writing.

In February the following year, he picked up his pen again, completing the eighth elegy, followed quickly by the seventh and ninth elegies. With the ten Duino Elegies seemingly complete, Rilke, still in a good writing state, rewrote the tenth elegy, incorporating his journey to Egypt a decade earlier. In this elegy, he follows a young, deceased person through the "plain of lamentation" until disappearing into the "mountains of primal pain."

Rilke was overjoyed, feeling the reward for his decade-long struggle had finally arrived. He wrote to friends, the duchess, and his publisher, announcing the completion of the Elegies, fulfilling his ten-year mission. This work now stood as a peak in twentieth-century poetry.

However, his Elegies were not yet finished. One night, recalling his experiences in Paris and a Picasso painting he had seen, Rilke couldn't suppress the urge to write, composing an elegy centered on a wandering performer. Satisfied with this new elegy, he replaced the original fifth elegy in the Duino Elegies, finally concluding the collection.

"Family of Saltimbanques" by Pablo Picasso

The Fifth Elegy and The Tenth Elegy are like twin stars, representing two extremes of human existence. The former depicts modern city dwellers controlled by fate, while the latter represents a more primitive, authentic survival space. As Paris and Egypt symbolize two opposing modes of existence, Rilke continually sought the wilderness within himself, as he wrote at the end of the Second Duino Elegy:

> *If only we could discover*
> *such a singular human place-*
> *pure, determined, self-contained,*
> *our own fruitful soil between*
> *the river and the stone!*
> *But our hearts outrun us.*
> *We cannot capture their essence by*
> *lingering before consoling statuary,*
> *nor by contemplation of those godlike*
> *forms*
> *containing all for which we yearn*
> *in monumental measure.*
>
> *(translated by Robert Hunter)*

About the author:

Cai Xiaole, a young poet and translator with a master's degree in German literature, is the author of *Annotations on Duino Elegies* and the translator of *Selected Short Stories of Kafka*.

Reflections on Reading "The Biographies of the Wealthy" in the Records of the *Grand Historian*

ZI Zhongyun

Since ancient times, China has held a tradition of looking down on merchants. The social hierarchy of "scholars, farmers, artisans, and merchants" places merchants at the bottom. But when did this tradition begin? I haven't researched it thoroughly. It seems that during the Spring and Autumn and Warring States periods, this saying did not exist. Even Confucius did not look down on merchants; several of his disciples were engaged in trade. It appears that the disdain for merchants in Confucianism came later. Legalists certainly looked down on merchants; Han Feizi listed them among the "Five Vermins." Since the Sui and Tang dynasties, with the establishment of the imperial examination system, the order of the four classes became fixed. Scholars occupied the top not merely due to their high status but because they were the only ones who could become officials. A poor scholar without any official titles might have a lower status than a wealthy local. Hence, the reality is that officials are above merchants. Merchants have always feared officials, and officials have always oppressed merchants—this is the true tradition.

Sima Qian (司马迁) dedicated a chapter in the Records of the Grand Historian (《史记》) specifically to merchants, "The Biographies of the Wealthy" (《货殖列传》). Previously, I merely noted that he differed from later official historians by writing biographies for various people, not judging heroes by their success or failure. His perspective was indeed unique. However, I was personally more interested in assassins and knights-errant and had never closely read "The Biographies of the Wealthy". Now, in a new reality, rereading this chapter, I suddenly realized that the Grand Historian of two thousand years ago had such an evaluation of merchants' roles. Some of his views are quite advanced, even by today's standards, at least in China.

This "biography" differs from others in that it does not focus on individuals but uses various cases to illustrate the author's viewpoints.

Viewpoint 1: Affirmation of Human Material Desires

The article begins by criticizing Laozi's (老子) famous statement: "In the utmost governance, neighboring countries see each other, hear the sounds of chickens and dogs, and the people enjoy their food, love their clothes, are content with their customs, delight in their work, and to old age and death, they do not visit each other." Sima Qian argues that if this were the case, modern people's senses would be almost useless. He then discusses that humans have an inherent nature to pursue sensory pleasures and delicious food, which cannot be suppressed. Thus, rulers should not suppress these desires. He proposes several approaches, from the best to the worst: "following it," "guiding it," "educating it," "regulating it," with the worst being "competing with it," meaning competing with the people for profit. He believes that rulers should allow the people's desires to manifest naturally without interference. This sharply contrasts with Zhu Xi's (朱熹) later idea of "preserving heavenly principles and eliminating human desires."

Viewpoint 2: Trade is Spontaneous

Sima Qian argues that the exchange of goods to satisfy one's desires is spontaneous among people. The specialties of different regions, "all of which the people of China love," are "produced by craftsmen and traded by merchants." People utilize their abilities and work hard to obtain what they desire, naturally engaging in trade and setting prices, "like water flowing downward, ceaselessly, coming without being summoned, produced without being sought." There is no need for any "political education." In modern terms, this suggests that the government should not excessively interfere in the market.

Viewpoint 3: Affirmation of Profit and Wealth

Sima Qian states, "The world bustling about is all for profit; the world jostling about is all for profit." This phrase is often quoted negatively to highlight human selfishness, but Sima Qian uses it to affirm its legitimacy. "Wealth is something that people naturally desire without learning." He lists various types of people—soldiers risking their lives in battle, hunters facing fierce beasts, petty officials manipulating documents, idle youths practicing martial arts, women beautifying themselves and learning skills, and even those committing crimes—all driven by profit. He agrees with Guan Zhong's (管仲) saying, "When granaries are full, people know propriety; when food and clothing are sufficient, people know honor and disgrace," and further develops it: "Propriety arises from abundance and disappears from want; the noble seek wealth to pursue virtue, while the common people seek wealth to meet their needs." Contrary to Mencius's (孟子) idea of opposing righteousness and profit, he argues,

"When people are wealthy, righteousness naturally follows." He concludes that the pursuit of wealth is a universal human nature, unimpeded by social status and consistent with practicing righteousness.

Viewpoint 4: Economic Development Strengthens the Nation

Sima Qian spends considerable space detailing the characteristics of different regions, including population, geography, products, customs, and the prosperity brought by trade. It is well known that Sima Qian traveled extensively across China in his youth, which influenced his writing style. In his self-narrative, he mentions beginning his travels at twenty, covering the north, south, east, and west, even reaching remote regions like Bashu (巴蜀) and Kunming (昆明). His travels were not mere sightseeing but thorough field research. Thus, his work serves as a valuable reference for studying the economic geography of his time. He emphasizes that economic development should be tailored to local conditions and not solely rely on agriculture.

The rise of the state of Qi was due to two individuals: Jiang Taigong (姜太公), who was enfeoffed in Yingqiu (营邱), a saline and sparsely populated area unsuitable for agriculture. He encouraged women to engage in weaving and developed the fishing and salt industries, leading Qi to attract external populations with its fish and salt while becoming a major exporter of clothing. This early prosperity was not due to force but persuasion and encouragement. The other was Guan Zhong, who revitalized Qi during its decline, establishing nine departments to manage the economy and finances, eventually leading to Duke Huan of Qi's hegemony.

The story of King Goujian of Yue (越王勾践) enduring hardship and ultimately defeating the state of Wu (吴) is well known. This text highlights his economic construction during his confinement in Kuaiji (会稽), assisted by two financial experts, the famous Fan Li (范蠡) and the lesser-known Ji Ran (计然). Ji Ran's comprehensive economic strategies covered coping with good and bad years, floods, droughts, and famines, and optimizing the pricing and profit distribution of agricultural products. Under his management, Yue (越) prospered over ten years, enabling generous rewards for soldiers, who then fought fiercely in battle, eventually leading to Yue's dominance over Wu.

Fan Li was inspired by Ji Ran's strategies. He noted that Yue had implemented five of Ji Ran's seven strategies with great success and decided to apply them personally. He resigned and ventured into business—"sailing on a small boat across rivers and lakes." It's uncertain if the modern term "going into business" stems from this anecdote. Fan Li, who later became known as Tao Zhugong (陶朱公), amassed great wealth, dispersing it to help impoverished friends, achieving wealth thrice over nineteen years. He is regarded as a philanthropist today.

During the early Han dynasty, the country prospered with open policies and lifted restrictions, allowing merchants to travel freely, facilitating trade, and meeting various needs, contributing to the stability of Emperor Wen (文帝) and Emperor Jing's (景帝) reign.

Viewpoint 5: Merchants as Talented Individuals on Par with Political Figures

The text highlights numerous wealthy individuals, from nobles like those in Yue (越) to commoners. It begins with Confucius's disciples, noting that while some like Yan Hui (颜回) lived in humble conditions, others like Zigong (子贡) achieved great wealth through trade. Zigong's opulent lifestyle and gifts earned him the respect of rulers, who treated him as an equal. Sima Qian suggests that Zigong's success helped elevate Confucius's fame.

In Wei (魏), Bai Gui (白圭) excelled in seizing opportunities, buying low and selling high, earning him a reputation comparable to renowned statesmen and strategists. Sima Qian fully acknowledges his achievements.

During the Qin dynasty, a man named Luo (倮), proficient in animal husbandry, became wealthy through trading livestock, earning him a noble title. Similarly, a widow named Qing (清) in Bashu managed her wealth effectively, receiving imperial recognition for her virtues. Sima Qian comments that their wealth enabled them to be honored and respected.

The article also mentions the "plain-clothed nobility" system, where individuals received honorary titles without salaries or lands, relying on their business acumen to maintain a lifestyle comparable to feudal lords. Examples include the Zhuo (卓) family in Shu (蜀), the Cheng (程) and Zheng (郑) families in Shandong, the Kong (孔) family in Nanyang, and the Cao (曹) and Bing (邴) families in Lu (鲁), all of whom thrived through various industries like iron smelting and fishing. These families achieved wealth through legitimate means, without official titles or illicit activities, exemplifying Sima Qian's ideal of wealth earned through talent and opportunity.

However, not all wealthy individuals were virtuous. Some profited from immoral or illegal activities, which Sima Qian criticizes. He distinguishes between legitimate wealth ("worthy wealth") and wealth gained through deceit or crime ("unworthy wealth"). He also criticizes those who, despite lacking abilities, live in poverty while boasting of their moral superiority, calling them "shameful."

In conclusion, Sima Qian believes that wealth can be amassed by those with capability and lost by the inept. Wealth comparable to that of rulers can be achieved.

This is Sima Qian's view on wealth. In his self-narrative, he states that the purpose of writing "The Biographies of the Wealthy" was to demonstrate that commoners could become wealthy without harming the state or people, making them worthy of admiration. This recognition of merchants, especially wealthy ones, was unconventional for his time. Sima Qian's forward-thinking extends beyond this; historian Ban Gu (班固) criticized him for deviating from traditional values, citing "The Biographies of the Wealthy" as an example of glorifying wealth and despising poverty. This criticism oversimplifies Sima Qian's nuanced perspective. Ban Gu may have misunderstood the depth of Sima Qian's insights due to different circumstances.

Sima Qian himself experienced the pain of poverty. After being sentenced, he could have avoided brutal punishment if he had money to buy his way out. However, his impoverished family and lack of support left him with no options. This personal experience likely influenced his reflections on wealth and poverty. Nonetheless, he did not resent the wealthy; instead, he recognized the importance of economic development for national strength and the value of merchants in achieving prosperity. His broad vision and insights were extraordinary.

About the author:

Zi Zhongyun, a translator and scholar, is an honorary academician of the Chinese Academy of Social Sciences. She formerly served as the director of the Institute of American Studies at the Chinese Academy of Social Sciences and as editor-in-chief of the *American Studies* journal.

The Influence of Friedrich Hayek on Humanity

YANG Xiaokai

Italian political thinker Niccolò Machiavelli wrote in *The Prince*, "The armed prophets have been victorious, and the unarmed ones have been destroyed." In his view, violence dictates the course of history.

However, can an armed prophet still be considered a prophet? Throughout human history, violence is ephemeral; only ideas endure. A prophet's sole weapon is his thoughts. The impact of Hayek's ideas on human history best exemplifies this statement. Hayek's influence on human thought may become as profound and pervasive as Confucius's influence on Chinese thought. As someone with a unique economic perspective, I've never felt a sense of worship for Nobel laureates in economics. In fact, I've often felt that some of them hardly deserved the honor. Additionally, as someone passionate about scientific methods, I've typically disregarded non-mathematical ideas. Hayek, however, was an economist who never used mathematical models, yet reading his works left me with an intense admiration and a sense of missed kinship. I can't precisely explain why, but I believe that most people, after reading his books, will experience a profound shift in their worldview.

In 1974, the Swedish King awarded Hayek the Nobel Prize, describing him as the most respected economist and moral philosopher since Adam Smith.

Human Society as a Spontaneous Order

Hayek's critique of 20th-century utopianism differs significantly from most critiques. Today, most critiques of utopianism in China focus on the inefficiency of its economic implementation. In contrast, Hayek's criticism targets the mechanism of institutional formation.

Hayek argued that the institutions of a free society emerge spontaneously rather than being deliberately designed. Thus, these institutions result from the competition and interaction of millions, encompassing diverse and disparate information known to different individuals. This competitive process prevents monopolization of institutional design, thereby minimizing the distortion of information during transmission.

In contrast, utopian institutions are the first to be comprehensively designed by certain thinkers. These systems are not spontaneously formed through competitive processes and therefore contain limited information constrained by the knowledge of those thinkers. They cannot integrate the diverse information derived from the interactions of millions.

The differences between a free society and a utopian state are clear. In a free society, institutions and order emerge spontaneously and cannot be designed by a few thinkers. Furthermore, institutions in a free society are merely rules of the game, judged solely on their fairness.

Utopian societies, on the other hand, predefine who should win and what specific goals society should pursue. Consequently, in utopian systems, some people will always impose their desires on others. Imagine a game where the winner is predetermined before it begins—how can there be any fair competition?

In a free society, there is no mandate to "eliminate utopian systems" or "implement capitalist systems." There are only fundamental rules of competition. The spontaneous development of institutions is based on the consensus of fairness in these rules. Whether utopianism, capitalism, or another system prevails is unpredictable.

Before reading Hayek's works, I thought the difference between utopianism and capitalism was not about planning versus lack of planning. There is more planning in capitalist economies than in utopian ones; for instance, McDonald's operations involve numerous directive plans from headquarters to its franchises.

The fundamental difference, however, is that planning in capitalist societies is voluntary and spontaneous, whereas planning in utopian societies is compulsory.

Before reading Hayek, I hadn't encountered his works but realized that my thoughts resonated with his ideas upon reading them. In hindsight, I was likely influenced indirectly by Hayek through reading works by Friedman and others.

Other scholars have noted that utopian economies are characterized by the visible hand. When these economies transition to market economies, people resist the market's discipline, complicating reforms.

These ideas originated with Hayek.

Hayek pointed out that in a free economy, the fairness of the game rules ensures effective enforcement. Losers have no choice but to accept defeat because the market, an invisible hand, is beyond debate and resistance, leaving no one else to blame.

In contrast, utopian systems rely on the visible hand for rewards and punishments. Losers can always seek government intervention, complaining about unfair or unreasonable rewards and punishments. Thus, game rules cannot be strictly enforced, leading to perpetually soft budget constraints. In such an environment, fair competition is unachievable.

The Misuse of Reason Leads to Disasters

Inspired by the scientific revolution, humans have grossly underestimated the complexity of society and human nature, misusing science and believing they can master destiny—a fatal arrogance that has brought severe utopian disasters.

In *The Counter-Revolution of Science: Studies on the Abuse of Reason*, Hayek wrote that humans can never attain omniscience; individuals will always be ignorant. Thus, it is crucial to curb the misuse of science and reason. Only by relying on the spontaneous decisions of individuals in a market division of labor can the most scarce resource—knowledge—be fully utilized.

Hayek's ideas diverge significantly from the mainstream economic schools that advocate "economic rationality." Represented by MIT, these schools emphasize the application of mathematical methods.

Many renowned economists in this school use mathematical models to prove market failures and justify government intervention. Others use mathematical models to demonstrate the superiority of the invisible hand.

Hayek's ideas differ from these. He emphasized that over-reliance on economic rationality could lead to institutional failure. He pointed out that human knowledge is limited, and often, we cannot judge or may misjudge what is rational and irrational.

Faith as an Antidote to the Misuse of Reason

Hayek's views on religion are particularly enlightening for Chinese intellectuals who venerate human reason and worship scientism. Hayek believed that enduring institutions throughout history did not originate from social science and human reason but from religion and ideology.

Religion and ideology, though not rational, dictate behavioral norms and game rules for human interactions. Ideology also provides a mechanism for commitment to these rules.

In a pluralistic society, competition among various religions and ideologies leads to the proliferation of those most conducive to spontaneous order.

During this process, followers of the prevailing religion or ideology do not choose them rationally, just as mothers do not love their children rationally. However, in the evolutionary process, mothers who do not love their children face extinction due to high offspring mortality rates, just as religions and ideologies that do not favor spontaneous social order will vanish. Hence, religions that have endured throughout history, while not rational, form the foundation for effective institutions.

Ensuring Greater Freedom

Hayek was a thorough pessimist. He believed that humanity could never escape the curse of utopianism, predicting that powerful governments would eventually plan to reduce populations to conserve resources.

Hayek devoted his life to proving that human prosperity, happiness, and dignity stem from individual freedom rather than any form of collectivism. Utopian systems trample private property and basic human nature, leading to endless scarcity, chaos, enslavement, and ultimately, economic collapse, moral decay, and the death of truth.

Hayek not only accurately predicted the future but also became part of history. Every tragedy and disaster after him has validated his ideas.

About the author:

Xiaokai Yang (1948-2004) was a Chinese-Australian economist. He was one of the world's pre-eminent theorists in China's economic analysis, and an influential campaigner for democracy in China.

The "Xiang Thinking" of Steve Jobs and Elon Musk

WANG Shuren

1

From the end of the 20th century to the present, America has gifted the world two remarkable inventors and entrepreneurs: Steven Jobs and Elon Musk. Their ability to transform the world is closely linked to their capacity to transcend traditional and habitual ways of thinking. "Transcendence" is easy to speak of but challenging to achieve. It requires an environment that provides freedom of time and space, and individuals must have a grand goal. Both were determined to change the world and transform humanity, making people more free. I've read Jobs' biography, and from his childhood, he was a rule-breaker, what one might call a rebellious child. Such children, characterized by their disregard for convention and instruction, follow their own free thoughts. These children need a discerning eye to recognize their genius. Jobs' adoptive parents supported him, criticizing teachers who failed to find a way to educate him. Fortunately, a math teacher saw his potential and became his first benefactor. Tradition and societal inertia stifle the development of genius.

Recently, Musk proposed the idea of the "first principles" as a mode of thinking. He believes that moving from experience to experience can never lead to innovation. Traditional analogical thinking is incompatible with innovation. The path to innovation requires a return to the first principles. Philosophically, this means returning to the irreducible origin, the ultimate point. I believe this path of thinking is about returning to the Dao, returning to nothingness, and reaching the ultimate point, expanding the space of thought to infinity and achieving maximum freedom. Only this power of freedom can support an individual in disregarding convention. Jobs and Musk both achieved breakthroughs in their thinking methods, enabling them to move toward their goals. Jobs is called a perfectionist; perfection is never attainable, but the effort of a perfectionist is a continuous pursuit of perfection. Musk's emphasis on returning to the first principles is about transcending the conventional and redirecting back to the origin. My reflections in this essay relate to this concept.

2

"Xiang thinking" (象思维) achieves spiritual transcendence through poetic association and creative activities. As a form of perceptive thinking, "Xiang thinking" is not entirely about abstract meditation. On the contrary, it always involves creative activities that break barriers and connect human with the Heavenly Dao (天道). These activities unfold both spiritually and materially, encompassing art, philosophy, religion, science, medicine, agriculture, industry, commerce, politics, military, and diplomacy. Despite varying degrees of innovation, all these creative activities must transcend existing experiential knowledge and preconceived notions. Innovation requires complete spiritual freedom, which is only possible by surpassing existing experiences and ideas, thereby opening up new avenues of thought. Thus, the transcendental nature of "Xiang thinking" lies in its necessity to first surpass the constraints of existing experiences and ideas, propelling the spirit into states described by Zhuangzi (庄子) as "I have lost myself" or "sitting and forgetting." This means breaking conventional experiential, logical, and linguistic constraints to enter a chaotic state of "nothingness." Only by breaking through the norm and entering this "chaotic noth-ingness" can one attain a vast spiritual realm of freedom, opening the "mystic gate" as described by Laozi (老子).

3

The concept of "Epoché" is borrowed from phenomenology. In phenomenology, how to "bracket" and enter a new spiritual realm is not entirely clear. In Chinese "Xiang thinking," "bracketing" is a practice towards enlightenment, a practice of self-negation or abandonment. Even with good potential, one must still cultivate it. This practice is described by Zhuangzi: "I kept still and let it be, and after three days, I was able to detach from the world; after detaching from the world, I kept still, and after seven days, I was able to detach from things; after detaching from things, I kept still, and after nine days, I was able to detach from life; after detaching from life, I attained clarity; clarity brought timelessness; timelessness brought entry into life and death" (*The Great Master*, 《大宗师》). The periods of three, seven, and nine days are metaphorical, indicating stages of enlightenment rather than actual durations. Throughout this process, each level is higher and involves continuous negation or sublimation. However, bracketing one's existing experiences and ideas to achieve continuous spiritual transcendence is incredibly challenging and requires significant effort, akin to Laozi's idea of "achieving utmost emptiness and maintaining profound stillness" or the Sixth Patriarch Huineng's (六祖 慧能) "no thought, no form, no abode." Here, "no" refers to the spiritual practice of elimination or negation, removing distractions that hinder enlightenment. Additionally, achieving such "bracketing" or transcendence depends on one's inherent potential or talent. Those with outstanding potential or talent find it easier, whereas others need strong willpower and long-term perseverance.

4

It is often said, "Effort will not disappoint the dedicated." This proverb usually refers to achieving practical goals, such as mastering a skill or gaining experience. Here, we discuss "effort" and "dedication" from the perspective of spiritual transcendence. In Zen Buddhism, "dedication" means returning to the "original mind," also known as the "ordinary mind." This seemingly simple task is incredibly difficult for those outside Zen because their minds are filled with mundane thoughts. Discarding these thoughts to return to the "original mind" or "ordinary mind," or as Daoism puts it, returning to a state of tranquility and non-action, is akin to "rebirth," which is extremely challenging. Historically, only a few people have achieved such overall enlightenment. For those engaged in creation or innovation, even if they cannot achieve total enlightenment, some degree of enlightenment is essential. This necessity means that during the act of creation or innovation, all other distractions are temporarily "bracketed." Whether a calligrapher freely brushes ink on paper, a scientist experiments and reasons, or a military leader commands in battle, they experience this state.

About the author:

Wang Shuren, a graduate of Peking University's Philosophy Department (1962), is a research fellow at the Chinese Academy of Social Sciences. Formerly the deputy director of its Academic Committee, his work has focused on Western philosophy and, more recently, on comparative studies of Chinese and Western thought.

Rebuilding the Foundations of Thought

Some Reflections on Conservatism

DU Hongwei

Liu Junning (刘军宁) is a leading figure among China's young political scholars, known for his unique insights into liberalism and conservatism. His numerous articles on conservatism in recent years have gradually introduced this concept to the Chinese public, though his views have received mixed reactions. Recently, I came across Liu Junning's article "The Divide Between Classical Liberalism and Conservatism" online and found myself differing with some of his points. At the beginning of his article, Liu Junning summarizes: "As atheists or agnostics, classical liberals believe that human order is spontaneous and evolutionary. In contrast, as theists, conservative believers in Jehovah view human order not as spontaneous but as divinely ordained. Thus, the fundamental divide between classical liberalism and conservatism becomes apparent: theism versus atheism, belief in Jehovah or not, which distinguishes classical liberals from orthodox conservatives. Classical liberals rely on rational choice and experience, while conservatives rely on transcendental faith and revelation, without excluding reason and experience." While I agree with Liu Junning's interpretation of conservatism, I believe his understanding of classical liberalism is incomplete, particularly his assertion that classical liberals rely on rational choice and experience, whereas conservatives rely on transcendental faith and revelation. This view misinterprets and distorts classical liberalism.

To better understand classical liberalism and conservatism, let's first trace their origins. Conservative thought stems from the late 18th-century Irish-British thinker Edmund Burke's *Reflections on the Revolution in France*. Many point out that during the Reformation, Anglican theologian Richard Hooker emphasized political stability for social harmony and public interest, displaying early conservative thought. However, conservatism became a systematic ideology only after Burke's work. The 20th-century American political theorist, historian, and social commentator Russell Kirk (1918-1994) is considered a modern representative of Anglo-American conservatism. Kirk's conservative ideas influenced presidents like Nixon and Reagan and earned him the Presidential Citizens Medal from Reagan. His notable works include "The Roots of American Order" and "The Conservative Mind." "The Roots of American Order" addresses the ideological foundations of American political society, crucial for understanding Anglo-American systems. "The Conservative Mind" outlines the intellectual history of Anglo-American thought, emphasizing the value of religious faith, which is essential for comprehending Western social systems.

Why have Americans enjoyed unprecedented freedom, opportunity, and prosperity in history? Historian Russell Kirk provides a compelling answer in *The Roots of American Order*: it is because America, not just a land of freedom and the home of the brave, also enjoys liberty under order. This order, often referred to as spontaneous order, is essentially divine order—an order designed by God for humanity. The term spontaneous order was coined by Friedrich Hayek to differentiate from human-constructed order. This foundation, rooted in divine order, was established nearly three thousand years ago by the Hebrews, who recognized a "moral purpose under God." The ancient Greeks solidified this foundation with their philosophy and political consciousness, followed by the Romans, who nurtured it with their legal and social awareness. This foundation is inseparable from Christian understandings of human responsibility, hope, and redemption, intertwined with medieval customs, scholarship, and courage. Ultimately, this foundation was enriched by two great experiments in law and liberty: one in London, home to the Magna Carta and the British Parliament, and one in Philadelphia, where the American Declaration of Independence and Constitution were born. Thus, Kirk's narrative can be described as a story of five cities—Jerusalem, Athens, Rome, London, and Philadelphia. The core of modern conservatism lies in the concept of "ordered liberty." Despite being nearly 200 years apart, Burke and Kirk share many similarities, including respect for customs and traditions, aversion to ideology and radicalism, and belief in prudent politics and policies.

Conservatism is often seen differently in various contexts and historical periods but typically emphasizes preserving established values or the status quo. Conservatism is usually contrasted with radicalism rather than progressivism, advocating gradual change over radical reform. Conservatism branches into cultural, religious, fiscal, and economic conservatism and ideologically into liberal conservatism, authoritarian conservatism, and traditional conservatism. Some also categorize conservatism into classical conservatism, ideological conservatism, neoconservatism, and paleo-conservatism. This complexity often leads to confusion and misuse of the term. Essentially, conservatism, as proposed by Burke in "Reflections on the Revolution in France", aims to preserve the ideas and traditions of classical liberalism represented by Locke. True conservatism seeks to maintain the spontaneous order and natural laws established by God while opposing human-constructed orders and utopian dreams. As the father of conservatism, Burke was a classical liberal, supporting Locke's political liberalism and Adam Smith's economic liberalism. Witnessing the radical political movement of the French Revolution, which pursued an omnipotent government, trampled individual freedom, destroyed tradition and order, and threatened human nature, Burke's conservatism primarily aimed to oppose such radical social change and preserve traditional British liberalism.

Burke's conservatism can be seen as opposing the rationalist social order of continental Europe and preserving the spontaneous order formed by British empiricism, following the mission God bestowed upon humanity. Locke's liberalism is rooted in the belief in God, particularly his concept of natural rights, stemming from divine rights. In his "Two Treatises of Government", Locke presented two fundamental concepts of liberty: economic liberty, meaning the right to own and use property, and intellectual liberty, including moral freedom. Locke defined these as "life, liberty, and property." His concept of natural rights became a precursor to modern human rights. In Western political philosophy, Locke's "Two Treatises of Government", particularly the second part, is seen as the establishment and completion of classical liberalism. Locke first described a state of nature different from existing human society, where individuals had no political power or obligations and were independent, free, and equal. This equality meant political equality, not excluding natural inequalities like height or strength. In this state, everyone had the inalienable right to their body, a premise derived from the theological belief that humans are God's creation and thus God's property, each with a divine mission and the duty to protect their body and life to honor God's ownership.

Locke argued that all resources in the state of nature, including animals and plants, were common to humanity. However, through labor, which is an exercise of ownership over one's body, these resources became private property. Thus, property rights stem from body ownership. Labor is the exercise of body ownership, and its fruits are the natural extension of this ownership, endowed by God and inviolable. Any infringement on these rights is an infringement on God's natural law. In this state, everyone has the right to enforce natural law against offenders. However, human nature is selfish, and individual cognition is limited. If everyone acted as their own judge and enforcer, it would lead to excessive enforcement and further injustice. Hence, people formed governments based on social contracts to have a neutral, objective, and transcendent standard for adjudicating disputes, leading to political society.

In Locke's social contract theory, people did not surrender any rights upon forming governments, including liberty, equality, and property rights. They only transferred the right to arbitrate natural law disputes to ensure better protection of their remaining rights, not to create a government with supreme authority over individuals. This is the moral basis for people's right to replace oppressive governments. Overthrowing oppressive governments is the enactment of God's natural law on earth, essential for maintaining spontaneous order designed by God. Spontaneous order contrasts with human-constructed order and represents the divine order manifested in natural states. The purpose of human-constructed governments is to adjudicate relationships, not to establish supreme authority. This constructed order must be based on individualism to avoid unchecked rulers and dictators. Locke's liberalism is premised on belief in God, and without this premise, concepts like freedom, equality, and the sanctity of private property would not exist.

Therefore, Liu Junning's assertion that "classical liberals rely on rational choice and experience, while conservatives rely on transcendental faith and revelation, without excluding reason and experience" misinterprets liberalism.

Why did Friedrich Hayek, often labeled a conservative economist, declare, "I am not a conservative," distancing himself from conservatism? Yet, both old and new conservative camps regard Hayek as a primary contemporary representative. According to "Hayek on Hayek," Hayek maintained that he was a Burkean liberal, while Burke was essentially a liberal and the father of conservatism. This paradox arises from the transformations within conservatism and liberalism. Conservatism is often criticized for degenerating into traditionalism, and liberalism for evolving into radicalism. Both conservatism and liberalism can be misused to substitute God's divine order with human-constructed order. Hayek's spontaneous order counters planned economies, representing divine order expressed through human practice.

Liu Junning's view that conservatism believes human order originates not on earth but in heaven is valid. Just as solar energy exists waiting to be discovered, the transcendental principles of human order await acceptance and application. Order is not spontaneous or designed by humans but prepared by the Creator. Human order is divinely created, preordained by God, known as divine order. While I agree with this, it does not justify labeling classical liberalism as rationalism, empiricism, utilitarianism, and evolutionism. Hayek's spontaneous order represents human practice following God's natural laws, embodying divine order in society. There is no fundamental difference between divine and spontaneous orders. Human society's laws, morals, and ethics should be based on spontaneous order, recognizing that society is not arbitrarily constructed but follows principles. To prosper, society must adhere to these principles, which reflect God's will.

Human rational arrogance leads to two issues: viewing society as "institutions" (morals, ethics, laws) rather than "spontaneous order" and misinterpreting or constructing institutions based on personal experience. These perceived "good" institutions or traditions may only maintain a given social order, conflicting with divine order, ultimately causing societal stagnation and collapse.

The world is divided into authoritarianism and liberalism, or collectivism and individualism. Collectivism and authoritarianism are human constructs, whereas individualism and liberalism align with God's purpose. God created Adam and Eve as concrete individuals, not abstract humanity or collectives. Other ideologies like Nazism, Communism, neoliberalism, neoconservatism, and progressivism are derivatives and distortions, created by those with ulterior motives to deceive. They promote dictatorship under the guise of freedom or equality. True freedom and equality are individualistic and liberal, inherently incompatible with collectivism and authoritarianism.

Conservatism is often misunderstood as preserving traditional social systems and values. Wikipedia and the Encyclopedia Britannica define conservatism this way. However, this definition fails to clarify whether conservatism seeks to preserve universally significant institutions and values, specific historical ones, or those adaptable to changing contexts. Political scientist Samuel Huntington offers three definitions of conservatism: aristocratic, autonomous, and situational. The aristocratic view sees conservatism as the aristocracy's reaction to liberalism and revolution, a historically specific movement. The autonomous view treats conservatism as abstract principles like justice, order, balance, and moderation, transcending historical evolution. The situational view sees conservatism as the ideology preserving established systems and values, varying with the times.

Clearly, the aristocratic definition does not apply to American conservatism, as America never had a fixed aristocratic system like pre-revolutionary France. The autonomous definition,

represented by thinkers like Russell Kirk, poeticizes, philosophizes, and mystifies conservatism, but faces criticism from historically minded political scientists. Huntington argues that conservatism lacks a model of an ideal society, unlike other ideologies like socialism, anarchism, and fascism. Without a societal ideal to pursue, the autonomous definition of conservatism fails. Consequently, only the situational definition fits American conservatism, reflecting the changing ideas and actions of conservatives across historical periods.

According to Huntington, American conservatism exists within specific historical contexts, not as abstract philosophical ideas. This view is confirmed by scholars like Patrick Allitt, who notes that "conservatism" means different things in different eras. American conservatives never had a consensus on what to preserve, responding passively to social changes. Thus, the roots of Anglo-American conservatism lie in liberalism, stemming from biblical traditions in Jerusalem. Without this foundation and its derivative natural and divine laws, modern Anglo-American liberalism and conservatism would not exist. Conservatism and liberalism in Anglo-American contexts are intertwined, with conservatism preserving liberalism's traditions. Discussing conservatism without this foundation often implies preserving harmful policies. For example, promoting "conservatism" in India might advocate for preserving the caste system. In China, lacking belief in God and liberal traditions, conservatism would imply preserving centralized authoritarianism, providing theoretical support for despots.

Japanese political thinker Fukuzawa Yukichi argued that a nation's rise requires three changes: in people's hearts, institutions, and economy. These must occur in this order—spiritual first, institutional second, economic last. Reversing this order may seem expedient but ultimately fails. Unfortunately, Fukuzawa's spirituality did not lead to God. A genuinely great nation is not defined by skyscrapers or authoritative forums but by every individual with faith and soul. Their beliefs create a new spiritual organism, whose thoughts and expressions form an atmosphere, gradually spreading and initiating a cultural movement. True elites will stand on this foundation, bringing hope to the entire nation.